RISK MANAGEMENT:
THE STATE OF THE ART

THE NEW YORK UNIVERSITY SALOMON
CENTER SERIES ON FINANCIAL MARKETS
AND INSTITUTIONS

VOLUME 8

1. I.T. Vanderhoof and E. Altman (eds.): *The Fair Value of Insurance
    Liabilities.* 1997   ISBN 0-7923-9941-2
2. R. Levich (ed.): *Emerging Market Capital Flows.* 1997
                                                         ISBN 0-7923-9976-5
3. Y. Amihud and G. Miller (eds.): *Bank Mergers & Acquisitions:
    An Introduction and an Overview.* 1997   ISBN 0-7923-9975-7
4. J.F. Carpenter and D.L. Yermack (eds.): *Executive Compensation
    and Shareholder Value.* 1998   ISBN 0-7923-8179-3
5. I.T. Vanderhoof and E. Altman (eds.): *The Fair Value of Insurance
    Business* 2000   ISBN 0-7923-8634-5
6. S.J. Brown and C.H. Liu (eds.): *A Global Perspective on Real Estate
    Cycles* 2001   ISBN 0-7923-7808-3
7. R.A. Schwartz (ed.): *The Electronic Call Auction: Market Mechanism
    and Trading, Building a Better Stock Market* 2001   ISBN 0-7923-7256-5

RISK MANAGEMENT:

THE STATE OF THE ART

Edited by
STEPHEN FIGLEWSKI
Stern School of Business
New York University

RICHARD M. LEVICH
Stern School of Business
New York University

KLUWER ACADEMIC PUBLISHERS
BOSTON / DORDRECHT / LONDON

Distributors for North, Central and South America:
Kluwer Academic Publishers
101 Philip Drive
Assinippi Park
Norwell, Massachusetts 02061 USA
Telephone (781) 871-6600
Fax (781) 681-9045
E-Mail <kluwer@wkap.com>

Distributors for all other countries:
Kluwer Academic Publishers Group
Distribution Centre
Post Office Box 322
3300 AH Dordrecht, THE NETHERLANDS
Telephone 31 78 6392 392
Fax 31 78 6546 474
E-Mail <services@wkap.nl>

 Electronic Services <http://www.wkap.nl>

Library of Congress Cataloging-in-Publication Data

Risk management: the state of the art/edited by Stephen Figlewski, Richard M. Levich.
    p.   cm.—(New York University Salomon Center series on financial markets and institutions; v.8)
    Includes bibliographical references.
    ISBN 0-7923-7427-4 (alk. paper)
    1. Risk management.   I. Figlewski, Stephen.   II. Levich, Richard M.   III. Series.
HD61.R572   2001
658.15′5—dc21   2001034440

Printed on acid-free paper.

Printed in the United States of America

TABLE OF CONTENTS

List of Contributors   vii
Acknowledgments   ix
Introductory Materials and Abstracts   xi

I. IDENTIFYING, MODELING AND HEDGING RISKS

1. Modeling Liquidity Risk   3
   ANIL BANGIA, FRANCIS X. DIEBOLD, TIL SCHUERMANN, AND JOHN D. STROUGHAIR

2. Credit Risk Capital: More Than One Way to Guard a Guarantee   15
   PAUL KUPIEC

3. Qualitative and Quantitative Derivatives Risk Management   27
   EMANUEL DERMAN

4. Remarks on the Legal Risks of Derivatives   35
   THOMAS RUSSO

5. The Evolving Market for Catastrophic Event Risk   37
   KENNETH FROOT

6. Industrial Risk Management with Weather Derivatives   67
   RICHARD JEFFERIS

7. Designing and Pricing New Instruments for Insurance and Weather Risks   79
   JOSEPH B. COLE

8. Measuring Credit Risk: The Credit Migration Approach Extended for Credit Derivatives   87
   MICHEL CROUHY, JOHN IM, AND GREG NUDELMAN

9. The Y2K Enigma   111
DAN GALAI, MENACHEM BRENNER, AND MICHEL CROUHY

II. MANAGING RISK IN FINANCIAL INSTITUTIONS

10. Payment and Settlement Risks in International Financial Markets   123
DARRYLL HENDRICKS

11. Risks, Regimes and Overconfidence   129
MARK KRITZMAN, KENNETH LOWRY, AND ANNE-SOPHIE VAN ROYEN

12. The Bi-Currency Balance Sheet Model of Latent Currency Risk   145
ANTHONY C. MORRIS

13. Does Contagion Exist?   163
ROBERTO RIGOBON

14. An Analysis and Critique of the BIS Proposal on Capital Adequacy and Ratings   167
EDWARD I. ALTMAN AND ANTHONY SAUNDERS

15. Hedge Fund Transparency is no Silver Bullet!   187
BRUCE BRITTAIN

16. Capital Adequacy in Financial Institutions: Basel Proposals   201
DARRYLL HENDRICKS

17. Risk Management: Where Are We Heading? Where Have We Been?   207
LESLIE RAHL

Author Index   215

Subject Index   217

LIST OF CONTRIBUTORS

Edward I. Altman, *NYU Stern School of Business*
Anil Bangia, *Oliver, Wyman & Company*
Bruce Brittain, *Lyster Watson & Company*
Menachem Brenner, *NYU Stern School of Business*
Joseph B. Cole, *John B. Collins Associates, Inc.*
Michael Crouhy, *Canadian Imperial Bank of Commerce*
Emanuel Derman, *Goldman Sachs & Company*
Francis X. Diebold, *University of Pennsylvania and Oliver, Wyman & Company*
Kenneth Froot, *Harvard Business School*
Dan Galai, *The Hebrew University and Sigma P.C.M. Investment Ltd.*
Darryll Hendricks, *Federal Reserve Bank of New York*
John Im, *Canadian Imperial Bank of Commerce*
Richard Jefferis, *Koch Supply and Trading Company*
Mark Kritzman, *Windham Capital Management Boston*
Paul Kupiec, *Freddi Mac*
Kenneth Lowry, *State Street Bank*
Anthony C. Morris, *UBS Warburg*
Greg Nudelman, *Canadian Imperial Bank of Commerce*
Leslie Rahl, *Capital Market Risk Advisors, Inc.*
Roberto Rigobon, *Sloan School of Management, MIT and NBER*
Thomas Russo, *Lehman Brothers*
Anthony Saunders, *NYU Stern School of Business*
Til Schuermann, *Oliver, Wyman & Company*
John D. Stroughair, *Oliver, Wyman & Company*
Anne-Sophie Van Royen, *Windham Capital Management Boston*

ACKNOWLEDGMENTS

This volume presents the proceedings of a conference held at the Stern School of Business, New York University on January 13–14, 2000. The conference was held under the joint sponsorship of the NYU Salomon Center and the Derivatives Research Project. This is the second conference aimed at assembling participants from academia, the financial sector, and government and regulatory bodies, all of whom are working at the forefront of risk management. It is our pleasure to thank Ingo Walter, the Director of the NYU Salomon Center, for his assistance and encouragement throughout the planning for this conference. Thanks are also due to Mary Jaffier and her staff for efficiently handling the many administrative tasks associated with this conference, especially as the feared Y2K problem loomed over our proceedings. Finally, we thank the authors of the papers and the discussants for contributing their energy and talents to this project.

Stephen Figlewski
Richard M. Levich

INTRODUCTORY MATERIAL: ABSTRACTS OF PAPERS IN THIS VOLUME

STEPHEN FIGLEWSKI AND RICHARD M. LEVICH

Part I: Identifying, Modeling and Hedging Risks

1. Anil Bangia, Francis X. Diebold, Til Schuermann, and John D. Stroughair, "Modeling Liquidity Risk"

   It is customary in empirical work with financial data to ignore the bid-ask spread in market prices. This is typically not through choice, but through necessity, due to lack of data. And for studies of the most active markets under normal circumstances, this simplification does not make much difference. But for assessing risk exposure, as in setting capital requirements under the new BIS guidelines, failure to take account of liquidity risk may cause overall exposure to be seriously understated. Bid-ask spreads in less liquid markets are larger and more variable than in broader and deeper markets, and tend to expand sharply during periods of market disruption that will fall into the extreme tail of the returns distribution. In this article, the authors propose an extended version of VaR that formally takes account of the probability distribution of the bid-ask spread along with the mid-market value of the underlying asset or portfolio. In a detailed example, they show that for some assets and portfolios, the liquidity component of overall risk exposure may be nearly 20% of total risk, and that taking it into account may substantially reduce the frequency of violations of calculated capital requirements.

2. Paul Kupiec, "Credit Risk Capital: More Than One Way to Guard a Guarantee"

The Bank for International Settlements June 1999 proposal to credit risk capital standards addresses the issue of how to align the credit risk exposure of banks with their regulatory capital requirements. Measuring the credit risk of bank exposures is challenging and various techniques from those based on external credit ratings, to internal approaches based on Value-at-Risk, among others have been proposed. These approaches have in common a "buffer stock" approach to capital adequacy whereby banks hold sufficient capital to meet the possibility of unexpected losses. In this article, Paul Kupiec describes an alternative credit insurance approach that could accomplish the same regulatory objective (i.e. shielding banks against unexpected loan losses) while at the same time be amenable to more objective pricing. Kupiec also discusses the impact of maturity on credit risk and describes how this dimension of credit risk could be handled within a credit insurance framework. Empirical estimates suggest substantial differences between credit risk capital requirements under the BIS proposal and those based on a credit risk insurance approach.

3. Emanuel Derman, "Qualitative and Quantitative Derivatives Risk Management"

Emanuel Derman begins this article with "The awful truth about derivatives," which is basically that the world in which all of our elegant option pricing theory really holds bears very little resemblance to the real world in which our financial markets reside. He observes that after taking into consideration that you can't continuously rebalance a delta hedge; you don't know volatility and in any case it is stochastic; you don't know future interest rates or dividends or stock borrowing costs or the shapes of implied volatility surfaces either; there are issues of credit risk, jump risk, volatility basis risk, subtle currency risks; and many more unsavory facts, "you could get seriously low-spirited and glum."

And yet, our models are all we have. So, after an eye-opening evaluation of all of the problems that affect the performance of Black-Scholes family models, Derman describes how they need to be used in practice, and some of the many other important facets of real world derivatives risk management at a sophisticated securities firm such as Goldman Sachs. The general thrust of the discussion is that one should not place too much faith in models alone, models need to be examined carefully to verify that they are both correct mathematically and also that they make sense in practical terms, and that risk management should incorporate careful consideration of *all* aspects of a trade and a trading operation, from every possible perspective.

4. Thomas Russo, "Remarks on the Legal Risks of Derivatives"

Academic work on derivatives risks focuses mainly on evaluating and hedging different aspects of market risk, as measured by the familiar collection of Greek letters. Banks have always been most concerned with evaluating and managing exposure to credit risk, and other financial services firms are increasingly aware of credit risk issues, as well. And yet, some of the largest losses in recent years from inadequate risk management have not come from these "traditional" sources, but from other quarters, more properly called operational risk, legal risk, and documentation risk. Today's risk manager needs to worry about the legal ability of counterparty to enter in a trade (as in the Hammersmith and Fulham case), the precise legal interpretation of all contract terms under all conditions, even in industry standard documentation (e.g., Procter and Gamble), and (of course), the ever-present possibility of a rogue trader (e.g., Barings). In this article, Thomas Russo gives some insights into the kinds of non-traditional risk questions that preoccupy him in his joint roles as Chief Legal Officer and Vice Chairman of Lehman Brothers.

5. Kenneth Froot, "The Evolving Market for Catastrophic Event Risk"

Catastrophic risks, associated with hurricanes, earthquakes, and other natural disasters, have traditionally been distributed through insurance and reinsurance systems. Insurance companies have retained some risks, and sold off the remainder to other insurance companies who then repeat the process. In 1997, the market for catastrophic event risk witnessed an important change with the first large and truly successful catastrophic ("cat") bond. Moreover, new exchange have opened with traded contracts based on the introduction of new cat loss indexes. In this article, Kenneth Froot presents an overview of this newly developing market. Froot examines the incentives for insurers and investors to enter the cat market, how the market and successful products are likely to be structured, and who can benefit through the growing array of cat products.

6. Richard Jefferis, "Industrial Risk Management with Weather Derivatives"

Financial risks are nearly all price risks of one kind or another, as are most of the other types of risks for which derivative markets exist. There is also typically a single broad index or market that can serve as a proxy for the particular price risks affecting a broad range of hedgers. These properties do not hold for an important class of risks that are determined by weather. Weather derivatives represent a significant and interesting innovation in the universe of risk management instruments. As Jefferis describes, use of a single broad index is often not feasible, because weather is a local phenomenon. This leads naturally to an OTC structure for this market. Moreover, to a large extent, weather-related risks involve a quantity component, such as the risk facing a gas pipeline operator whose service will be in demand as a direct function of the temperature (e.g., unusually cold weather increases the amount of gas needed for heating). The particular character of the kinds of risks for which weather derivatives are useful and the important features of this market are explained in a series of examples, involving pipeline transport, agricultural production and operation of an electricity generation facility.

7. Joseph Cole, "Designing and Pricing New Instruments for Insurance and Weather Risks"

The theme of this paper stands in contradiction to the claim that people always talk about the weather but nobody ever does anything about it. Financial instruments for dealing with insurance, weather and other catastrophic risks have been a theoretical idea for some time, but it is only quite recently that functioning markets for these products have developed. In this article, Joseph Cole presents an introduction to insurance and weather derivative instruments, beginning with the characteristics of successful futures contracts and the design impediments that face contracts based on weather and other catastrophic phenomenon. Using several examples, Cole illustrates the general nature of how insurance or weather contracts could be structured and priced, as well as the similarities and linkages between these insurance-style contracts and traditional financial futures, options and swaps. Trading insurance risks of these sorts may become more appealing to a wider array of investors, and perhaps just in time as consolidation hits the insurance industry and the need for risk transfer increases.

8. Michel Crouhy, John Im, and Greg Nudelman, "Measuring Credit Risk: The Credit Migration Approach Extended for Credit Derivatives"

Efforts to bring credit risk into the same framework used for derivatives pricing have followed tow different paths. The structural approach attempt to model the evolution of firm value over time, in order to gauge the probability that it will fall to a level that will precipitate default. The credit migration approach models, instead, a firm's transition probabilities over time among a set of credit states, typically taken to be bond rating classes. This technique is more easily implemented because it depends on more readily observable factors. Even so, transition probabilities that can be estimated from historical default data are "true" or "natural" probabilities, while those used in derivatives valuation are the risk neutral probabilities. This article describes the credit migration approach to valuing credit derivatives developed at CIBC. The crucial steps involve the procedures for estimating the risk neutral transition probabilities from market (natural) data.

9. Dan Galai, Menachem Brenner, and Michel Crouhy, "The Y2K Enigma"

One nonstandard risk that briefly became a matter of major concern throughout the world was the "Y2K" risk, related to the transition to the new millennium on January 1, 2000. When we were putting together the conference program during the spring and summer of 1999, it seemed like an interesting idea to hold a "post mortem" discussion of Y2K risk in early January 2001. The possibility of substantial disruption of the financial system from computers software that did not handle the one-time rollover to the new date system properly was hard to evaluate and harder to hedge. Brenner, Crouhy, and Galai had the idea of using the options markets around the world to obtain the "market's" assessment of the magnitude of Y2K risk, by examining the implied volatilities from options maturing before and after the turn of the year. In this article (written prior to the event), they show that despite widespread concern over

Y2K risk in the popular imagination, the financial markets did not manifest any obvious increase in expected volatility over the turn of the millennium. And once again, market rationality was borne out by actual events.

Part II: Managing Risk in Financial Institutions

10. Darryll Hendricks, "Payment and Settlement Risks in International Markets"

    "The plumbing" is how we sometimes refer to the systems that enable payment and settlement of financial transactions. These systems are used to settle commercial and financial transactions in foreign exchange, equities and fixed-income securities, as well as derivative transactions. Most of these transactions are typically of very high value, and daily volume in some individual markets run into the trillions of dollars with many transactions linking counterparties across borders. In this setting, a technical failure or counterparty default can have ripple effects that extend around the globe. In this paper, Darryll Hendricks offers an overview of the kinds of payment and settlement risks that haunt international financial transaction, and he sketches some of the steps underway to reduce these risks. One of the steps is the development of a new Continuous Linked Settlement (CLS) Bank that will provide a payment vs. payment settlement alternative for foreign exchange transactions. Once in place, the CLS bank could substantially reduce the risk of full payment of one leg of a transaction in one time zone followed by non-payment of the second leg of the transaction in a later time zone.

11. Mark Kritzman, Kenneth Lowry, and Anne-Sophie Van Royen "Risks, Regimes and Overconfidence"

    An investment's risk exposure is commonly expressed in terms of the distribution of market value at the end of an investment horizon, as in Value at Risk, for example. But focusing exclusively on the probability distribution on a single terminal date essentially assumes, contrary to common sense, that a serious loss that develops during the holding period will be ignored until the end. A more relevant risk measure for an investor may be the probability that a loss of a given magnitude will develop at *any* time over the horizon. As Kritzman, Lowry and Van Royen show, these probabilities can be substantially larger than the point probabilities on maturity day. Another property of the asset returns process that can induce incorrect risk assessments is the possibility that there are multiple regimes, e.g., calm periods and turbulent periods. Treating a historical sample of returns as if there were only one regime leads to underestimating exposure in the turbulent period.

    This article presents useful and practical techniques for handling both of these problems. The probability of a loss of a given size any time during the holding period can easily be modeled as the "first passage time" problem of determining the probability that the first time the asset value falls to the critical level or below will occur sometime before the fixed terminal date. A way to allow for calm and turbulent regimes is first to fit a single regime model and then focus on the outliers. These are assumed to come from the turbulent regime, and the "inliers" from the calm regime. Once the sample is separated in this way, the risk parameters of the two regimes can easily be estimated. Simulation results show how much difference these factors can make in a practical setting.

12. Anthony Morris, "The Bi-Currency Balance Sheet Model of Latent Currency Risk"

With the wave of financial crises that swept through Mexico and Latin American countries, Asia, Russia, and then back to South America in the 1990s, sovereign credit risk has taken on greater importance for international investors. Rating agencies prepare credit ratings for the sovereign debt of emerging market countries, but notably there are often significant differences between the pricing of emerging market debt and debt issued by corporations from industrial countries, even when both share the same credit rating and both are denominated in U.S. dollars. Is this empirical regularity indicative of a market inefficiency, and if not, what factors might explain the observed pricing difference? In this chapter, Anthony Morris tackles these questions using principles of contingent claim analysis. Morris argues that the credit ratings of emerging market sovereigns may not adequately reflect a latent currency risk for their external debt denominated in U.S. dollars. Emerging market sovereigns are much more exposed to this type of risk than corporate issuers from industrial countries, and less likely to have access to adequate hedging products to mitigate this risk. Moreover, foreign holders of emerging market debt might play the role of junior creditors in comparison to local investors who, in practice, are more senior. A contingent claim approach predicts that investors would require a higher yield spread if sovereigns retain an option to default on obligations to foreigners, that domestic corporate issuers are unable to exercise. The contingent claim approach offers a useful paradigm for assessing sources of emerging market credit risks.

13. Roberto Rigobon, "Does Contagion Exist?"

Diversification is a cornerstone of modern portfolio theory. And diversification is usually judged to be more powerful in international investing, because the linkages among countries may be weaker typically than the linkages among shares within an individual financial market. This common precept began to be questioned in the wake of the 1987 U.S. stock market crash when markets around the world responded in sympathy. With the financial crises of the 1990s hitting Mexico, Asia, Russia and several South American countries, the possibility of "contagion" and rolling crises began to be taken even more seriously. If contagion exists, investors are subject to additional risks, or put differently, they are not likely to enjoy all of the benefits of international diversification that they would otherwise expect. Contagion, however, is a slippery concept that requires a precise definition in both economic and statistical terms. In this paper, Roberto Rigobon reviews alternative notions of contagion, and argues that contagion is not a short-run phenomenon that can be based on a similarity in market spikes over a few days, but it measures a much longer run pattern of co-movement. In looking at the empirical evidence, Rigobon points out that the common statistical measure of correlation can be biased by the presence of extreme outcomes, that need not coincide with a change in the rate of propagation of shocks from one country to another. This is an extremely useful, but disconcerting finding because it places tests of contagion in the same category as efficient market tests that test a joint hypothesis. Finding similarities in market spikes, Rigobon concludes, need not signal an increase in interdependence relative to the analysts prior beliefs.

14. Edward I. Altman and Anthony Saunders, "The BIS Proposal on Capital Adequacy and Ratings: A Critique"

In June 1999, the Bank for International Settlements released a proposal for reforming the standard 8% risk-based capital ratio for credit risk. In part, the proposal calls for risk weightings based on the external credit rating of the borrower, with less capital backing required for stronger credits and more for weaker credits. The proposal is intended to address some of the adverse "risk-shifting" incentives inherent in the old standard, whereby banks were encouraged to shed highly-rated loans and replace them with lower-rated loans in order to earn a higher return on the same regulatory capital at risk. Using the actual default and recovery experience for a large sample of corporate bonds, Edward Altman and Anthony Saunders analyze whether the risk weights under the BIS proposal conform with actual experience for various risk categories. The authors find some significant discrepancies between risk weightings and categories based on their analysis and the initial BIS proposal.

15. Bruce Brittain, "Hedge Fund Transparency is No Silver Bullet!"

As one of the largest, best-known and most respected hedge funds, the Long Term Capital Management (LTCM) debacle in the fall of 1998 damaged both the financial capital of LTCM and other hedge funds, and the intellectual capital of the hedge fund industry. What went wrong in the underlying strategy of LTCM and what might regulators have seen and done in order to prevent its collapse and the contagious effects that swept through financial markets ultimately leading to a centrally orchestrated rescue for LTCM? One commonly voiced prescription is a call for greater transparency. After observing the positions taken by LTCM, it is argued, a red flag associated with LTCM's positions or leverage would have been seen by either investors or regulators, leading to actions that would have made the collapse far less likely. Is this a credible interpretation and viable policy direction? Bruce Brittain analyzes the events leading up to the LTCM collapse, and puts forward a case that it was unlikely that investors might have spotted the systemic risks for the financial community as a whole, that ultimately brought down LTCM. This is a sobering tale. Brittain suggests, however, that transparency could have been a powerful tool for macro-economic policymakers, had they been able to assess the risks facing various hedge funds and the collateral requirements consistent with those risks. Clearly this is a tall order. Transparency is essential for hedge fund investors to understand the risks they are facing, and hedge fund transparency could possibly assist policymakers. But transparency itself, Brittain concludes, cannot help us predict the system-wide events of 1998 that ultimately brought down LTCM.

16. Darryll Hendricks, "Capital Adequacy in Financial Institutions: Basel Proposals"

The Basel Committee on Banking Supervision issued its first so-called capital accord in 1988. The accord set minimum capital adequacy requirements for banks to meet contingencies for unexpected losses due to counterparty failure. The objectives were to have standards that were fair and had a high degree of consistency across countries. While the original accord was a crude first step, it started national supervisors and banks along the path to a more level playing field and a more rational treatment of banking risks and capital requirements. The original accord was amended five times through 1996, but in June 1999, the Basel Committee put forward a new proposal for sweeping changes in the scope and methodology for measuring bank exposure the credit risks and setting appropriate capital requirements. The new proposal rests on three "pillars"—one devoted to minimum capital requirements, a second to a supervisory review of capital, and a third based on market discipline relying on greater information disclosures.

In this paper, Darryll Hendricks outlines the new Basel Accord and analyzes some of its key recommendations. Among these are the role of credit ratings, and the impact that internal ratings constructed by banks versus ratings from external rating bodies might have. Hendricks also touches on other issues, such as capital requirements for interest rate risk, operational risks, and guaranteed or collateralized loans. The linkages between capital adequacy and macroeconomic performance are another important dimension for Basel policymakers to consider. Will the new accord encourage banks to build up capital in good times, so that capital is in place and can be depleted in bad times without threatening the banking system? These complexities, combined with the inevitable evolution of financial markets, suggest that the Basel Committee may have its hands full for years to come.

17. Leslie Rahl, "Risk Management: Where Are We Headed?"

Leslie Rahl has been involved in assessing and managing financial risk exposure for many years, from her early days trading caps, when volatility was treated as a single input parameter to be arbitrarily chosen by the head trader, to her current role as President of Capital Market Risk Advisors (CMRA), at a time when stress testing for "twists" in the volatility curve is only the beginning of risk evaluation. In this chapter, she recalls the rudimentary risk controls that were felt to be adequate in the early 1980s and discusses some of the major new types of risks, and the techniques that have been devised during the 1990s to deal with them. The Russian debt crisis and the collapse of Long Term Capital Management provided a rich source of new lessons to be learned about unexpected risk exposure. But there is evidence, at least from a CMRA survey of large banks and brokers, that these lessons have not yet been fully assimilated.

RISK MANAGEMENT:
THE STATE OF THE ART

I. Identifying, Modeling and Hedging Risks

1. MODELING LIQUIDITY RISK, WITH IMPLICATIONS FOR TRADITIONAL MARKET RISK MEASUREMENT AND MANAGEMENT

ANIL BANGIA

Oliver, Wyman & Company

FRANCIS X. DIEBOLD

University of Pennsylvania, N.B.E.R and Oliver Wyman Institute

TIL SCHUERMANN

Oliver, Wyman & Company

JOHN D. STROUGHAIR

Oliver, Wyman & Company

ABSTRACT

Market risk management has traditionally focussed on the distribution of portfolio value changes produced by changes in the midpoint of bid and ask prices. Hence market risk is traditionally assessed under the assumption of an idealized market with a negligible bid-ask spread. In reality, however, spreads can be both wide and variable; hence a superior approach would recognize that positions will *not* be liquidated at the mid-price, but rather at the mid-price less the uncertain bid-ask spread. Liquidity risk associated with the uncertainty of the spread, particularly for thinly traded or emerging market securities under adverse market conditions, is an important part of overall market risk and is therefore important to model. We do so, proposing a simple liquidity risk methodology that can be easily and seamlessly integrated into standard value-at-risk models. We show that ignoring the liquidity effect can produce underestimates of market risk in emerging markets by as much as thirty percent. Furthermore, we show that because the BIS is already implicitly monitoring liquidity risk, banks that fail to model liquidity risk explicitly and capitalize against it will likely experience surprisingly many violations of capital requirements, particularly if their portfolios are concentrated in emerging markets.

R.M. Levich and S. Figlewski (eds.). RISK MANAGEMENT. Copyright © 2001. Kluwer Academic Publishers. Boston. All rights reserved.

We thank Steve Cecchetti, Edward Smith and two anonymous referees for helpful comments and suggestions. All remaining errors are ours. This paper was written while the second author visited the Stern School of Business, New York University, whose hospitality is gratefully appreciated. An abridged version was published as "Liquidity on the Outside," *Risk Magazine*, 12, 68–73, 1999.

"Portfolios are usually marked to market at the middle of the bid-offer spread, and many hedge funds used models that incorporated this assumption. In late August, there was only one realistic value for the portfolio: the bid price. Amid such massive sell-offs, only the first seller obtains a reasonable price for its security; the rest lose a fortune by having to pay a liquidity premium if they want a sale. . . . Models should be revised to include bid-offer behavior."

Nicholas Dunbar ("Meriwether's Meltdown," *Risk*, October 1998, 32–36)

I. INTRODUCTION

Experts and laymen alike often point to liquidity risk as the culprit responsible for the recent turmoil in world capital markets. Both sophisticated and inexperienced players were surprised when markets evaporated and spreads widened drastically. More generally, it is widely acknowledged that the standard Value-at-Risk (VaR) concept used for measuring market and credit risk for tradable securities suffers from failure to account for liquidity risk. At best, VaR for large illiquid positions is adjusted upwards in an *ad hoc* fashion by using a longer time horizon that reflects a subjective estimate of liquidation time.

Motivated by the defects of VaR as traditionally implemented, we present in this article a framework for incorporating liquidity risk in market risk measurement and management. In section 2, we present our conceptual framework for understanding market risk and its components, one of which is liquidity risk. We make an important distinction between *exogenous* liquidity risk, which is outside the control of the market maker or trader, and *endogenous* liquidity risk, which is in the trader's control and usually the result of sudden unloading of large positions that the market cannot absorb easily. In section 3, we describe the various components of overall market risk and techniques for their measurement, with emphasis on the neglected liquidity risk component and our approach to modeling it. Our liquidity risk adjustment uses readily available data and is easily integrated with traditional VaR calculations, and we provide several worked examples. In section 4, we broaden the analysis from one instrument to an entire portfolio, and we display backtesting examples that reveal the very different results that can be obtained depending on whether liquidity risk is or is not incorporated. We conclude in section 5 with additional discussion of selected issues.

II. CONCEPTUAL FRAMEWORK

"Risk" refers to uncertainty about future outcomes. Traditional market risk management deals almost exclusively with portfolio value changes driven by trading returns. Trading returns are calculated from mid-price, and hence the assessed market

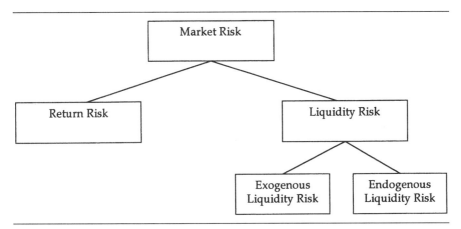

Figure 1. Taxonomy of Market Risk

risk corresponds to an idealized market with no friction in obtaining the fair price. However, risk in many markets possesses an additional liquidity component: traders do *not* realize the mid-price when liquidating a position quickly, or when the market is moving against them. Instead, they realize the mid-price less the bid-ask spread. Marking to market mid-price therefore yields an underestimation of the true risk in such markets, because the realized value upon liquidation can deviate significantly from the market mid-price. If one wants an accurate assessment of overall market risk, it is important to model the distribution of the deviation of the liquidation price from the mid-price, which is sometimes called the cost of liquidity.

More precisely, we conceptually split market risk into two parts: return risk, which can be thought of as a pure market risk component, and liquidity risk. We further split liquidity risk into endogenous and exogenous components, as summarized in Figure 1.

*Ex*ogenous illiquidity is the result of market characteristics; it is common to all market players and unaffected by the actions of any one participant. Markets with very low and stable levels of exogenous illiquidity, such as G7 currencies, are typically characterized by heavy trading volumes, stable and small bid-ask spreads, and stable and high levels of quote depth. *En*dogenous illiquidity, in contrast, is specific to one's position in the market, depends on one's actions, and varies across market participants. It is mainly driven by position size: the larger the size, the greater the endogenous illiquidity. A good way to understand the implications of the position size is to consider the relationship between the liquidation price and the total position size held, which we depict qualitatively in Figure 2.

If the size of the order is smaller than the quote depth, the order transacts at the quote, and the cost of immediate execution is half the bid-ask spread. Such a position possesses only exogenous liquidity risk. If the size of the order exceeds the quote depth, the cost of immediate execution is greater than half the spread. The excess over the half-spread reflects endogenous liquidity risk, which can be partic-

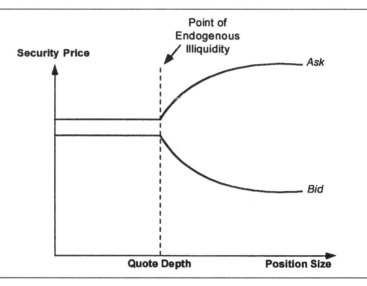

Figure 2. Effect of Position Size on Liquidation Value

ularly important in situations when normally fungible market positions cease to be fungible. Quantitative methods for modeling endogenous liquidity risk have been proposed recently by Jarrow and Subramanian (1997), Chriss and Almgren (1997), Bertsimas and Lo (1998), Longstaff (1998) and Krakovsky (1999), among others. Such methods, however, typically rely on models whose key parameters (e.g., relevant elasticities) are unknown and extremely difficult to gauge, due to a lack of available data.

In this paper we approach the liquidity risk problem from the other side, focusing on methods for quantifying *ex*ogenous rather than endogenous liquidity risk. Our approach is motivated by two key facts. First, fluctuations in exogenous liquidity risk are often large and important, as will become clear from our empirical examples, and they are relevant for all market players, whether large or small. Second, in sharp contrast to the situation for endogenous liquidity risk, the data needed to quantify exogenous liquidity risk are widely available. The upshot is that we can incorporate exogenous liquidity risk into VaR calculations in a simple and powerful way.

III. MODELING UNCERTAINTY IN MARKET VALUE

A. Incorporating Exogenous Liquidity Risk in VaR Calculations

Asset returns are the log difference of mid-prices:

$$r_t = \ln[P_t] - \ln[P_{t-1}] = \ln\left[\frac{P_t}{P_{t-1}}\right],$$

Taking a one-day horizon over which the change in asset value is considered, and assuming that one-day returns are Gaussian, the Value-at-Risk at 99% confidence level is

$$VaR_t = P_t\left(1 - e^{(E_t[r_t] - 2.33\sigma_t)}\right),$$

where $E_t[r_t]$ and σ_r^2 are the first two conditional moments of returns. With no loss of generality, we set $E_t[r_t]$ to zero.

The above expressions for VaR consider only the distribution of the mid-price, whereas on average we would expect the bid to be less than the mid-price by half the average spread, $\frac{1}{2} \cdot \overline{S}$. Moreover, risk managers are interested not in average spreads but rather in extreme spreads associated with extreme market conditions. We define the (exogenous) cost of liquidity, COL, based on a certain average spread, $\overline{S}$, plus a multiple of the spread volatility, $a \cdot \tilde{\sigma}$, to cover most (say 99%) of the spread situations:

$$COL_t = \frac{1}{2}[P_t(\overline{S} + a\tilde{\sigma})],$$

where P_t is today's mid-price for the asset or instrument, $\overline{S}$ is the average *relative spread* (where relative spread, a normalizing device which allows for easy comparison across different instruments, is defined as ([Ask–Bid]/Mid), $\tilde{\sigma}$ is the volatility of relative spread, and a is a scaling factor that produces 99% probability coverage.

Because spread distributions are typically far from normal, we cannot rely on Gaussian distribution theory to help determine the scaling factor a. Empirical explorations indicate that a ranges from 2.0 to 4.5 depending on the instrument and market in question. For illustration, we show in Figure 3 the densities of relative spreads (in basis points) for three currency returns, with the best-fitting normal superimposed. As we move to anecdotally less liquid markets, the densities become less normal. Moreover, spread distributions are not nearly as well behaved as return distributions; sometimes, for example, they appear multi-modal. We seem to be seeing different regimes, some of high liquidity, others of low liquidity.

In order to treat the return risk and liquidity risk jointly, we make the conservative simplifying assumption that extreme return events and extreme spread events happen concurrently. The correlation between mid-price movements and spreads is not perfect, but it is nevertheless strong enough during extreme market conditions to enable and encourage us to view return risk and exogenous liquidity risk as experiencing extreme movements simultaneously. Hence when calculating liquidity-risk adjusted VaR we incorporate both a 99% mid-price return on the underlying and a 99% spread, as we summarize graphically in Figure 4.

To translate from returns back to prices, we simply define the 1% worst-case price (P') and parametric liquidity-adjusted VaR for a single asset as

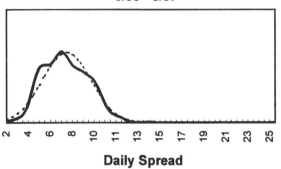

Spread Distribution, Japanese Yen
5/95 - 5/97

Daily Spread

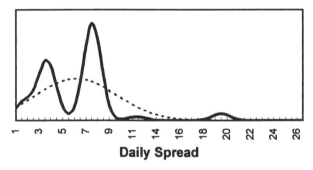

Spread Distribution, Thai Baht
5/95 - 5/97

Daily Spread

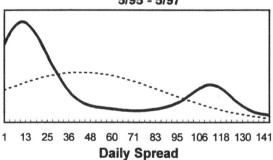

Spread Distribution, Indian Rupee
5/95 - 5/97

Daily Spread

Figure 3. Distribution of Spreads for Three Currencies

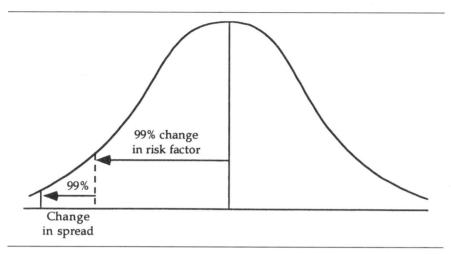

Figure 4. Combining Return Risk and Liquidity Risk

$$P_t = P_t e^{(-2.33\sigma_t)} - \frac{1}{2}[P_t(\overline{S} + a\tilde{\sigma})]$$

$$L - VaR_t = VaR_t + COL_t = P_t(1 - e^{(-2.33\sigma_t)}) + \frac{1}{2}[P_t(\overline{S} + a\tilde{\sigma})].$$

B. A Detailed Example

We examine two exchange rates against the U.S. dollar, one highly liquid (the Japanese Yen, JPY) and the other much less so (the Thai Baht, THB). We first examine basic asset-return risk, and then we consider the exogenous liquidity component. We split the sample period into pre and post May 1997, which corresponds to the onset of the Asian crisis.

For the pre-crisis period we calculate the risk measures as of May 2, 1997. The U.S. dollar exchange rates for the Yen and Baht were 126.74 and 26.11, and the volatilities were 1.12%, and 0.19%. Hence we calculate the 99% worst case prices as:

$$P\star_{JPY} = ¥126.74 \cdot e^{-2.33 \cdot 1.12\%} = ¥123.47$$

$$P\star_{THB} = B26.11 \cdot e^{-2.33 \cdot 0.19\%} = B25.99.$$

In other words, we calculate that on May 2, 1997, the probability of a one-day movement in the Yen from ¥126.74 to ¥123.47 is 1%. Next, we incorporate exogenous liquidity risk by adding the 99% bid values, computed using our estimates of spread means, volatilities, and scaling factors, yielding

$$Bid_{JPY} = ¥123.47 - \frac{1}{2}[¥126.74 \cdot (6.6bp + 2.5 \cdot 1.7bp)] = ¥123.40$$

$$Bid_{THB} = B25.99 - \frac{1}{2}[B26.11 \cdot (6.3bp + 3.5 \cdot 4.1bp)] = B25.96.$$

Table 1a. FX return risk and liquidity risk, pre-crisis

	JPY	THB
Price on May 2, 1997 (P_t)	¥126.74	B26.11
Average return volatility (σ_t)	1.12%	0.19%
Mean and volatility of relative spread ($\bar{S}$, $\tilde{\sigma}$)	6.6 bp, 1.7 bp	6.3 bp, 4.1 bp
Return risk component of VaR, $P_t(1 - e^{(-2.33\theta\sigma_t)})$	¥3.26	B0.12
Liquidity risk component of VaR, $\frac{1}{2}[P_t(\bar{S} + a\tilde{\sigma})]$	¥0.07	B0.03
Total liquidity adjusted VaR	¥3.33	B0.14
Liquidity component %	2.1%	19%

Table 1b. FX return risk and liquidity risk, post-crisis

	JPY	THB
Price on January 22, 1998 (P_t)	¥127.17	B53.55
Average return volatility (σ_t)	2.0%	5.48%
Mean and volatility of relative spread ($\bar{S}$, $\tilde{\sigma}$)	7.1 bp, 2.7 bp	76.4 bp, 47.4 bp
Return risk component of VaR	¥5.79	B6.42
Liquidity risk component of VaR	¥0.09	B0.65
Total liquidity adjusted VaR	¥5.88	B7.07
Liquidity component %	1.5%	9%

In Table 1a we summarize the progression of market risk calculations, which account for both the return risk and exogenous liquidity risk components of total market risk. The difference in liquidity risk contribution is strikingly different for the two currencies: the marginal impact of the liquidity component is only 2% for the Yen, but 19% for the Baht. This makes good sense, because the JPY/USD spot market is arguably one of the most liquid in the world, whereas the THB/USD market most definitely is not. Hence, at least during the period at hand, one could have safely ignored Yen liquidity risk, whereas ignoring Baht liquidity risk would have resulted in substantial underestimation of overall market risk.

In Table 1b we present the analogous calculations for the post-crisis period. Comparison of the results for the two periods reveals that the proportion of exogenous liquidity risk in total market risk dropped from 19% to 9%, as the floating of the Baht and subsequent heavy trading increased return risk substantially. Thus, although both return and liquidity risk increased with the crisis, the share of return risk increased.

IV. ADJUSTING PORTFOLIO VAR FOR EXOGENOUS LIQUIDITY RISK

We have discussed return risk and exogenous liquidity risk, and their combination, at the level of a single financial instrument. Now we move to the level of an entire portfolio. In traditional portfolio VaR analysis, which ignores liquidity risk, the covariance matrix of asset returns is the key bridge from single-instrument to portfolio risk. A liquidity-adjusted portfolio VaR analysis could proceed in similar

Table 2. Compositions of four equally-weighted portfolios

S.E. Asian telecoms	Emerging Mkts. mixed	US equities/bonds	G7 currencies
Singapore Telecom	Indonesian rupiah	IBM 5 yr issue (6.375%)	Japanese yen
Telecom Asia (Thai)	Polish zloty	IBM 10 yr issue (7.25%)	British pound
Telekom Malaysia	Telecom Asia (Thai)	AT&T	French Franc
Singapore dollar	Genting (Malaysia)	DuPont	Deutschemark
Thai baht	City Devs (Singapore)	GE	
Malaysian ringgit			

Table 3. BIS capital multiplier

# of VaR violations in a trading year	PR (violation) if true 99% VaR		BIS zones	Capital multiplier
0	8.1%			3.0
1	20.5%			3.0
2	25.7%	89.2%	Green Zone	3.0
3	21.5%			3.0
4	13.4%			3.0
5	6.7%			3.4
6	2.7%			3.5
7	1.0%	10.8%	Yellow Zone	3.65
8	0.3%			3.75
9	0.08%			3.85
10 or more	0.01%		Red Zone	4.0

fashion, but it would require an assumption of multivariate normality of the spreads and estimation of the spread covariance matrix. Unfortunately, as we have seen, spread distributions are not nearly as well behaved as return distributions, which renders the approach of dubious value.

An alternative and more credible approach is to compute a portfolio-level bid and ask series by simply taking a weighted average of the individual instrument bids and asks, and then to use the instrument-level L-VaR methodology to adjust standard portfolio VaR for exogenous liquidity risk. We will now illustrate this approach using four portfolios, which range from Asian telecom equities to G7 currencies, from January 1995 to March 1997, as detailed in Table 2.

Recall that BIS assigns regulatory capital according to the number of VaR violations experienced over the course of a trading year, as illustrated in Table 3. Based on violations, banks are assigned regulatory colors with corresponding capital multipliers. From a bank's perspective, both over- and underestimation of VaR results in misallocation of capital. Overestimation produces too few violations, which indicates inefficient capital use, and underestimation produces too many violations, which result in capital charges.

In Figure 5 we display VaR backtesting results for the four portfolios considered. We show the number of violations during a trading year for two models: a standard VaR model, and the same model with our adjustment for exogenous liquidity

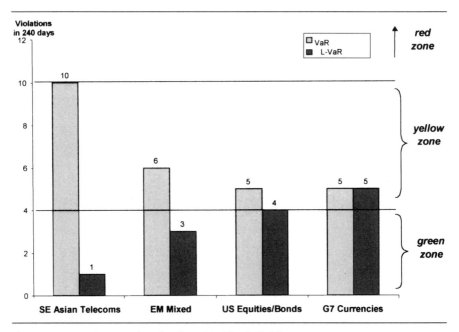

Figure 5. VaR Violations with and without Liquidity Risk Adjustment

risk. The liquidity risk adjustment never worsens performance, and it typically produces substantial improvement. As one moves from right to left in Figure 5, liquidity of the underlying assets decreases, and the risk assessment gains from incorporating a liquidity adjustment increase dramatically.

V. CONCLUDING REMARKS AND DIRECTIONS FOR FUTURE RESEARCH

Traditional VaR measures are obtained from the distribution of portfolio returns computed at mid-market prices, which underestimates risk by neglecting the fact that liquidation occurs not at the mid-market price, but rather at mid-market less half the spread, and the spread may fluctuate widely. Hence we developed and illustrated a simple measure of exogenous liquidity risk, computed using the distribution of observed bid-ask spreads. Our results suggest that ignoring exogenous liquidity risk can produce substantial underestimates of overall market risk, particularly for portfolios containing emerging market securities.

The insight that a simple liquidity adjustment can produce substantial accuracy gains in assessed VaR has wide-ranging implications for best-practice financial risk management, and it also has a number of more specialized implications. An immediate implication for trader compensation, for example, is that performance evaluation should be based on returns adjusted for risk—*including* liquidity risk. In recent years, many financial institutions have seen growth in their emerging markets trading activity due to higher margins. A risk-adjusted view of performance in those markets should account not only for return risk, but also for liquidity risk. Otherwise, performance will be incorrectly assessed and dealer compensation will be distorted.

A second implication involves regulatory capital guidelines. BIS regulations stipulate that the number of VaR violations be monitored, but not the way that VaR is computed. Neglecting liquidity risk will produce spuriously low estimates of overall market risk, under-capitalization, and too many violations. Hence the regulator, whether intentionally or not, *is* quite appropriately monitoring liquidity risk. The regulated need to do so as well.

REFERENCES

Bertsimas, D. and A.W. Lo (1998), "Optimal Control of Execution Costs," *Journal of Financial Markets*, 1, 1–50.

Chriss, N. and R. Almgren (1998), "Optimal Liquidation," Manuscript, Department of Mathematics, University of Chicago, Goldman Sachs & Co., and Courant Institute of Mathematical Sciences.

Dunbar, N. (1998), "Meriwether's Meltdown," *Risk*, 11 (October), 32–36.

Jarrow, R. and A. Subramanian (1997), "Mopping up Liquidity," *Risk*, 10 (December), 170–173.

Longstaff, F. (1998), "Optimal Portfolio Choice and Valuation of Illiquid Securities," Manuscript, Department of Finance, UCLA.

Krakovsky, A (1999), "Gap Risk in Credit Trading," *Risk*, March, 65–67.

2. CREDIT RISK CAPITAL: MORE THAN ONE WAY TO GUARD A GUARANTEE

PAUL KUPIEC*

In June 1999, the Basle Committee on Banking Supervision issued a consultative paper that outlines a set of proposed changes to the credit risk capital standards set in the 1988 Basle Accord.[1] The consultative paper, "A New Capital Adequacy Framework," proposes to reclassify bank credits among the Accord's original 0, 20, 50 and 100 percent risk buckets using external credit ratings to replace the Organization for Economic Cooperation and Development (OECD) membership criteria. It also includes a 150% weight and an asset-backed category that are included to discourage "regulatory arbitrage" activities. The proposal suggests that regulators may consider allowing banks to use internal risk rating systems to allocate credits into the Basle credit risk categories.

The amendments are motivated by regulators' desire to alter the incentive structure created by the original Basle Accord. The existing risk weighting system reduces banks ability to lever the returns on credit risky investments. In many instances, the leverage restriction reduces a bank's return on equity below targeted thresholds. Because the underlying equilibrium expected returns on high quality credits are modest, the existing risk weighting system discourages banks from retaining high quality (low default risk) instruments. In response to these limits, banks have in some cases sold their high quality credit exposures in securitization transactions and

* Director, Financial Research, Freddie Mac. Contact information: email paul_kupiec@freddiemac.com; phone 703-903-3945; postal address 8200 Jones Branch drive, McLean, VA, 22102. An edited version of this article appeared in the February 2000 issue of *Risk*.

R.M. Levich and S. Figlewski (eds.). RISK MANAGEMENT. Copyright © 2001. Kluwer Academic Publishers. Boston. All rights reserved.

retained exposures to more risky counterparties and to the residual credit risk associated with securitization. The Basle amendments are intended to stem the trend toward increased concentration in risky counterparty exposures.

The proposed amendments will at best only marginally improve the alignment between credit risk exposure and regulatory capital. The changes are unlikely to stem regulatory arbitrage as the number of risk buckets is limited to selected discrete ratings, and the risk buckets largely ignore the tenure of the exposures. Such an approach is inherently ineffective as credit risk is continuous in both dimensions. Indeed it is unlikely that modifications to the bucket-based approach to capital can remove regulatory arbitrage incentives as credit ratings alone are not sufficient to measure credit risk exposure.[2]

Recognition of the shortcomings in the Basle approach has led some to call for the use of internal bank credit risk models to set regulatory capital. Regulators have yet to embrace an internal models approach for credit risk because of well-founded concerns with model integrity and comparability. Credit risk modeling techniques— so-called credit VaR models—are less standardized than the techniques used to measure market risk. Not only do individual credit exposure measurement techniques differ among banks, model calibrations are often influenced as much by an institution's tolerance for risk as they are by objective data. The approaches used to measure diversification benefits also vary by institution. Because of data limitations, there can be only limited confidence that credit risk model calibrations measure exposures that are consistent with an "average" credit cycle. Moreover, data considerations limit the capacity for statistical validation of unexpected loss exposure estimates.

The series of consultative papers released by the Basle Supervisors suggest that regulators' preferred approach for measuring risk and setting capital is to design procedures that mimic the measurement processes they observe in financial institutions. Following the procedures used in banks, regulators have decided that market and credit risk capital requirements should be set according to a buffer stock theory of capital where capital is set with the objective of limiting the probability of financial distress over some relatively short-term horizon.[3] While the risk bucket approach of the Basle Accord is far removed from a credit value-at-risk capital system, the collective writings of the Basle Supervisors Committee suggest that the requirements associated with each bucket are intended to roughly approximate those that would be suggested by more formal credit modeling techniques.

While the buffer-stock view of capital may be a useful paradigm for measuring credit risk exposures in some business applications, there is no economic argument that suggests that the buffer stock approach is the *only* way to measure credit risk exposure. Indeed, notwithstanding its current popularity in the commercial market, there is no evidence that suggests that the buffer stock approach is the optimal approach for measuring risk exposures or setting regulatory capital requirements.

An alternative approach for setting credit risk capital requirements can be designed using a measure of risk capital proposed by Merton and Perold (1993). The market value of the credit risk embedded in a contract with default risk can be estimated and used to set an economically appropriate capital requirement for an individual contract's credit risk exposure. Credit risk and capital are measured using an estimate of the equilibrium market value of the insurance contract that will eliminate the credit exposure at issue. The insurance valuation measure of credit risk capital will generally not equal the capital suggested by a buffer stock measure, nonetheless it can be used to effectively control the moral hazard problem in financial contracting.[4]

At the most basic level, the insurance value approach requires that shareholders have an equity interest that is proportional to the market value of the credit risk in the assets acquired by an institution. If bank management decides to add additional credit risk exposures, the equity holders' investment must rise in proportion. Such a capital rule limits shareholder ability to expropriate wealth from stakeholders with risk-insensitive compensation structures. Under the insurance valuation approach, it is not necessary to measure default probability directly. By measuring the market value of the credit risk in an asset, and setting equity risk capital in proportion, stakeholders are shielded from the credit risk exposure in existing and new asset acquisitions. The degree of safety accorded stakeholders (including regulators) is related to the proportionality factor used to set capital under the insurance value method and the length of the monitoring period used to assess capital adequacy.[5]

The credit insurance approach for measuring capital has a number of significant benefits when compared to the buffer stock view of capital. The proposed measure is transparent and comparatively insensitive to the technical modeling assumptions that bedevil credit VaR models. It is objectively measurable, sensitive to the tenor of the underlying credit exposure, sensitive either to the tenor of the institution's funding sources or the horizon chosen to monitor capital, and completely consistent with market based insurance costs. Consequently, if applied uniformly across the credit risk spectrum, the credit insurance approach is less likely to distort business unit behavior and encourage regulatory arbitrage activities and structures in response to poorly calibrated capital requirements. The proposed measure produces capital requirements that are additive, as individual asset capital requirements completely account for the diversification benefits that are appropriately recognized in a well-diversified portfolio. In contrast to buffer stock capital measures, the credit insurance approach is easily verified as it does not require estimation of the potential credit loss distribution.

The intuition that underlies the insurance value approach for setting credit risk capital requirements can be introduced by considering the credit risk component of a simple insurance contract. Assume that investors are risk neutral and as a consequence assets are valued according to the present value of their expected future cash flows discounted at a known risk free interest rate. The arguments generalize to a more complicated set of contracts, to a market with risk averse investors, and to settings with a time-varying risk free term structure.

Consider an insurance contract with a simple payoff structure illustrated in Figure 1. At the end of T years, the contract pays $1,000 if a certain specific set of events

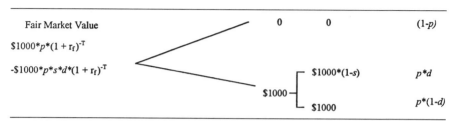

Figure 1. Simple Insurance Contract with Credit Risk

materializes, and pays nothing otherwise. Assume that the probability of experiencing the specific set of events that trigger an insurance payment is given by p, and so the probability of receiving no payment from the contract is $(1-p)$. In the event the insurance contract is scheduled to pay \$1,000 at maturity, there is some probability that the insurer fails to make the \$1,000 payment. Assume that this conditional probability of default is d, and default severity is s. When credit risk is recognized, the contract's potential payoffs at maturity can be enumerated as: 0 with probability $(1-p)$; $1,000 * (1-s)$ with probability of $(p * d)$, and \$1,000 with a probability of $p * (1-d)$.

The market value of the insurance contract can be decomposed into two components: the market value of an equivalent insurance contract without default risk less the market value of the default risk in the contract. It can be shown that the second term is equal to the equilibrium market value of an insurance contract that completely protects against the credit risk in the underlying contract. The second term—the implied market value is credit risk insurance—is a market based measure of credit risk exposure generated by the contract. It can be used as a basis for setting credit risk capital allocations.

The insurance approach for calculating credit risk exposures and capital requirements is easily illustrated for corporate bonds. The market value of the implicit credit risk is estimated by discounting the bond cash flows implied by the corporate bond par yield curve for selected rating categories using contemporaneous Treasury spot (zero coupon) interest rates.[6] The difference between the sum of the cash flow values discounted at Treasury rates and the par value of the bond is an estimate of the market value of the insurance contract necessary to insure the credit risk in the bond. In the case of corporate bonds, the credit risk insurance contract is the value of the implied put option in a Merton (1974) so-called "structural model" of risky debt. If actual market prices of individual bonds were available, the ratings-specific par coupon yield curves would not be necessary to estimate the market value of credit risk insurance and name-specific exposures could be calculated.

Panel a of Table 1 reports the implied market value of credit risk insurance expressed as a percentage of the market value of bonds as of January 3, 2000. The implied credit risk insurance value is calculated using contemporaneous quotes on Treasury strip securities to determine the risk free rate of interest.[7] The estimates

Table 1. Implied market value of credit risk (measured as percent of par value)

January 3, 2000

Maturity	AAA industrial	AA1 & AA2 industrial	A1 industrial	BBB1 industrial	AAA bank/fin	AA3 bank/fin	A1 bank	A2 bank	BBB1 bank	A1 finance	agency
1	0.40	0.46	0.59	0.88	0.55	0.64	0.60	0.65	0.90	0.67	0.18
2	0.90	1.01	1.27	1.89	1.17	1.41	1.43	1.48	1.98	1.48	0.50
3	1.38	1.54	1.85	2.81	1.80	2.12	2.07	2.57	3.15	2.17	1.03
4	1.70	2.08	2.49	3.76	2.32	2.60	2.67	3.11	4.11	2.91	1.43
5	1.92	2.33	2.91	4.45	2.91	3.16	3.08	3.37	5.20	3.37	1.05
6	2.30	2.71	3.58	5.32	3.46	3.91	3.99	4.20	5.92	4.16	1.74
7	2.68	3.18	4.39	6.30	4.11	4.83	5.10	5.21	6.69	5.10	2.69
8	3.08	3.44	4.47	6.95	4.65	5.38	5.14	5.56	7.98	5.38	2.66
9	3.37	3.70	4.76	7.33	4.89	5.55	5.55	5.88	8.06	5.62	2.12
10	3.35	3.92	4.99	7.55	5.34	6.06	5.34	5.98	9.12	6.70	2.92

October 28, 1998

Maturity	AAA industrial	AA1 & AA2 industrial	A1 industrial	BBB1 industrial	AAA bank/fin	AA3 bank/fin	A1 bank	A2 bank	BBB1 bank	A1 finance	agency
1	0.41	0.44	0.62	0.98	0.43	0.66	0.58	0.58	0.73	0.71	0.37
2	0.95	1.01	1.37	2.12	1.18	1.61	1.24	1.27	1.65	1.69	0.80
3	1.33	1.41	1.94	2.93	1.69	2.55	2.13	2.24	2.93	2.60	1.08
4	1.85	1.95	2.93	4.44	2.32	3.36	3.07	3.36	3.76	3.76	1.49
5	2.07	2.21	3.84	5.78	2.52	4.10	3.80	3.84	4.24	4.41	1.77
6	2.51	2.67	4.22	6.92	3.13	5.13	4.90	4.90	5.34	5.41	2.28
7	2.96	2.76	4.10	7.60	3.40	5.79	5.68	5.62	6.09	6.03	2.47
8	3.63	3.83	4.95	9.18	4.68	7.19	7.33	7.39	7.86	7.39	3.36
9	3.77	3.98	5.51	10.01	5.58	8.05	8.49	8.49	9.50	8.41	3.62
10	3.00	3.23	4.87	9.79	4.56	7.84	8.77	8.85	10.88	8.38	2.61

Table 2. Proposed credit risk weights (and percent capital requirements in parenthesis)

Counterparty	S&P Rating AAA to AA−	A+ to A−	BBB+ to BBB−	BB+ to B−	Below B−	Unrated
Sovereigns and	0%	20%	50%	100%	150%	100%
Central Banks	(0%)	(1.6%)	(4%)	(8%)	(12%)	(8%)
Corporate	20%	100%	100%	100%	150%	100%
	(1.6%)	(8%)	(8%)	(8%)	(12%)	(8%)
Maturity	20%	50%	50%	100%	150%	50%
>6 months	(1.6%)	(4%)	(4%)	(8%)	(12%)	(4%)
Banks, GSEs						
Maturity	20%	20%	20%	50%	150%	20%
<6 months	(1.6%)	(1.6%)	(1.6%)	(4%)	(12%)	(1.6%)
Banks						
Asset Backed	20%	50%	100%	150%	deduct value	
Paper	(1.6%)	(4%)	(8%)	(12%)	from capital	
					(100%)	

show a monotonic pattern for the value of credit risk insurance. The value of credit risk insurance is increasing in term to maturity and decreasing in credit quality (highly rated credits have smaller implied premia).

For comparison purposes, panel b of Table 1 report estimates of the implied value of credit risk insurance as of October 28, 1998, a close-of-business snapshot of insurance values during a period of significant market turmoil. Notice that lower rated banking and financial credits have significantly higher implied market values for credit risk insurance during the turbulent third quarter of 1998.

Table 2 reports the credit risk weights and implied percentage capital requirements that will prevail under the proposed amendments to the Basle Accord. A comparison of the capital requirements proposed by the Basle Supervisors with estimates of the market value of the credit risk insurance reported in Table 1 do not suggest that these alternative credit risk measures are strongly aligned. The risk weights recommended by the Basle proposal are not consistent with the market's view of credit risk. The discordant alignment of the capital measures is more apparent when viewing time series estimates of the market value of credit risk insurance for selected ratings categories. Figures 2 through 8 plot quarterly estimates of the implied market value of credit risk insurance for alternative ratings categories of corporate bonds. The times series are constructed from estimates of the implied market value of credit risk insurance for selected bond ratings categories at (roughly) quarterly frequency beginning on April 15, 1994 and terminating with estimates from close of business data on January 3, 2000.

An explicit assumption that underlies the proposed Basle risk weighting scheme is, holding constant credit rating, a banking counterparty will have equal or less credit risk than an equivalently rated corporate counterparty. The estimates of credit risk insurance values pictured in Figures 2 through 6 show that, on average, the market views banking/financial credits to be more risky than equivalently rated industrial counterparties. This generalization appears to be true regardless of the

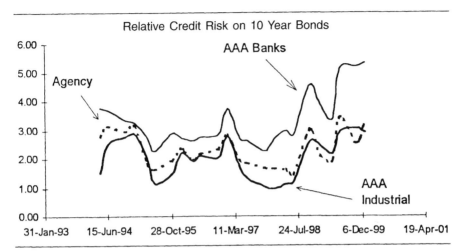

Figure 2. The Implied Market Value of Credit Risk Insurance on Selected 10-Year Corporate Bonds

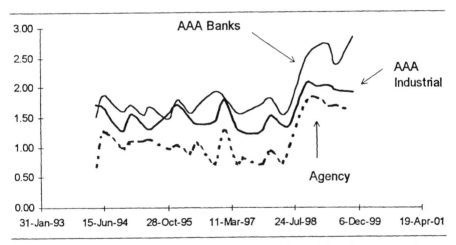

Figure 3. Implied Market Value of Credit Risk Insurance on Selected 5-Year Corporate Bonds

market conditions and the tenor of the credit exposure. For highly-rated long maturity exposures (e.g., Figures 2 and 5), it is not uncommon for the market to assess an average banking/financial counterparty exposure to be almost twice as risky as an equivalently rated industrial credit. Figures 3 and 4 suggest that the exposure differences diminish as the maturity of the bonds decreases.

Under the Basle proposal, a corporate counterparty with a AA rating would be subject to a 1.6% capital charge whereas a A-rated corporate counterparty would require 8% capital. Figure 7 suggests that, while the market clearly does view an A-rated industrial issuer as riskier than an AA-rated industrial credit, the additional risk exposure recognized by the market is minor when compared to the capital differ-

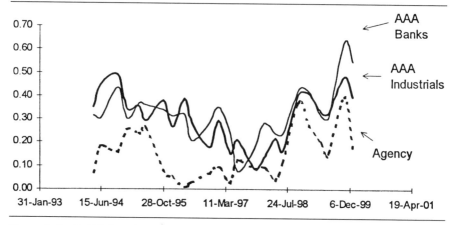

Figure 4. Implied Market Value of Credit Risk Insurance on Selected 1-Year Corporate Bonds

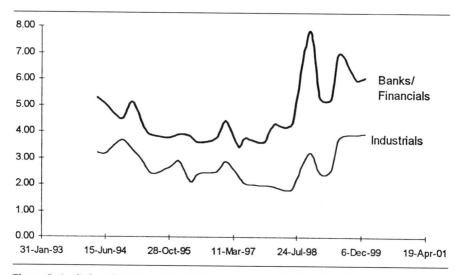

Figure 5. Implied Market Value of Credit Risk Insurance for AA-Rated Bonds

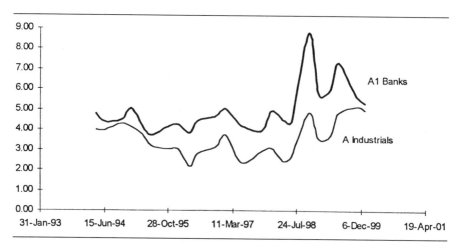

Figure 6. Implied Market Value of Credit Risk for A-Rated Bonds

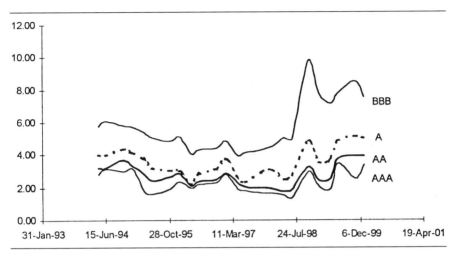

Figure 7. Implied Market Value of Credit Risk Insurance on 10-Year Industrial Bonds

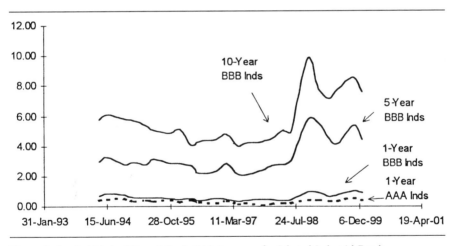

Figure 8. Implied Market Value of Credit Risk Insurance for Selected Industrial Bonds

ential proposed by the Basle Supervisors. Indeed, the market insurance value estimates suggest that if a sharp ratings-based distinction is to be recognized, it should
be associated with an industrial credit falling from an A to a BBB rating.

The Basle capital proposal is—excepting highly rated bank credits with less than
6 months to maturity—completely insensitive to the tenor of the credit risk exposure. Figure 8 illustrates the market's view of the importance of tenor in determin-
ing credit risk. The estimates suggest there is relatively little difference between the
credit risk in a 1 year AAA-rated and 1-year BBB-rated industrial bond, whereas
the market value of the credit risk insurance for BBB-rated industrials increases

markedly as maturity lengthens. Longer-term exposures carry not only a significantly elevated probability of default, but the uncertainty of recovery rates (default severity) is in many instances an increasing function of a credit's tenor. If the Basle Supervisors intention is to align credit risk and regulatory capital, it appears that the maturity of the counterparty exposure must somehow be reflected in the regulatory risk weight.

The estimates of the market value of credit risk insurance present an overall picture of credit risk that is in many respects at odds with the risk weighting scheme proposed by the Basle Supervisors. Regardless of whether the Supervisors or the profession at large wish to embrace a credit risk insurance based approach for setting credit risk capital, the estimates do provide a useful benchmark for comparison—for credit VaR estimates or for regulators proposed capital schemes. Using the credit insurance approach as a yardstick, it seems apparent that the supervisors need to recalibrate their credit risk capital measures if they are to achieve their stated objectives of aligning capital with risk and eliminating regulatory arbitrage.

NOTES

1. The Basle Accord refers to, "International Convergence of Capital Measurement and Capital Standards," Basle Committee on Banking Supervision, 1988.

2. Credit spreads and the market value of the default option reflect the probability of bankruptcy, the severity of anticipated loss, and the state(s) of nature (e.g. level of aggregate consumption levels) in which default may occur. Credit rating agencies seem to focus on expected loss (measured under physical default probabilities) and cannot control for firm variation in the price of default risk. As a consequence, equivalent credit ratings do not imply equivalent default option values. A clear example is seen when comparing the yield curves for a single rating among industrials, financials, and utilities.

3. See for example the discussion in, "Credit Risk Modelling: Current Practices and Applications," Basle Committee on Banking Supervision, April 1999.

4. Moral hazard is associated with situations in which management has the ability to substitute into higher risk assets and benefit shareholders by expropriating wealth from the firm's creditors and stakeholders including those associated with the provision of miss-priced government guarantees.

5. The technical development of this approach to capital, including a discussion of the appropriate multiplication factor, are presented is a separate paper by the author.

6. The bond data are taken from Bloomberg. The 6, 8 and 9 year maturity data are linearly interpolated.

7. The use of an "on-the-run" Treasury yield curve to measure risk free rates will upwardly bias the credit risk valuation owing to the rate effects associated with "specialness" in the repo market. See Duffie (1996) for further discussion. Another issue, not addressed here, is the state tax exempt status of Treasury securities. Because the income from Treasury securities is exempt from state taxes, it is possible that the rates on general collateral Treasury issues may be slightly understated relative to the true underlying risk free rate. This effect will tend to upward bias the estimate of the value of the credit risk in securities. The analysis also abstracts from any ill-liquidity premium differences that may exist between corporate bonds and off-the-run Treasury issues.

REFERENCES

Basle Committee on Banking Supervision. "Internal Convergence of Capital Measurement and Capital Standards," The Bank for International Settlements, Basle Switzerland, July, 1988.

Basle Committee on Banking Supervision. "Credit Risk Modelling: Current Practices and Applications," The Bank for International Settlements, Basle Switzerland, April, 1999.

Basle Committee on Banking Supervision. "A New Capital Adequacy Framework," The Bank for International Settlements, Basle Switzerland, June, 1999.

Duffie, Darrell (1996). "Special Repo Rates," *The Journal of Finance*, Vol. 51, No. 2, (June), pp. 493–526.

Merton, Robert (1974). "On the Pricing of Corporate Debt: The Risk Structure of Interest Rates," *The Journal of Finance*, Vol. 29, (May), pp. 449–70.

Merton, Robert and Andre Perold (1993). "Theory of Risk Capital in Financial Firms," *Journal of Applied Corporate Finance*, Vol. 6, No. 3, (Fall), pp. 16–32.

3. QUALITATIVE & QUANTITATIVE DERIVATIVES RISK MANAGEMENT

EMANUEL DERMAN

THE AWFUL TRUTH ABOUT DERIVATIVES

For a long time I worked in the area of equity derivatives, building models and systems for valuing the desk's book. I want to take a backward look at the almost invisible problems you can run into in using the Black-Scholes model and its extensions to hedge a portfolio of options.

Standard options theory made a brilliant discovery. It says that volatility trading is all about capturing the value of curvature in a security's payoff. In theory, at every instant, if you can hedge or replicate an option, you can earn the weighted difference between realized and implied volatility. If you are long an option, you are trading realized future volatility against current implied volatility.

What assumptions lie beneath this result? The Black-Scholes theory proves that you can replicate an option perfectly if

- You can know the single lognormal volatility;
- You can hedge continuously;
- You can transact at zero cost; and
- You know the future level of interest rates, dividends and stock borrowing rebates.

Standard options theory is a brilliant idealization. What happens in practice? Here's a brief sketch of the realistic circumstances we faced in running an equity derivatives book.

R.M. Levich and S. Figlewski (eds.). RISK MANAGEMENT. Copyright © 2001. Kluwer Academic Publishers. Boston. All rights reserved.

- Let's start with one option on one stock. First of all, riskless hedging is an oxymoron. Even if you could hedge at no cost, and even if you could forecast volatility perfectly, you still wouldn't be able to hedge continuously. Just the act of hedging discretely, N times over the life of the option, means that the P&L you capture is uncertain because of the sampling error. This error is of order $(2N)^{-1/2}$. Hedge 50 times on a three-month option rather than continuously, and your percentage error is 10%. It could be in your favor, could be against. Your Black-Scholes hedge is certainly wrong!
- Even if you could hedge continuously, there are transactions costs at each rehedging. This makes a long position worth less to you, and a short position costs you more. Your BS value is wrong!
- Even if there had been no transactions costs (but there are), and even if you could hedge continuously (but you can't), you have no idea about what value of the future volatility to use to calculate your hedge ratio. So, your hedge is even more off!
- Furthermore, you don't know future interest rates, or dividend yields, and you can occasionally be very wrong about the cost of borrowing stock. There are no term repos for stock loans, only overnight rates, and there may be future squeezes. So, forgetting about volatility-dependent options, even the value of the volatility-independent forward contract may be wrong. This is worse than having the wrong volatility.
- Now we get into subtleties. First, real and implied stock evolution isn't exactly lognormal anyhow, so Black-Scholes is using the wrong distribution to price and hedge.
- In fact, in more and more markets, there is a volatility skew and a volatility smile. What causes it? Which model should you use to hedge your option?
- And the volatility smile is sometimes a reflection of the possibility that jumps may occur. Jumps are unhedgeable and lead to losses because of discontinuous changes in delta. Does delta even make sense?
- And the smile or skew may also reflect the correlation of volatility with stock level, as well as stochastic volatility, all much more complicated. And the correlation of stock returns with volatility and with volatility of volatility aren't well known or predictable either.
- And volatility surfaces aren't stable; they move much like yield curves. The best you can do is look at their patterns or principal components, and most people don't.

So far, I've just been talking about simple single stock options, one expiration, one strike.

- The instruments we really trade involved hundreds of underlyers, indexes and single stocks and baskets thereof, over many strikes and expirations for each underlyer. We hold index options, stock options, vanilla and exotic options, basket options, currency-linked and currency-neutralized options, convertibles, hybrids that combined currency, interest rate and equity risk, etc. Now the problems begin to multiply, or perhaps exponentiate.

- For barrier and many other exotic options, near the barrier the curvature becomes so great that hedging is impossible in practice.
- There are subtle currency risks—what's the right skew for a compo or quanto?
- There is all kinds of volatility basis risk. You can't simply hedge one kind of volatility with another. You can't hedge long-term volatility with short-term volatility, or out-of-the-money volatility with at-the-money volatility. You can't hedge single stock volatility with index volatility.
- OTC options have credit risk, a relatively new area of exploration.
- There are liquidity limitations. Who really knows how to value that?
- As for long-dated volatility: no-one has a very good idea about how to price long-dated options, where the current skew is not a good indicator of future volatility levels.
- And, so far I've ignored other more complex derivatives areas like yield curve modeling, Bermudan swaptions or the relatively new field of credit derivatives.

The Moral: You should really be depressed at the recalcitrance and contempt that security prices have for options theory. If you're a trader and you let slip your usual belief in your supernatural predictive powers or your luck, or if you're a typical academic and you drop your naive belief in the possibility of finding the "right" model and using it happily ever after, you could get seriously low-spirited and glum, and perhaps even ask whether the Black-Scholes model is a BS model. But it's not, it's what we've got and the world goes on. So, what do you do when your responsibility is managing derivatives risk?

SOME PRINCIPLES FOR MANAGING DERIVATIVES RISK

You cannot naively depend on a fully quantitative approach. Managing derivatives portfolios, from either a desk perspective or an enterprise-wide perspective, is at least as much art (in the sense of craft) as science. Models are all you have, but you have to have a love-hate relationship with them. You have to be sceptical about any particular model, but trusting in a cautious way of the use of models as a whole.

These are some of the principles we have come to employ from a firmwide point of view in dealing with all these issues.

1. Adopt a **qualitative as well as quantitative** approach. You should be quantitatively accurate only after you've been qualitatively sensible.
2. Verify values and hedging strategies **before deals are done** rather than after.
3. Try to model **the realistic behavior of the underlyer** as best you can.
4. Recognize that **there is no absolutely correct model**. For the social sciences, under whose roof a good part of derivatives trading falls, the "right" model is a holy grail or unobtainable *fate morgana*. Many academics foolishly think that models can be fit to the world once and for all, and then used over and over again while the world stays the same. That's not what happens in reality.

The purpose of these models is to interpolate smoothly, from the prices of known liquid instruments to illiquid or exotic ones for which there is incomplete price discovery. But even if you have completely liquid prices in a complex world, without a model you don't know how to hedge, so you still need a theory.

No-one has the luxury of knowing which model is right, and the environmental factors aren't stationary. One year it's oil that drives interest rates, then the Fed. So, the best thing is to look at a variety of plausible but consistent models, all representing possible market styles, and see how vulnerable you are by relying on one of them. A good way to use models is as a tool for exploring parallel universes, one of which may turn out to be the one we live in for a little while.

I'm **NOT** saying models are just a matter of convention. I'm saying it's hard to know what's right, and there may be **NO** long-term right. As Andy Warhol might have said, one day every model will be right, but only for 15 minutes.

5. Therefore, use models **to determine relative value**, as intuitively reasonable interpolating devices to get from liquid market prices through the model parameters to illiquid OTC deals. Financial models work much better for finding relative values, once calibrated, than for computing absolute rational values.

6. In view of the fact that markets and traders violate so many of the Black-Scholes assumptions, it makes sense to estimate what will actually happen. So, we like to **rely on the realistic simulated replication** of the behavior of our whole options portfolios to determine the statistical distribution of the P&L given some attainable replication strategy that includes discrete hedging and actual transactions costs. The mean of this distribution generates a reasonable mark. The standard deviation or uncertainty generates a reasonable estimate of the uncertainty or reserves or valuation adjustments that may ultimately be lost or gained during the lifetime of the position.

7. Finally, to look at worst cases, **scenario analysis** of an underlyer and its volatility in previous disasters is a good way to understand major risks. For example, in a sudden equity market decline, index volatilities usually rise, correlations between stocks rise, and short-term put volatilities rise the most.

A MULTI-FACETED APPROACH TO RISK MANAGEMENT

Because of all this, in Firmwide Risk at Goldman, we try to take a multi-faceted approach to handling derivatives risk management.

I'm in charge of the Derivatives Analysis group within the Firmwide Risk department. We don't belong to any particular product area. Our job is to ensure, from the firm's point of view, that the firm's derivative books, in all product areas, but especially the long-term illiquid OTC positions, are marked and hedged *appropriately*.

Given what I said in the previous section about the shortcomings of Black-Scholes, "appropriately" is a tricky word, because no-one knows what's right in valuing a derivative. You're always talking about the future behavior of volatility and correlation and jumps. By appropriately, we mean neither conservatively nor excessively, just as sensibly and honestly as one can.

We concentrate on long-term illiquid positions that are marked by model, where most of the uncertainty lies. Liquid listed positions are less of a problem or focus.

Organizationally, each business has its own traders, its own quantitative strategists, and its own software developers. We don't buy much in the way of models or software. There are tens of thousands of trades, hundreds or thousands of models and model variants being used.

From a practical point of view, our group lives in the space between the traders who do the deals, their strategists who help build the models to value and hedge them, and the controllers who are responsible for the certification of the marks. Sometimes we investigate prices and valuation adjustments for controllers, sometimes we build more detailed models and give them to the desk strategists, and sometimes we analyze the risks and models of whole areas.

Hiring

Here our theme is qualitative as well as quantitative. Traditionally, we hired mostly classic Ph.D. quants, preferably with some front office experience. Lately, we've also hired some (tired, but not totally exhausted) former traders with a quantitative background who can get beyond the mathematics and help us improve the link between traders and quants, and who can give us some insight into what is believable in market prices and what achievable in hedging. It's very important to get rid of some of the either/or barrier between traders and people with quantitative skills. We try to use these ex-traders in our group as a sort of Maxwell's demon to pass information in both directions between the traders and the modelers.

Control

Our first line of defense is the quality of the work done by the traders and strategists them-selves. We work closely with each product area and controllers to institute formal procedures for the production, validation, modification and maintenance of models by the quantitative strategists in each division. We do this to encourage care and to preserve a communal knowledge and history of what's being used and how reliable it is.

Most of the onus is on the product areas' strategists. Every model developed must have at least two people involved, one to create it and one to then analyze and test it. Groups that create the models must describe and justify their use. They must report model changes and code changes.

There are too many models. Each is carefully built but not everyone can be rigorously validated by us. So, in order to focus, we concentrate on those models that bear the greatest dollar risk for the desk. For example, for equity derivatives, we start with the models whose total volatility sensitivity *vega* summed over all deals in the book is largest. That's the model that most needs checking. Ideally, desk strategists then write a report that describes the logical underpinning of the model, its implementation, and the results of some tests that test the behavior of the model, showing that in certain simple limits the model pastes smoothly onto well-known results, that it produces smooth hedge ratios, etc.

We also have strict policies about moral hazard. We separate model-building and trading. We don't want traders marking their own deals with their own unverified models. But even if traders don't explicitly write their own models, they often do so implicitly in booking subtly exotic trades by shoe-horning them into simpler products and simpler models. This too is dangerous. Some honest mistakes have been made by traders on subtle quanto-style hybrid products, where the trader knows enough to understand that the drift on the underlyer must be modified to get it into Black-Scholes form, but does it incorrectly himself. It's best to have a defined product type for everything you trade.

Price Verification and Valuation Adjustments

Controllers, who see every new deal, let us know about anything non-standard and questionable. We look at the deal, the model being used, the data and calibration, and try to verify not just the numbers, but the thinking and the approach. Obviously, this still doesn't catch everything, but controllers are pretty smart about what they query.

Let me give two examples of the way in which we do price verification: (1) a long-term (20-year) swaption with quanto features, and (2) a long-term (4-year) equity derivative collar bought by someone who wants to protect a technology stock they cannot sell. Traders typically assign a single volatility in a reasonable way to model to each of these products, or perhaps two volatilities, in the case of the collar, one to each strike. In verifying this we want to understand more carefully what would happen to our investment in this illiquid position if it were held to expiration. In that case we would hedge it periodically over its lifetime.

We simulate the discrete hedging strategy over the life of the option, over all scenarios, including hedging cost, and look at the distribution of P&L that follows from hedging mismatches. Then we mark at the expected value including cost, and assign a reserve or valuation adjustment of, say, one standard deviation of uncertainty in the replicated value. This theoretically computed reserve varies with volatility and market level, as it should, and prevents traders from taking estimated and perhaps unrealistic profits before they are realized.

We believe that for illiquid positions, these simulation methods really do provide a more realistic and accurate mark than putting a single volatility or correlation into a simple model. Ultimately, we want the desks to use these slower but more careful models for pricing and hedging.

Investigating Product Areas and Their Models In General

Finally, when circumstances demand it, we try to operate at the highest level, looking at risk factors and models for whole product areas. Skew is a good example.

Before I came to work in Firmwide Risk earlier in the year, I knew only about the volatility skew in equities, which had been visible since the '87 crash. Now, during the last ten years, options markets have become more scared of sharp regime changes and more savvy about reflecting these regime changes in their valuations. There is now a volatility skew in the swaption market, in caps, in currencies, in commodities, and most recently in precious metals, usually with higher volatilities on the side in which people fear the large move. Every desk attributes a different cause to it and uses a different corresponding model. Even if you calibrate all models to the same vanilla options prices, different models produce different hedge ratios. In equities the skew might be mostly due to jumps and a negative correlation of volatility and index level. In swaptions, jumps may matter less and stochastic volatility more. It's important to use the model with the right explanation in that market to get the right exotic options prices, and the right vanilla hedge ratios.

When a new market feature like skew suddenly appears, we try to take a view from the high ground. We try to form an independent analysis of what the major risks are, what causes the skew, and then evaluate whether the models used reflect those risks accurately, not just numerically but in spirit. We try to look "through" the models, rather than at them.

Secondly, as I mentioned before, we like to repeat the same process for different imaginary but nevertheless still **self-consistent** worlds. No one knows exactly how clients and market makers will behave in the future, or even what's the right models today. So, we like to perturb not just parameters, but models too, doing imaginary experiments on the world itself. We might value options in a sticky-local-volatility world, then in a stochastic-volatility world, then a jump-diffusion world, each world calibrated to the skew and term structure. We want to see the right price in each of these regimes or market modes, to get a sense of how sensitive our positions are not just to the parameters in our model, but to our model itself.

If the range of values we get is very different from the desk's mark, it's a sign that thought and caution are required.

CONCLUSION

I began by pointing out just the shakiness of the foundation on which the details of vanilla options valuation rest. Nevertheless, models are all we have for valuing structured products and illiquid deals that don't have easily accessible market prices, and so use them we must.

Traders use options models as a device for generating prices. Put in a volatility, get your option price in dollars! But in my experience traders don't always have a good feel for the multiple ways in which the real world disrespects and violates the assumptions that underpin the models.

Our role in risk management is find the time to go one better—to deconstruct the models into their assumptions, to understand to what extent the models are just approximations, and then to make them more realistic in the details. We want to simulate over what traders actually do and how they actually hedge in real life in order to understand the proposed distribution of portfolio P&L, and then behave accordingly. Initially we do this to understand the accuracy of their marks and hedges, and to estimate valuation adjustments against the marked P&L. Ultimately, we want traders to mark in this more accurate way too.

But even as we use these models in more realistic simulations, we have to remember that there's more than one possible reality too. The worst catastrophes occur when traders or risk managers become idolators by believing more faithfully in their man-made formulas than in the diversity of human behavior, by assuming that they can capture it all in a circumscribed model. So for risk management, we have to use models seriously, but also to remember not to take them too seriously. We have to think of the variety of models that might be right, and do risk analysis across models as well as across model parameters.

4. REMARKS ON THE LEGAL RISKS OF DERIVATIVES

THOMAS A. RUSSO

Good morning. I'm pleased to be addressing the topic of risk management today and the ways in which I deal with risk management issues in my capacity as both Chief Legal Officer and Vice Chairman of Lehman Brothers, a global investment bank.

Let me begin by noting that the concept of risk management has evolved significantly in the seven and a half years since I joined Lehman Brothers. In the early 1990's, risk management meant simply market risk management and involved using quantitative tools, such as models, to predict market movements. As the global financial markets grew increasingly integrated through technological advances and the widespread use of over-the-counter derivatives, it became clear that financial market participants and the markets themselves faced a panoply of risks far beyond market risk. These additional risks, such as credit, documentation, legal and operational risks, are those that I wish to discuss today.

To effectively address risk management in this broad sense, it is essential to understand how each type of risk arises and how the risks relate to each other. In most high-profile financial crises, the problem begins with a market movement that adversely affects a market participant and ultimately highlights lapses in other risk areas. For example, in the Barings debacle, market losses on Japanese arbitrage trades led to the downfall of the bank, not because the bank had faulty risk models, but rather, because the bank lacked sufficient operational risk controls to prevent a rogue trader from mismarking his positions. Similarly, in the Hammersmith and Fulham case, a court permitted an English municipality to walk away from its losing derivatives position based on its lack of authority to enter into the trade, thus underscoring the necessity of obtaining adequate documentation regarding authority and capacity. In the 1994 Bankers Trust actions involving Proctor and Gamble, legal risk took center stage, as regulators and courts struggled to determine whether the swaps BT sold to P&G were securities subject to the U.S. securities laws or commodities futures or options subject to the federal commodities laws, or both. More recently, the Asian and Russian crises of 1998 and the losses associated with those irregular markets cast a spotlight on contract documentation and how important it is that documents cover all material terms and that they be properly executed. The crises of 1998 also precipitated the phenomenon of "documentation basis risk", in which economically identical transactions documented on different industry form documents could be valued differently on close-out due to differing notice and grace periods, as well as disparate valuation methodologies.

With respect to risk issues at Lehman Brothers, I'm often called on to wear either or both of my Chief Legal Officer and Vice-Chairman hats. My experience has revealed that when counterparties lose a lot of money on trades, they seek any avenue possible to avoid fulfilling their obligations—and these potential avenues out always seem to be risk areas that are controllable. To that end, counterparties seeking to renege often point to a lack of documentation or incomplete documentation as a way to avoid paying. They sometimes seek to recharacterize a trade as unauthorized or unenforceable. In all such instances, they waste time, money and legal resources that could be put to better use. It is these types of risk problems that are handled mainly in my Chief Legal Officer role.

As a senior executive, by contrast, my role proves far more interesting and productive in terms of risk management. In that connection, I am Chairman of Lehman's Operating Exposures Committee, which is composed of senior business and control leaders and seeks to mitigate a variety of ongoing risks Firmwide. As Chairman of that Committee, I am able to leverage the Firm's resources to tackle risk areas that are easily ignored or marginalized, such as documentation and operational risks. This Committee has strengthened numerous risk controls, ranging from creating comprehensive credit data and reporting systems, to establishing cutting-edge documentation policies and related technological processes, to rationalizing the Firm's entity structure, to enhancing the audit function. These risk control measures have worked well, thereby reducing the possibility that Lehman will be sued and that money will be lost. The less often I need to be troubled with such counterproductive litigation, the more time I can spend on actually reducing risk—a far more desirable endeavor, in my view.

The transformation from simply reacting as a lawyer to problems, to pro-actively preventing potential risks, marks a major evolution in my professional life—one that has brought me great satisfaction and, I believe, substantially heightened my firm's ability to effectively limit risk. For me, risk management is one of the most important aspects of my dual roles at Lehman Brothers and one that I am committed to pursuing so long as money is lost in markets and crises can arise at any time.

5. THE EVOLVING MARKET FOR CATASTROPHIC EVENT RISK

KENNETH FROOT

THE DISTRIBUTION OF CATASTROPHIC EVENT RISK

The distribution of catastrophic (cat) event risk is highly unfavorable without insurance and reinsurance. Individual households and companies are significantly exposed to their own property damage; and because they are not exposed to others' property damage, these entities are not rewarded with a financial gain if no cats occur. Households and corporations dislike this situation; they face a large potential downside from cats that affect them yet receive no upside when no cats occur.

Insurance, reinsurance, and the capital markets provide an obvious redistribution mechanism whereby those who are exposed can protect themselves against cat loss. Households and companies are risk averse; therefore, they will pay more than actuarial losses for insurance. This demand then translates into an upside for others. When there are no catastrophes, each entity's premiums are redistributed to others in the form of financial gains.

The Inefficiency of Catastrophic Event Risk Distribution

Clearly, a catastrophe risk distribution mechanism exists. But how well has it functioned historically? The answer is mixed. Many entities, particularly businesses, have large assets that remain greatly exposed to cat risk. This is because large insurance and reinsurance policies are difficult and sometimes costly to obtain. Indeed, even insurance companies that underwrite policies affected by cat events have, at times, experienced difficulty transferring substantial quantities of cat risk to reinsurers.

R.M. Levich and S. Figlewski (eds.). RISK MANAGEMENT. Copyright © 2001. Kluwer Academic Publishers. Boston. All rights reserved.

To demonstrate this, Figure 1 shows the fraction of cat losses that insurers protect through reinsurance, averaged across insurers.[1] Note that the fraction of protection is high for relatively small cat losses but low for moderate-sized cat events. For example, for cat events generating an $8 billion industry loss, only about 20 percent of marginal insurer losses would have been covered by reinsurance as of 1994.[2]

A well-working risk distribution mechanism would have an insurer, like any other company, ceding most of its own cat exposure. By self-insuring, companies are requiring their equity holders implicitly to provide the insurance.[3] After all, equity returns are the first to suffer when there is a cat event loss. Self-insurance is likely to be inefficient for several reasons.

First, equity investors typically expect high average returns. This is largely because equities have large amounts of undiversifiable risk—they move strongly with the entire stock market, and the stock market is volatile. By contrast, catastrophe risks can, for all intents and purposes, be fully diversified when embedded in standard portfolios of stocks and bonds.[4] As a result, both the returns and risks associated with cat exposures are likely to be lower than those associated with equities. Equity investors would prefer a pure high-risk/high-return investment and would rather not have the "reward dilution" associated with cat exposures.

Second, equity investors typically expect a long-lived, complex risk. (Even if their trading horizons are short, equity investors know that the current stock price telescopes back both short-horizon as well as long-horizon perceptions about the firm's prospects.) Equity risks are, therefore, not targeted to precise events over precise periods of time. Rather, they tend to be fuzzier and evolve over time. Their precise nature is, at least partially, opaque.

Cat risks, by contrast, can be analyzed as event risks. Writers of cat reinsurance receive a predetermined premium in exchange for protection against a prespecified event, with a predetermined maximum loss over a predetermined period of time. Whether embedded in a traditional reinsurance contract or in a cutting-edge cat bond, the event's nature is clearly defined. Even though the probability of the event may be uncertain, the risk doesn't evolve much and the scenarios that produce losses and gains are fairly transparent. The event risk is studied more when it has to stand alone. Modeling firms attempt to quantify the likelihood and severity of dollar damages and the models are then reviewed by specialists and investors. Much more light is cast on the risk than if it remained—unquantified and amorphous—embedded in equity.

Event-risk exposures' clarity and specificity make it easy to separate cat risks from other risks imbedded in equity, such as management risk, firm-specific product risk, firm-specific cost risk, industry-specific product risk, industry-specific cost risk, and general macroeconomic risk. It is fundamentally inefficient to take a clearly defined event risk and embed it into an ambiguous, multipurpose instrument like equity.

Closed-end mutual funds are a good example of the costs of clouding up clearly defined risks. Closed-end funds invest in publicly traded securities and then sell stakes in their portfolio to shareholders, much as open-end mutual funds do. The difference is that open-end funds allow shareholders to sell their shares back to the

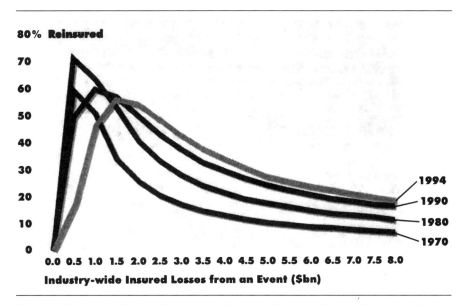

Figure 1. Percentage of Marginal Exposure that Insurance Companies Reinsure (by event size)

fund at a price dictated by the net asset value of the portfolio. Closed-end funds do not automatically buy and sell their shares. Rather, a shareholder wishing to sell must find another investor who wishes to purchase the shares. The price of the closed-end-fund shares, like the price of most traded stocks, must find its own value in the market-place in accordance with supply and demand.

There is, however, a puzzle associated with closed-end fund shares. Their prices are, on average, considerably below the net asset values of the shares they own. This cannot happen with open-end fund shares. Closed-end share discounts average about 10 percent to 20 percent and are pervasive across funds. Why is there such a discount? The reason is that share-holders can't observe or control what managers do next with the portfolio. If managers make bad trades, an investor would prefer to liquidate the portfolio at its net asset value. Investors will pay a lower price for a manager-controlled portfolio of stocks—that is, they demand a higher return on their capital when its control is given to a manager. The lack of transparency, clarity, and control associated with managerial discretion creates these higher capital costs. Closed-end funds are therefore expected to pay average returns in excess of what the underlying assets earn.

In this example, the underlying stocks in closed-end fund portfolios are analogous to clearly defined cat risks: the risks they represent are transparent and specific. Closed-end fund equity is analogous to other companies' equity. Just as closed-end funds could raise their market value by selling off a portion of their portfolios and returning the cash to investors, companies with cat risk could maximize their value by taking the cat risk out of their equity and letting it trade on a separate market for cat event risk.

Not incidentally, a direct implication of the closed-end fund argument is that reinsurers may be inefficiently funded and, therefore, that their reinsurance is expensive. Reinsurers underwrite pools of cat risk, retaining most and effectively self-insuring through their equity holders. Pooling helps diversify the cat risk, but it does not give equity investors the high-octane risk and reward they seek, nor does it retain the clarity of the component event risks. Reinsurers who are currently struggling with the need to earn "equity-like" returns on their underwriting activities increasingly have too much equity and too little event risk protection to be fully efficient.

Reasons for Inefficient Distribution of Catastrophe Risk

The above arguments suggest that cat event risk sharing is currently inefficient. Why is this the present state of affairs? Reasons include the following:

- *Lack of objective information.* Technology and computer modeling of natural perils have only recently reached the point where the risks can be cheaply and objectively clarified. If little can be said objectively about the risk of an event, then risk sharing is less likely to occur, because buyers (i.e., assumers) of the risk worry that they will be sheep and that sellers will be wolves. Cat risk tends to accumulate and firms self-insure.

- *High cost.* A second but related reason for the inefficient distribution of cat risk is that it is costly to back cat protection with capital. These "frictional" costs can add up to be a significant portion of the premium. For example, suppose that financial technology is such that the cost of assembling a pool of funds from investors is two percent of the size of the pool. These "deadweight" costs of creating the pool can be large relative to the premium the pool can be used to generate. Thus, these costs make it expensive to provide protection for unlikely events. Of course, as financial technology improves so that it is cheaper to assemble the pool, the inefficiency diminishes.

- *Barrier to entry caused by lack of objective information.* Another reason the institutional arrangement may be inefficient is that the lack of objective information acts as a kind of barrier to entry. When objective information is costly to assemble, a greater investment is required to get into the underwriting business. Indeed, when objective information is in short supply, markets tend to be organized around relationships and reputation. By contrast, when objective information is plentiful, markets tend to be organized around transactions, with the players being more interchangeable. Because newcomers are discouraged from entering the market, the incumbents who specialize in underwriting cat risks (e.g., cat risk reinsurers) can more easily charge high prices.

Competition and innovation are making today's markets more efficient. It is therefore useful to understand where this greater efficiency will take us. As we have

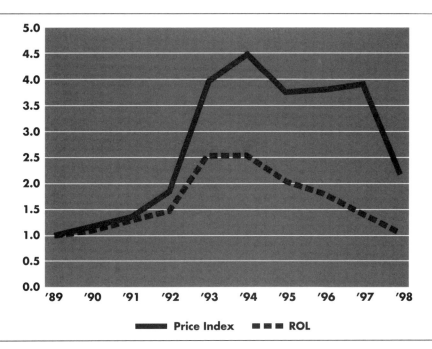

Figure 2. Price Level of Reinsurance Contracts (1989–1998)

argued, we are likely to see that companies will maximize their market values best by ceding cat event risks into a cat event risk market and nonspecific risks into the equity market. As Adam Smith saw centuries ago, specialization is the key to greater efficiency.

Evidence of Improving Efficiency

Cat risk distribution has been, and to a degree still is, inefficient. But our real emphasis is on the forces of change. The recent increase in efficiency is, of course, hard to measure. However, considerable evidence exists that is consistent with recent improvement.

Most important is the evidence that the price of cat event protection has fallen for the past four years. Figure 2 shows the average rate on line (ROL) of catastrophe excess-of-loss contracts for the decade from 1989 to 1998.[5] ROL increased substantially following Hurricane Andrew in 1992. By 1993, ROLs averaged 2.5 times the 1989 level. Then, beginning in 1993, rates began to fall. ROL fell steadily from 1994 through 1998. As indicated in Figure 2, the ROL of today's market is at approximately the same level as in the late 1980s—before the impact of Hurricane Andrew and the Northridge earthquakes.

However, it is important to remember that ROL can be a misleading measure of the price of reinsurance. For example, suppose ROL stays constant, but the retention (i.e., deductible) specified in the reinsurance contract falls. All else being equal, this means that the reinsurance is invoked more frequently. In effect, more protection has been purchased for the same overall cost, so the price per unit has actually fallen.

In addition to showing ROL, Figure 2 provides an improved measure of price. The price index, compiled and calculated by Guy Carpenter & Company, Inc., adjusts ROL for changes in retention. Clearly, the price index shows an even more dramatic change in price, upwards in the immediate aftermath of Hurricane Andrew, then downwards thereafter. Thus, the basic impression that comes out of Exhibit II is not due to mismeasurement—prices did indeed fluctuate substantially in the 1990s, as it first appears.

Capacity fluctuations are one explanation for these price changes. Prices rose in the early 1990s because capacity was reduced (i.e., the supply of reinsurance fell as a result of catastrophe losses from events). Subsequently, there were few large cats, which led to a regeneration of capacity. Of course, aficionados will point out this "supply-side" story is not the only possibility. There is a second explanation: price changes might also have been demand driven. That is, demand for reinsurance increased following the occurrence of Andrew and Northridge and then fell with the paucity of additional cats. It is not immediately clear which force—supply or demand—was more important in generating the prices shown in Figure 2.

However, we can distinguish between these two explanations by examining the two curves in Figure 2 more carefully. The fact that the price index amplifies the movements in ROL implies that less reinsurance was purchased as prices rose and more was purchased later when prices fell. This pattern is not consistent with a demand effect, which would say that more (less) reinsurance would be purchased during times of increasing (decreasing) prices. Only supply shifts could generate the price and quantity patterns we observe.

In other words, over the last four years, the price of reinsurance has fallen, while the quantity of reinsurance purchases has risen. (Note that the quantity purchased has increased particularly strongly in the last year of the sample. This suggests that for the years immediately preceding 1997, prices declined less rapidly than suggested by the ROL.) Only changes in supply could account for this pattern. And increases in supply come from greater competition and efficiency in production. In some sense, the reinsurance market is like the computer chip market—increasing efficiency allows prices to decrease even while quantities soar.

There is also evidence that the improved efficiency in the provision of reinsurance has affected the reinsurance buying patterns of insurers. Figure 1 shows that over time insurers have come to purchase greater amounts of coverage for midsized and large events. Beginning in 1994, the fraction of large losses being reinsured may be low, but it is nevertheless much higher than before. Greater competition in the reinsurance market seems to have improved the sharing of cat event risk.

FINANCIAL INNOVATIONS

Financial innovation permits greater competition among capital suppliers. In the last few years, clear and well-defined cat event risks have been brought directly to investors for the first time. This direct sourcing of investor capital can improve efficiency by removing layers of management, separating cat risk from equity risk, and improving the information with which those who bear the cat risk have to work. In this section, we discuss several of the mechanisms that have been used thus far to securitize cat event risk.

Table 1 provides a listing of most of the important securitized cat event risk transactions to date. Because these are the first transactions to occur, there is as yet little standardization. Each transaction is different and challenging in its own way. The purpose of this section, however, is not to uncover the fine details of each. Examples are used from Table 1, but the goal is to convey a broad characterization of the securities and the way they work. With an emphasis on the functional characteristics of these innovations, it is possible to think about the opportunities and limitations for new, yet-to-be-completed transactions.

There are two basic methods of delivering cat event risk directly to investors: financing transactions and risk-transfer transactions. Financing transactions are those that, upon the occurrence of an event, exchange funds from investors with securities. In a financing transaction, the securities require the insured to repay investors over time, and the exchange of securities for cash is done at fair value at the time of the exchange. Thus, when the cat event occurs, the investor loses no money: $100 worth of securities is received in return for $100 in cash. The main risk faced by investors, therefore, is that they are obliged to come up with the cash quickly. A standard credit facility with a bank is an example of a pure financing transaction (however, drawdown on a credit facility is generally not tied to cat events).

Risk transfer transactions are different. Here, the investor loses when the cat event occurs. Specifically, the investor purchases securities with predetermined event-linked payments. This exchange occurs before the cat event. If and when a cat event occurs, investors receive less than full or no repayment. In this way, investors share in the event-linked loss of the insured. If no event occurs, investors share the insured's upside. With risk transfer, the insured company and its stockholders bear less cat event risk than they otherwise would. Reinsurance and insurance are examples of more of less risk-transfer arrangements, though they are not capital market instruments and they sometimes contain financing elements.

Risk transfer solutions are likely to be a richer area for innovation than risk financing transactions. Better risk sharing—which is critical—can be accomplished only through better risk transfer. On the other hand, contingent risk financing can be accomplished in a number of ways. For example, the ability to perform straight financing operations (through debt, equity, or any other instrument) whenever desired obviates any strong need for contingent financing. Moreover, financing methods for general-purpose contingencies—such as bank credit facilities—are close substitutes and are widely available.

Financing Catastrophic Event Risk: Contingent Surplus Notes

In terms of financing linked to cat events, there are two main prototypes. The first is an event-linked issuance of debt. Insurers who have done this have typically issued

Table 1. Overview of major catastrophe securitization issues 1995–1998

Issuer	Date closed	Amount ($mm)[5]	Maturity	Trigger type	Coupon	Probability of attachment
Normandy Re[1]	prior to 95	25+	3yr	PCS Index	LIBOR + 550	1%
ACE Ltd.[1]	1995/96	45	14mo	PCS Index	UST + 450	2%
Cat Ltd.[1]	1995/96	50	5mo	UNL	LIBOR + 1075	1.1%
CA Earthquake Authority[2]	1995/96	1000	4yr	UNL		1.27%
AIG, PX Re	5/96	10	20mo	Index	0	25%
Georgetown Re (notes), St. Paul Re	12/96	44.5	11yr	UNL	6.097%	Various
Georgetown Re (pref. shares), St. Paul Re	12/96	24	3yr	UNL	14.15%	Various
Hannover Re II	12/96	100	5yr	UNL	50% profit	20%
Winterthur	1/97	SF399.5	3yr	Index	2.25% SF	20%
SLF Re,	4/97	10	16mo	Index	LIBOR + 900	15%
Reliance National						
USAA, Residential Re A-1	6/97	163.8	12mo	UNL	LIBOR + 273	.7%[4]
USAA, Residential Re A-2	6/97	313.2	12mo	UNL	LIBOR + 576	.7%[4]
Reinsurer Swap	7/97	35	11mo	Index	LIBOR + 519	.7%[4]
Swiss Re A-1	7/97	42	2yr	PCS Index	LIBOR + 255	.41%[4]
Swiss Re A-2	7/97	20	2yr	PCS Index	8.645%	.41%[4]
Swiss Re B	7/97	60.3	2yr	PCS Index	10.493%	.68%[4]
Swiss Re C	7/97	14.7	2yr	PCS Index	11.952%	Approx. 1%
Parametric Re—Notes	11/97	80	10yr	Parametric	LIBOR + 430	.70%[4]
Parametric Re—Units	11/97	10	10yr	Parametric	LIBOR + 206	.70%[4]
Trinity Re A-1	2/98	22.036	9mo	UNL	LIBOR + 182	.83%[4]
Trinity Re A-2	2/98	61.533	9mo	UNL	LIBOR + 436	.83%[4]
USAA, Residential Re	6/98	450	11.5mo	UNL	LIBOR + 416	.60%[4]
Yasuda, Pacific Re	6/98	80	5–7yr	UNL	LIBOR + 370[3]	.94%
Reliance National II	6/98	20	9mo	Index	LIBOR + 925	11.06%[4]
USF&G, Mosaic Re Tranche 1—Class B Notes	7/98	21	1yr	UNL	LIBOR + 820	2.75%[4]
USF&G, Mosaic Re Tranche 2—Class A Notes & Units	7/98	24	1yr	UNL	LIBOR + 440 / LIBOR + 210	.61%[4]

Sources: Goldman Sachs, Sedgwick Lane Financial, Guy Carpenter & Company, Inc., Morgan Stanley & Co.

[1] Deal not closed—data represents proposed plan.

[2] Deal withdrawn and replaced with a traditional reinsurance contract closed with Berkshire Hathaway.

[3] The Pacific Re terms also included a second-event drop down mechanism which pays LIBOR + 950bps and has a 5.12% attachment probability.

[4] Percentages represent expected loss.

Table 2. A sample of large surplus note issues

Issuer	Issue date	Maturity (Years)	Principal ($mm)	Offer yield	New issue spread to comparable U.S. Treasury (bp)
Anthem	3/26/97	30	$200.0 mm	9.04%	204
Jackson National	3/13/97	30	250.0	8.18	120
Lumbermens Mutual	6/19/96	30	400.0	9.18	206
Equitable	12/13/95	10	400.0	6.98	124
Equitable	12/13/95	20	200.0	7.73	181★
Metropolitan Life	11/08/95	30	250.0	7.00	75
Metropolitan Life	11/08/95	20	200.0	7.73	143
Minnesota Mutual	9/21/95	30	125.0	8.25	169
Prudential	7/17/95	13	100.0	n.a.	
Prudential	6/29/95	30	250.0	n.a.	
Prudential	6/29/95	12	350.0	n.a.	
Liberty Mutual	5/11/95	30	150.0	8.52	153
Liberty Mutual	4/27/95	12	250.0	8.24	117★
Nationwide (Contingent)	2/13/95	30–10	392.0	n.a.	220
Farmers	7/25/94	10	100.0	n.a.	
Farmers	5/11/94	30	300.0	n.a.	
Principal Mutual	3/03/94	50	100.0	8.09	125★
Principal Mutual	3/03/94	30	200.0	7.94	110
John Hancock	2/25/94	30	450.0	7.44	71
Massachusetts Mutual	2/22/94	30	300.0	n.a.	
Nationwide	2/14/94	30	300.0	n.a.	103
Nationwide	2/14/94	10	200.0	n.a.	68
New England Mutual	2/03/94	30	150.0	7.94	163
General Amer. Life	1/14/94	30	107.0	7.72	142
New York Life	12/08/93	30	300.0	7.52	120
New York Life	12/08/93	10	150.0	6.40	73
Metropolitan Life	10/28/93	30	300.0	n.a.	130
Metropolitan Life	10/28/93	10	400.0	n.a.	95
Prudential	4/21/93	10	300.0	n.a.	112

Note: Spreads for 12 yr and 20 yr issues are calculated from interpolated yields (straight line) using 10 yr and 30 yr Treasuries. 50 yr issue is shown as spread to 30 yr Treasury.
Source: Securities Data Corporation and USAA.

surplus notes, which are basically debt instruments that for regulatory purposes may be treated as capital. In spite of their status as statutory surplus, surplus notes generally oblige the issuer to repay the funds on a fixed schedule. As a result, these transactions cannot transfer risk; cat event losses are still borne by the company and its equity holders. The contingent part of contingent surplus notes is that the investors agree to accept the surplus notes not when the deal is struck, but when a particular event, such as a cat event, occurs.

Table 2 lists surplus note issues. Most of these issues are straight surplus notes: insurers borrowing funds directly, which they then use as statutory capital. Investors receive the repayment in the form of interest and principal, or if the issue is structured as a preferred stock, in the form of dividends and principal.

Only a few companies have issued contingent surplus notes: Nationwide, Hannover Re, and Arkwright. In these transactions, investors place funds into a safe account and receive account-ownership certificates. Initially, the account holds U.S. Treasury bills. Interest on the Treasuries passes through to investors, so it is as though investors are holding safe government securities. However, there is an additional wrinkle: under a set of pre-established conditions, the insurer (or reinsurer) can withdraw the liquid Treasury securities from the account and replace them with its own surplus notes. At that point, investors would receive interest and principal from the issuer, so they would bear the credit risk associated with potential issuer default. Investors are compensated in two ways for this added risk. First, the surplus notes pay a higher coupon than U.S. Treasuries; second, starting at the time the safe account is established, the issuer pays investors a premium for the right to "put" its own surplus notes into the account and withdraw the funds. In a pure financing transaction, the higher coupon on the surplus note would by itself be sufficient to compensate investors for the possibility of issuer default. In that case, the "put" premium would be compensation only for liquidity—that is, for knowing that the facility is there when it is needed.

Financing Catastrophic Event Risk: Contingent Equity

An alternative to contingent debt is, naturally, contingent equity. The setup is similar: the insurer pays a fee to investors for the right to issue equity later in return for cash. When issued, the equity would fetch the going market price, so that investors would receive $100 worth of stock for $100 of cash. What makes contingent equity different from a vanilla equity issue is the modifier "contingent": the trigger for the issue is cat-related event losses incurred. As long as investors receive the stock issue at the then-fair price, contingent equity is a pure financing vehicle. Although investors do not lose money when the equity is "put," they require nevertheless a payment in return for the contingency. This payment can be thought of as compensation for the investor remaining sufficiently liquid to purchase the put equity on demand.

In practice, the transactions involving contingent equity have been slightly more complex. Partly as a result, they may include elements of risk transfer as well as risk financing. A good example of a contingent equity transaction was a $100 million issue by a Bermuda reinsurer. The reinsurer paid approximately $2.4 million per year to investors for the right to sell them $100 million in preferred shares. The reinsurer was entitled to exercise this right if its losses from a single cat event exceeded $200 million or if its aggregate losses for any year exceeded $250 million. The preferred shares paid dividends of LIBOR plus a spread. The spread was set according to a predetermined schedule—higher if the reinsurer's credit rating was low at the time of the issue and lower if its credit rating was high at the time of the issue. This helped insure that investors would suffer only minimally if cat losses reduced the reinsurer's creditworthiness. Once issued, the preferred shares were convertible to the reinsurer's common equity. The conversion was to be effected at the 30-day average stock price prior to conversion.

In order to be predominantly a financing vehicle, this structure attempts to minimize any risk transfer component. The dividends on the preferred stock are set according to the credit rating at the time of the contingent issue. And the preferred stock is converted to common at the current fair price. Thus, while cat losses may trigger the reinsurer's need for financing, they are unlikely to impose a loss on investors. Just as in the contingent surplus note transactions, investors need only supply the cash to buy fairly priced securities in the aftermath of cat event losses.

Thus far, there have been relatively few contingent-risk financing transactions—debt or equity—even in the presence of a large market in finite reinsurance. There are apparently too many close substitutes available at competitive cost. Reliable financing in the aftermath of a cat event can be found either through an on-the-spot ex post issue of a debt or equity or through a prearranged ex ante contract that allows drawdown at any time. Indeed, the distinction between even the ex post and ex ante solutions is blurred by conventions such as shelf registration, which allows for very rapid access to commercial paper or other medium funds.

Transferring Catastrophic Event Risk: Act-of-God Bonds

In most instances, however, financing cat event risk is not enough. Suppose, for example, a cat loss occurs that is larger than the going-concern value of an insurer. Could the insurer arrange a pure financing transaction in anticipation of that loss? The answer is no. Investors would not provide contingent financing because their securities would be dead on arrival, worth less than their purchase price. The going-concern value would be lost if the insurer had to rely only on risk financing. Risk transfer, however, can preserve the going-concern value. By ensuring that its cat event exposures are shared, the firm can safeguard its future.

Standard insurance and reinsurance contracts are reasonably elegant techniques for transfer of cat risk. But like any real-world technique, they are not perfect. First and foremost, the cedent bears the credit risk of the insurance or reinsurance counterparty. There is usually no ironclad "quadruple A" guarantee that the insurance protection will be there when the insured becomes entitled to it. The problem can be diminished—though not eliminated—by buying reinsurance from a collection of reinsurers. Moreover, dividing the transaction up into pieces at times can be costly.

Second, in the past, cat reinsurance agreements included the tacit understanding that there was a financing element to the transaction. The traditional reinsurance transaction was in fact not pure risk transfer, and this was a shortcoming. After a cedent declared a loss under the contract and the loss was paid, it was assumed that the cedent would continue buying reinsurance from the same provider and that it would voluntarily do so at a higher price. The higher price didn't so much reflect an increase in the probability of loss as it provided the reinsurer the opportunity to recoup paid losses. Pure risk transfer transactions, by contrast, are "memoryless"—their terms are set according to the risk at hand and are otherwise independent of previous outcomes. Of course, there is nothing about the reinsurance contract itself that requires consideration be paid for past claims. So this "shortcoming" is more a matter of industry culture. And, perhaps as a consequence, this aspect of reinsurance is likely to change going forward.

Cat bonds perform a risk transfer function similar to that of insurance and reinsurance. They also avoid the shortcomings mentioned above. With a cat bond, investors place cash into a safe account from which they receive interest. This account is normally structured as a safe trust. The proceeds of the account are available to the cedent only if a cat event loss occurs. In return for this benefit, the cedent pays into the account a premium, which is transferred (in addition to interest) directly to investors. If there is no event loss, the safe account remains just that—safe. After interest and premium is paid to investors for a prespecified period of time (usually from one to three years), the full principal is returned to investors. However, should there be an event loss, the investor will receive only that portion of principal and interest that is left after paying the cedent's event losses.

The first thing to note about this structure is that it resolves some of the shortcomings of traditional insurance and reinsurance contracts. The cedent bears no credit risk. The funds are remote from any other claims or possible uses while in the safe account; they are there for the sole purpose of paying cedent event losses in case there is an event. Also, because the cat bond is purchased in the capital markets, it is a memoryless transaction with no judgements about past events. There is no relationship to manage between investors and the insured. Investors cannot extract a "repayment" for the losses of prior cat bond investors. Prior losses may raise the perception of future losses, but in no sense would the cedent in a transaction be paying back the investors who lost last time around.

The second thing to note about cat bonds is that they may have an unexpected and surprisingly widespread positive side effect: improving the general clarity of corporate bond analyses and ratings. With cat models serving as reference points, a given cat bond will have a certain likelihood of paying in full and an average recovery payment when payment isn't full. The promised yield on the bond will depend on both. This is, investors require a higher yield to compensate either for a lower probability of full repayment or for a lower recovery amount, given default. The rating, too, will need to take both probability and recovery into account. Figure 3 shows how Fitch summarizes the relationship between rating, probability, and recovery. Each rating curve in the exhibit is generated by a set of probabilities and recovery rates. The higher the probability of full repayment, the lower the recovery rate must be if the same rating level is to be maintained.[6]

In the past, rating agencies have never been precise about the exact combinations of probability and recovery that result in a given rating for any kind of bond. In fact, some rating agencies (e.g., Standard & Poor's) have maintained that they evaluate only probabilities and not net recovery when assigning ratings. In the context of cat, this makes little sense. And, when one thinks about it, this makes little sense in any context. Recovery rates clearly affect investor risk and reward, so they should also affect ratings. It seems that precision modeling of cat events (however rudimentary it may be) has generated additional clarity on what ratings mean. Over time, this will lead to improvements in the transparency of the ratings process.

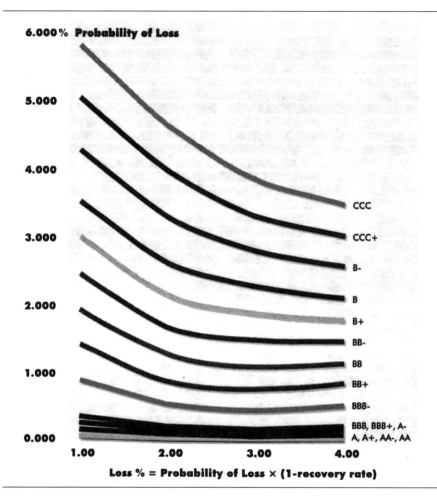

Figure 3. Fitch Iso-Rating Curves

The third thing to note about in the cat bond approach is that it, too, has short-comings. Clearly, it is costly to set aside enough in an account large enough to pay the largest possible loss under the cedent's contract, no matter how unlikely that loss is. Consider the fact that approximately $186 billion in capital and surplus backs all worldwide property/casualty reinsurance contracts issued by the world's top 100 reinsures.[7] If these traditional contracts were alternatively structured as cat bonds, they would require the sum of all limits—nearly one trillion in capital. While it is not unthinkable that such a large sum of money could be raised, it is certainly a very large amount—on the order of the amount tied up in securitized mortgages. It would seem inefficient to raise the maximum potential loss for each and every risk, especially those risks for which the probability of loss is tiny. To the extent that the losses are unlikely and uncorrelated, it becomes more efficient to pool the risks together in a fund. That looks more like the traditional solution, reinsurance.

To demonstrate in greater detail how a cat bond works, it is useful to examine the 1997 USAA transaction, the largest single securitized risk transfer to date.[8] In this case, the safe account was a trust, administered by an offshore special purpose reinsurer (SPR) called "Residential Re." The SPR had no business purpose other than to sell a one-year $400 million reinsurance contract to USAA and to issue $400 million in risk-transfer securities to fully collateralize that reinsurance.[9] The proceeds of the issuance were held in a trust and invested in highly rated, short-term investments such as commercial paper. In the event of a catastrophe, the trustee would have sold the investments to cover 80 percent of USAA's losses in excess of $1 billion (until the $400 million is exhausted). In return for this reinsurance, Residential Re received a premium from USAA of 600 basis points ($24 million). The premium, along with virtually all of the interest on the commercial paper, went directly to investors, regardless of whether USAA experienced a loss.

To fund the reinsurance, Residential Re issued securities of two types: principal variable and principal protected. If there was a loss, principal variable investors would have lost some or all of their initial investment. These notes paid interest at a rate of LIBOR plus 575 basis points (this is essentially interest plus the reinsurance premium of 600 basis points, less about 25 basis points for costs).[10] The principal protected securities would have had their principal repayment delayed for ten years in the event of a loss, with a reduction in interest along the way. The principal protected securities paid LIBOR plus 273 basis points. Figure 4 and Table 3 provide additional details of the transaction structure.

Transferring Catastrophic Event Risk: Standardized Contracts

Cat event bonds are not the only vehicles for transferring risk. Swaps and forward contracts can be linked to cat losses in much the same way, as can bonds. However, these "derivative" contracts have an important short-coming that bonds do not share—credit risk. Much like traditional reinsurance contracts, the cedent has a claim only on a counterparty, not a safe account. So it isn't surprising that securitized contracts that simulate insurance or reinsurance tend to be structured as bonds.[11]

However, full collateralization is not the only way to reduce credit risk. Exchanges can reduce credit risk by marking to market frequently and by standing in between buyer and seller to guarantee contract performance. With this problem solved, the exchanges are positioned to offer another benefit: the liquidity associated with trading standardized instruments. This is a benefit, indeed, because high-volume, low-cost trading in standardized cat event linked contracts would seem an effective means of improving risk sharing.

To achieve standardization, exchanges have linked cat event futures and options contracts to aggregated measures of cat losses. The payoffs on these contracts are therefore tied to industry, rather than individual, losses. The Chicago Board of Trade

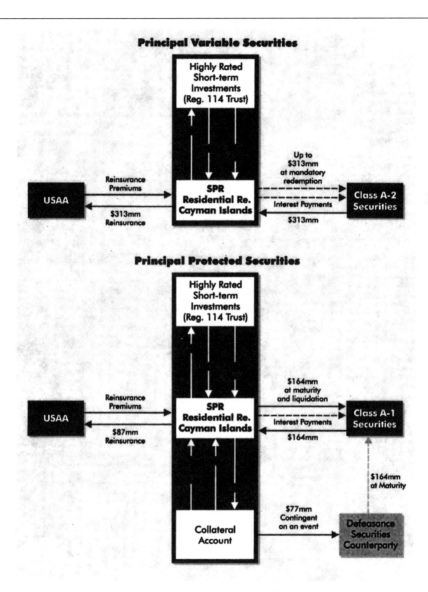

Source: Kenneth A. Froot and Markus F. Mullarky, "Mid Ocean Limited—Trading Catastrophe Index Options," Harvard Business School, case no. 9-298-073, April 1998.

Figure 4. USAA Cat Bond Transaction Structure

Table 3. Cat bond contract specifications

Obligor:	Residential Reinsurance Limited, a Cayman Island reinsurance company, whose sole purpose is to provide reinsurance for USAA		
Amount:	Class A-1:	$164 mm	$87 mm principal variable
			$77 mm principal protected
	Class A-2:	$313 mm	100% principal variable
Yield:	LIBOR plus: 575 basis points for the Class A-2 notes; 273 basis points for the Class A-1 notes. Interest is paid semiannually.		
Loss Occurrence:	A Category 3, 4, or 5 hurricane		
Reinsurance Agreement:	Residential Reinsurance Limited will enter into an reinsurance agreement with USAA to cover approximately 80% of the $500 mm layer of risk in the excess of of the first $1,000 mm of USAA's Ultimate Net Loss		
Ultimate Net Loss:	Ultimate Net Loss = amount calculated in Step 6 (below)		
	Step 1 All losses under existing policies and renewals		
	Step 2 All losses under new policies		
	Step 3 9% of the amount calculated in Step 1		
	Step 4 Add the amount from Step 1 with the lesser of Step 2 & 3		
	Step 5 Multiply Step 4 by 1.02 for boat and marine policies		
	Step 6 Multiply Step 5 by 1.02 to represent loss adjustments		
Coverage Type:	Single occurrence[1]		
Coverage Period:	June 16, 1997 to June 14, 1998		
Ratings:	Class A-1:	Rated AAA/Aaa/AAA/AAA by S&P, Moody's, Fitch, and D&P, respectively	
	Class A-2:	Principal variable notes are rated BB/Ba/BB/BB by S&P, Moody's, Fitch, and D&P, respectively	
Covered States:	Alabama, Connecticut, Delaware, Dstrict of Columbia, Florida, Georgia, Louisiana, Maine, Maryland, Massachusetts, Mississippi, New Hampshire, New Jersey, New York, North Carolina, Pennsylvania, Rhode Island, South Carolina, Texas, Vermont, and Virginia.		

[1] Unlike traditional reinsurance, the form of reinsurance offered by Residential Re was limited to one occurrence. If there was a hurricane that caused $1,300 mm of damage, the contract covered 80% of $300 mm. If there was another storm that produced USAA losses of more than $1,000 mm, USAA would no longer be covered.

is trading futures and options linked to the Property Claims Service (PCS) index, and the Bermuda Commodities Exchange is trading contracts linked to the Guy Carpenter Catastrophe Index (GCCI).[12] Table 4 provides data on the exchange-traded contracts.

Standardized contracts have several important features worth noting. First, because of the aggregated nature of the indexes, they are not designed to indemnify—that is, to match the losses of—any particular entity. As a result, any given insurer, reinsurer, or corporation ceding risk through these contracts will experience "basis risk" deviations between cedent losses and those paid by the contract. Sometimes when the cedent experiences a loss, the contract will not pay as much as the loss; sometimes it will pay more. All else being equal, this makes aggregate standardized contracts less attractive.

But the size of the basis risk varies considerably. It depends in part on the nature of the insurance portfolio being hedged and the choice of index. Clearly, lumpy portfolios that contain a few large industrial assets will not show losses that are tightly linked to total cat losses across a large area like a state or region. Portfolios that contain homes evenly dispersed across an area will perform more like the area aggregate. Furthermore, most portfolio concentrations vary geographically. That is, market share changes considerably with location for insurance carriers. Indeed, market share varies not only across regions and states but also across counties and zip codes. Thus, the greater geographic disaggregation of the GCCI index proves valuable for many portfolios.

Second, although standardized contracts generate basis risk for hedgers, they simplify life for investors. Imagine if investors were to buy diversified portfolios of cat event risks by purchasing individual bonds. One at a time, investors would have to evaluate facilities such as Residential Re and the underlying risks of companies such as USAA. This is hard work and, even worse, redundant work. Each investor would need to separately analyze each individual risk. It is far more efficient for these risks to be bundled first into something that looks like an aggregated index before being marketed to investors. That way, each investor needs to understand only one kind of contract. The implication is that standardization makes it far less costly to distribute cat event risks widely.

Along these lines, it is interesting to note that in 1998 USAA placed a layer of reinsurance through Residential Re in a new securitized transaction. This layer had similar risk characteristics to the one placed in 1997, also through Residential Re, yet the pricing of the 1998 bonds was considerably lower. On a comparable basis, the 1998 bonds provided a one-year return over LIBOR of 416 basis points, compared with 576 basis points for the 1997 bonds. This decline in return partly represents savings by investors and intermediaries. They needed to expend far less time and energy understanding the transaction, having studied the same underlying package of risks one year earlier.

Third, it is worth distinguishing the role of standardization from that of the exchanges. Strictly speaking, standardization does not require an exchange, or for that matter even securities, to work. Traditional reinsurance contracts can (and are) standardized by adding triggers responsive to aggregated industry losses. However, the value of standardization is greater the more liquid the underlying contracts. With greater liquidity, standardized contracts can be sold and traded more widely. As with any other standard, the value is that everyone is on it.

THE FIVE KEY INGREDIENTS FOR A SUCCESSFUL CAT BOND ISSUE

When are cat bonds and other securitized forms of risk financing likely to work best? Of the structures we have seen so far—contingent surplus notes, contingent equity puts, and cat bonds—the bonds are the purest. They provide true risk transfer, which unlike pure financing alternatives does not merely prolong the day of reckoning. They avoid use of all-purpose equity financing, even on a contingent basis. They focus in on the cat event risks at hand, promoting greater transparency and helping to reduce the costs of capital. They provide large capacity with zero-credit risk protection funded by competitive capital markets.

Table 4. Comparison: the proposed Bermuda Commodities Exchange (BCOE) catastrophe linked options and the Chicago Board of Trade (CBOT) PCS options

	BCOE	CBOT
Membership		
Membership requirements:	• By application—no specific restrictions	• By application—no specific restrictions
The Contracts		
Index used:	• GCCI Index	• PCS Index
Reported metric:	• 1 unit = .01% industry loss-to-value ratio[1]	• 1 unit = $100,000,000 of industry losses
Geographic coverage:	• 7 geographic areas available: Northeast, Southeast, Gulf Area, Mid/West, Florida, Texas (subject to data availability) and National	• 9 geographic areas available: Northeast, Southeast, East Coast, Midwest, West, California, Florida, Texas and National
Types of coverage:	• Aggregate losses • Single and second loss	• Aggregate losses
Duration of loss periods:	• Semi-annual	• Annual/Quarterly[2]
Payoff structure:	• Digital/Binary[3]	• Graduated depending on ending value of index
Operations		
Clearinghouse used:	• Bermuda Commodities Exchange Clearing House	• Board of Trade Clearing Corporation
Clearing member requirements:	• No specific restrictions	• $1 million of BOTCC stock • $1.5 million of Memberships
Fees:	• $20 round trip transaction fee per trade • LIBOR −100bp interest on cash margin (after first $250,000) • 200bp/annum utilization fee on securities or letters of credit posted as margin	• Roughly $15 round trip transaction fee per trade[4] • Short term U.S. Treasury interest on cash margin (less ~50bp)[4] • Zero utilization fee on securities or letters of credit posted as margin
Margin requirements:	• 100% posted up front and held through the term of the contract ($5,000 per contract written) • Variation margin only posted if the market value of margin drops below $5,000	• Approximately 20% posted initially[5] and adjusted daily on a mark-to-market basis • Clearing firms may require Members to post additional trading margin
Settlement timeline:	• Variable—up to 13 months from the end of the contract	• Last business day of 12th month following end of loss period

Source: BCOE, CBOT.
[1] For example, it the industry is estimated to have suffered a loss to value ratio of 1.5%, the index will be published with a value of 150.
[2] California & Western contracts are annual, all others are quarterly (National contract available in both).
[3] Contract pays 100% of value ($5,000) if the ending index value is above the option strike value, and pays $0 otherwise.
[4] Includes the brokerage fee charged by clearing firms to process Members' trades.
[5] CBOT cat option participants post margin equal to the greater of the normal margin maintained by other CBOT option traders (and based on a 20% volatility) and 20% of their maximum potential losses.

However, as we have noted, cat bonds have weaknesses, and may not be appropriate in many circumstances. When, therefore, are cat bonds likely to be economically advantageous over traditional reinsurance? What conditions need to be present in order for cat bonds to be the preferred choice? In this section, we try to answer these questions by providing a list of ingredients—preconditions, really—that are likely to make cat bonds the risk-transfer mechanism of choice.

Ingredient #1: The Retention Should Be Substantial

Like traditional reinsurance, cat bonds need to cut possible losses into layers, so that each contract has an associated limit, or maximum possible loss. Low layers are those that are impacted frequently, as many cat events generate at least a low loss level. High layers—like the USAA example above—are those that are impacted relatively infrequently, as few cat event losses breach the contract retention (i.e., deductible). Most of the cat bond transactions in Table 2 have low probability of loss and therefore translate into relatively high reinsurance layers. Indeed, the highest likelihood of loss among all the transactions is only 25 percent, and most have been completed at a probability of loss closer to one percent—a one-in-a-hundred likelihood of loss.

Several factors make this the case. First, there are institutional issues associated with fixed-income investing that bias choice toward higher layers. This is because many institutional fixed-income investors are restricted in their mandates: they must hold predominantly bonds that are rated; and they must hold bonds that have minimum credit ratings.[13] The demand for higher-rated bonds is greater than for "junk" debt, which is deemed less than investment grade. In assigning a rating for bonds, credit-rating companies examine the probability of less than full repayment of principal and interest. A bond with an actuarial risk of loss of about two percent or greater is likely to generate a rating below investment grade, reducing the number and types of investors who can buy it.

Of course, with a little financial engineering, it is always possible to satisfy the rating agencies, improving the rating on relatively low-layer protection. The most common method is called "principal protection," which was used for the USAA Class A-1 notes. Under principal protection, some of the money raised from investors is never put at risk. Instead, it is used to purchase long-term zero-coupon U.S. Treasuries at a deep discount. Since these securities will eventually pay their principal with certainty, cat bonds can be designed to pay back their principal with certainty too. If there is a cat event, investors lose money because they have to wait a relatively long time to get their principal back; and along the way, interest payments are at less than market rates. Using this feature, the Residential Re Class A-1 notes received the highest rating, AAA, while the Class A-2 notes were judged as being below investment grade at BB (see Table 3).

Naturally, there is a cost to this method: it waters down the cat event risk embedded in the bond. Principal protection requires that much more than a dollar be raised for every dollar of risk transfer. The extra money finances the purchase of the principal protection. For example, in the USAA transaction, $164 million of Class

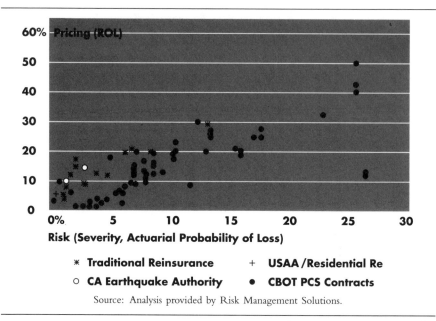

Figure 5. Comparison of Pricing and Riskiness of Different Types of Cat Risk Contracts

A-1 notes were issued. But of this amount, only $77 million went toward backing USAA's reinsurance. The rest went toward the purchase of zero-coupon U.S. Treasuries. As a result, the Class A-1 notes paid only 273 basis points above LIBOR, compared with 575 basis points for the Class A-2s. If USAA had wanted to protect a lower layer, this ratio would have been worse, with risk transfer making up an even smaller fraction of the money raised. Since marketing and distribution (and sometimes fee) costs of an issue depend critically on the amount raised, the costs of a low-layer cat bond become problematic.

There is a second, entirely different reason why low layers are not naturally transferred through cat bonds. Among insurers, reinsurers, and capital market investors, none like to bear the first dollar of loss from a risk. As a result, most contracts stipulate a deductible or retention. The reason is to give high-powered incentives to the original owner of the cat risk. If a loss is declared, the owner pays the first dollars. This encourages good cedent behavior—better risk mitigation, loss-evaluation monitoring, and so forth. It also protects risk writers against private information cedents may have about their risk. The lower the layer, the worse the pool of cedents to come forward. Cedents who privately know the risk is bad are the ones who most want a low deductible.

These issues—formally referred to as moral hazard and adverse selection—are particularly important for cat bonds because the capital markets are at arms' length from the cedent. Traditional insurance and reinsurance methods bring the risk writer much closer. This is accomplished through ongoing information conveyed by

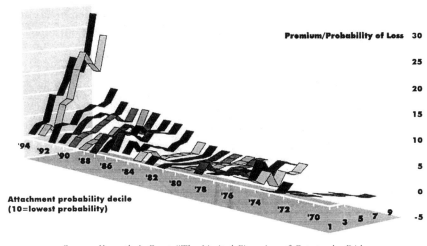

Premium/Probability of Loss

Attachment probability decile
(10=lowest probability)

Source: Kenneth A. Froot, "The Limited Financing of Catastrophe Risk:
An Overview," Harvard University, 1997.

Figure 6. The Ratio of Premium to Actuarial Probability of Loss, by Layer

brokers, by relationships, and by greater oversight and control over the cedent's risk-assumption process.

Over time, as arm's-length disclosure of information improves, lower-layer cat bonds may become more common. But as we discuss in Ingredients 4 and 5 below, techniques for managing moral hazard and adverse selection are crucial, and disproportionately so for lower layers.

The final reason that layers are likely to be high has to do with reinsurance pricing. So far, cat bond returns have more or less mirrored those of the reinsurance market. This is shown in Figure 5, which compares the pricing of cat bonds with traditional reinsurance contracts and options traded on the CBOT.[14] And the pricing in the reinsurance market has been the most attractive in the highest layers. While this is apparent in Figure 5, it is clearly seen in Figure 6, which depicts the historical pricing of lower versus higher layers. Basically, large cat risks are the risks most destructive to insurers and reinsurers because they create a large need for additional capital. The return for providing this additional capital is thus most generous relative to the risk. Thus, it is perhaps not surprising that cat bonds have been targeted to compete with upper reinsurance layers.

Ingredient #2: The Layer of Protection Shouldn't Be Too High

By itself, Ingredient #1 suggests that cat bonds are relatively more attractive as the layer becomes higher. This seems natural, given the limited capacity of traditional markets. Why not go out into the vast liquid capital markets for funding not just the next higher layer, but three or four layers beyond that? The answer, of course, is as layers become higher, risk transfer ultimately becomes less economical. As the layer becomes too high, the probability of loss becomes too low. With very low probability of loss, the premium ought to be very small. But a small premium will be insufficient to afford the costs of establishing the safe account, the SPR, or marketing and distributing the cat bond. Moreover, the risks embedded in each bond, however small, are still unique. This forces investors to spend costly time understanding each risk. Very low risk cat bonds simply do not pay.

To get a sense of how low premiums can go to be economical, it is worth considering several of the more precise costs of a cat bond issue:

- *Underwriting fee.* Bankers will charge an underwriting fee, which could range between 50 and 250 basis points of the risk transfer amount, depending on the complexity of the structure and the quality of the underwriter. Given the state-specific regulatory nature of insurance, in some cases considerable travel expenses need to be paid by the cedent in addition to the fee.
- *Legal costs.* The legal costs of establishing the SPR and trust account are likely to be considerable. The legal work is complex, because the SPR must have the ability to write insurance or reinsurance protection and issue claims that are designated as securities and not as insurance or reinsurance policies. So it is not a standard (and less-expensive) type of special purpose vehicle used to create asset- or mortgaged-backed securities. For cat bonds, the legal costs are likely to decline as the necessary legal expertise becomes more of a commodity. But currently this is not the case.
- *Cost of producing information on the risk.* Clients incur the cost of producing information on the risk for investors and rating agencies—in particular, fees to cat risk modelers. This cost can vary tremendously, depending on the risk. But it also can be a substantial expense.
- *Fees to the rating agency.* These are still somewhat higher than fees on normal corporate or asset-backed securities because of cat bonds' still novel nature.
- *Costs associated with capitalizing the SPV.* These costs include directors' fees, licensing fees, claims and reserve consultant retainers, insurance fees, and so forth.

Taken together, these costs can easily exceed 150 basis points on a $100 million issue. To see what this does to the economics of a high-layer cat bond, consider a bond with a one percent risk of loss. The actuarially fair premium on such a bond would be 100 basis points. Even if investors were willing to buy bonds that paid only actuarially fair rates, the bare minimum charge—premium plus issue costs to the cedent—for such a bond would be 250 basis points. The cost is 2.5 times the minimum rate that investors are willing to receive.

It may be that cedent demand for protection is very great, but at some point the amount of protection gets too small relative to costs. At increasingly higher layers, the probabilities of impact fall. Clearly, at a layer so high as to have an actuarial risk of one basis point, the cedent costs would total 15 basis points—more than 150 times as large! Unless the demand for protection is extremely inelastic, there is too little cedent protection in such a contract to make it worth the premium.

Ingredient #3: The Dollar Amount of Risk Transfer Shouldn't Be Small

Because a large portion of the costs enumerated above are fixed, the 150 basis point threshold grows as the limit shrinks. A $50 million issue would almost certainly require more than 200 basis points in cost. And the $400 million Residential Re risk transfer was done for at least 100 basis points. These costs must either be paid in addition to the premium or must come out of investors' take. Clearly, small issues quickly become uneconomical.

The fixed-cost problem can be handled in part by using multiyear contracts. Although these are currently difficult to engineer, over time they will get easier. Today, participants are very unsure about how cat risks and the associated premiums should evolve over time. Cedents may need to pay a higher premium to successfully launch a multiyear issue.

The fixed-cost problem can also be reduced through an increase in the market-wide volume of cat bond issues. Legal, modeling, and investment banking fees are all prone to competition. A larger volume will support more competitors and allow fixed costs to be better amortized. Costs will therefore decline. But cat bond volume will probably never grow large in comparison with that of other fixed-income markets such as corporate debt, asset-backed bonds, or mortgage-backed securities. So, at least for now, the prospect of razor-thin margins is a dim one.

Finally, over-the-counter transactions can be a partial solution to the costs above. The required level of underwriting fees, legal expenses, and modeling work can be reduced in small private transactions. This creates greater leeway in finding cat bond possibilities. However, small private deals are by definition small and poorly advertised. The cost to a cheap distribution network can be that there is less competition among buyers.

Ingredient #4: The Loss Trigger Should Be Beyond Cedent Control

Cedent control of the loss trigger is known as moral hazard. Moral hazard tends to keep markets from developing. No one will come to trade when the outcome of a contract can be determined by the entity on the opposite side of the trade. In most insurance market instances, however, control is partial and often minor (e.g., workers compensation, product and environmental liability, errors and omissions). In such circumstances, it is not so much that moral hazard precludes exchange; it is more that the disadvantaged side must be paid sufficiently. The greater is the moral hazard—the control a cedent has of its losses—the greater the cedent payment must be.[15]

The first point to make about moral hazard is that cat event risks provide relatively limited scope for it. Cat event risks are highly exogenous. So it is not surprising that they have been among the easiest insurance risks to trade. But, in spite of the exogenous nature of cat events, cedents may nevertheless exert some degree of control over their losses. For example, the benefits of aggressive mitigation measures and loss cost and payment monitoring may not inure to the cedent once cat risk has been transferred. As a result, the cedent may undertake less, increasing potential losses. Superior cat bond structures are those that reduce opportunities for cedent control.

Dual triggers are a second way in which the scope for moral hazard is reduced. Many cat bond triggers are linked to individual insurer losses (referred to ultimate net loss) as a first trigger, but there is almost always a second trigger as well.[16] One obvious second trigger is that the claimed losses be associated with a cat event as defined by Property Claims Service (PCS). In other instances, the second trigger adds a severity condition to the simple event trigger. Examples would be that a qualifying event must be a hurricane of class three or above, or an earthquake of magnitude 5.5, with an epicenter within a specific area.

A third way to reduce moral hazard is to eliminate the ultimate net loss triggers in a client trigger contract, leaving the company protection triggered off the size of industry losses associated with an event. A given company cannot manipulate industry cat losses as much as it can its own cat losses. So moral hazard with respect to industry losses is reduced.

Industry losses can be thought of as a kind of index to which individual company contracts can be benchmarked. The practical problem is that it is not easy to measure industry losses. Collecting data on losses that are directly related to a cat event is difficult. It requires sophisticated information technology to classify claims (and paid losses) as specifically associated with a cat event. Consolidating information across companies is difficult and slow, because each company collects and maintains information in its own way. As a result, existing indexes do not directly measure total industry-wide cat event losses, even though the concept seems straightforward enough.

In practice, different indexes measure different things. An index published by PCS polls insurers in the aftermath of a cat event, asking for estimates of their losses. This index has several virtues. Surveys can be conducted immediately after an event, making the result timely. The surveys are redone as claims come in, allowing for more accurate measures for a given cat over time.

However, the PCS index has major disadvantages. Because it is based on surveys rather than hard data, it is difficult—indeed, impossible—to verify the results. Manipulation by reporting companies is possible, and error is likely. Moral hazard therefore remains a concern with the PCS index. In addition, large companies sustain a large proportion of losses. This means that estimation errors by large companies will remain important in the overall industry result. Finally, and most important, the index is computed on a state-by-state basis. States are large areas in comparison with cat event footprints. Because many insurers' exposures are unevenly distributed throughout a state, individual insurer losses may correlate poorly with statewide losses. The index therefore provides less desirable protection for an insurer than would a contract linked directly to its ultimate net loss.[17]

A second approach to indexing is taken by the newly developed Guy Carpenter Catastrophe Index. It has several advantages as well. the GCCI is based on actual data from participating insurers. This removes guess-work and eliminates the scope for manipulation. These are advantages from the investors' perspective. The GCCI also makes it feasible to calculate disaggregated indexes on a zip code level. This is an advantage from the insurers' perspective, because it affords insurers better correlation with their own losses. Insurers can design a portfolio of zip code indexes to match their portfolio rather than rely on a one-size-fits-all statewide index.

The disadvantages of this index are a direct consequence of its use of hard data. Because the data collection requires time and considerable aggregation, GCCI results are available quarterly at prespecified times. More frequent updates are not yet possible. Also, not all insurers report their data to the GCCI. Thus, the index uses a sampling approach, estimating loss-to-value ratios from participating companies within a zip code. These loss-to-value ratios can be aggregated across companies within any zip code, then grossed up to estimate losses within the zip code. Of course, since the sampling approach is what actually makes the hard-data index computation feasible, it may be better to think of it as an advantage. Indeed, statistical work suggests that the sampling errors are reasonably small, especially in view of the index's geographic disaggregation. Finally, the index currently reports only homeowner losses on atmospheric cat events. Commercial/industrial losses and other events (such as an earthquake) are not covered.[18]

Some cat bonds have been tied to index outcomes rather than ultimate net losses. For example, Swiss Re set up an SPR to provide it with $112 million in California earthquake protection. The protection and the bonds issued by the SPR were linked to industry losses—measured by the California PCS index—associated with a single earthquake in California. For more details, see Table 1.

As already mentioned, indexes help reduce moral hazard on the part of the insurer. They also help standardize cat event risks, helping investors avoid analyzing the properties of each company's individual cat event risk. These features should, in principle, make index-linked protection cheaper (for the cedent) than indemnification through an ultimate net loss trigger. Currently, because there have been so few transactions, there is not much evidence that indexes are cheaper. But as investors begin to use indexes as benchmarks, a cost disparity should emerge.

Ingredient #5: The Loss Trigger Should Be Symmetrically Transparent

The last important ingredient concerns asymmetric information. It is clearly difficult to cede a risk to another party when it is known that the cedent has superior information. In that case, the buyer (the assumer) is a sheep and the seller a wolf. Cedents who wish to lower the costs of protection have an interest in credibly providing information and transparency about the risk to be sold. However, investors will be concerned that some cedents will not worry so much about the cost of protection. They worry that those cedents who view the cost as cheap are those who know that their risk is worse than appreciated. The effect becomes worse as the cost of protection is higher. Thus, the greater the information asymmetry, the greater the "adverse selection" of transactions against the investor.

There are several points to be made about adverse selection. First, indexes can help reduce informational asymmetries in much the same way that they reduce moral hazard. Investors may credibly know as much about index losses as any particular company would know. A company with risks that are worse than appreciated by investors has no particular incentive to link its protection to an index. The reason is that if the company loses more than the index, the company would suffer, not investors.

The second point about adverse selection is that it depends on an asymmetry in buyer-versus-seller information and not on the level of available information. There are no sheep without wolves. For example, it may be impossible for anyone to know how the courts will handle certain environmental or health liabilities in the future. But as long as cedents know as little about the risks as do investors, protection can be obtained, even if very little is known in an absolute sense about the risk. Indeed, earthquakes and hurricanes are this way. We know very little about when and where the next big event will occur. Yet because much of the ignorance is common to buyers and sellers, protection for such events can be obtained.

The third point is that adverse selection can be mitigated in several ways. First, a high level of disclosure is helpful. Given a cedent's information, it is on average better to raise buyers' information level. Second, companies can incur more damage by being seen as preying on sheep than by paying the cost of protection. For example, faulty products ruin a company's reputation and can severely reduce its market value. Managers, whose compensation is increasingly tied to stock price performance, have little incentive to produce faulty products; because writers of product liability insurance do not bear the full cost of damage to a firm's reputation. They would prefer to buy product liability insurance for unforeseen matters, but to do everything possible to mitigate the scope for, and effect of, product imperfections.

LOOKING TO THE FUTURE

Several of the five key ingredients for a successful bond issue are likely to evolve over time. For example, the importance of having a high retention (Ingredient #1) will likely decline. The cause will be a reduction in institutional barriers to issuing lower-rated cat bonds. There is, after all, nothing that says low-rated cat bonds must pay less than high-rated corporate bonds. Certainly, low-rated cat bonds will offer greater yields and commensurately greater risk. But, as with any cat risk placed into a fund, much of the risk is diversifiable. This is true even within catastrophes: combining the risks of California earthquake, East Coast hurricane, and North American freeze together with those from outside the U.S. can reduce pooled risk enormously. Funds whose mandates allow them to buy low-rated bonds—perhaps dedicated entirely to cat—will create a market for securitization at lower retention levels.

This institutional evolution is likely to be important in a number of ways. The costs of issuing cat bonds are in large part a function of the volume of issue. If there is little volume, few investment banking groups specializing in these bonds can be supported, and competition will be low. Few investment managers will specialize in the area, so the general level of investor expertise will be low. This will make funds generally less willing to purchase new risks and will raise the cost to potential issuers considering the capital markets. For these reasons, the market for cat bonds is subject to increasing returns—it will run smoother and more efficiently if the volume of cat issues is relatively high. And, of course, this is self-reinforcing— if the volume of cat issues is higher and costs are lower, more companies will want to use them.

We are already seeing additional investment pools today that will specialize in taking insurance risk. A first group of these will look like traditional reinsurers— raising equity from investors, forming a company, and using the money to write insurance risks. A second group will do something similar, but specifically from tax havens such as Bermuda. This permits an investment that allows funds to compound tax-free, and tax-free compounding is valuable to investors. These firms will pursue investment strategies that are particularly tax-disadvantaged, in order to maximize the value of the tax-free compounding they can offer. Note that because such firms can add value by virtue of tax-free compounding of their investments, they do not need to add much—or even any—value in their insurance/reinsurance operation.[19] Thus, these firms will be a potent source of competition, helping drive down prices of insurance and reinsurance. This is one way of increasing the amount of low-cost capital willing to provide cat event risk capacity.

A third group will emerge looking more like mutual funds, where investors put money into a fund (not a company) and own shares of the fund assets. For open-ended funds, these shares will be priced daily on a marked-to-market basis. The fund assets go toward buying cat bonds and other insurance risk securities. Such fund structures will help to reduce the cost of capital. However, this structure also reduces efficiency somewhat, since each fund investment will be on a fully collateralized basis, and the "lever-age" employed by insurers and reinsurers is lost. Still, the fund structure will be very important for providing a potentially large and rapidly expandable pool to discipline prices.

Together, these three institutional prototypes will provide easier access to capacity when needed. By historical standards, prices will be low. And, in spite of any uncertainty about the absolute level of issuance, a more basic truth emerges: because of these developments, the insurance cycle is fundamentally and permanently changed. In the past, large events depleted balance sheets and triggered enormous increases in prices. Afterward, the high prices encouraged an increase in the amount of capital willing to write risk; but the increase occurred slowly, over several years. As capacity increased, prices fell again.

These new sources of insurance risk transfer undercut this cycle by disciplining prices. Capital will rush in quickly if prices rise substantially, and this keeps prices from rising in the first place. Prices may rise after a cat, but not nearly to the extent that we have seen in the past. The days of large cycles and extremely profitable underwriting opportunities appear to be coming to a close. Competition for capacity is coming to insurance and reinsurance, just as it has come to every other financial services business over time.

If insurers and reinsurers are to succeed in the world just described, they must reduce their costs of capital. One way to do this is to make their businesses and balance sheets more transparent. Increasingly, investment portfolios of these firms are marked-to-market. Bad news is reflected immediately. This means that problems cannot as easily be swept under the rug and be allowed to build, unobserved, for a long period of time (e.g., the banking crisis of U.S. savings and loans, Japan's real estate loans, etc.). By extension, marking-to-market of liabilities will help to shrink surprises, reducing moral hazard and adverse selection. Insurers and reinsurers will increasingly be under competitive pressure to do this. Interim trading of cat event risks will facilitate—even force—this development.

Thus, cat bonds are going to be a powerful force even if we don't see many dedicated bonds issued. The analogy is the way Saudi oil output affects U.S. pump prices, even though the United States buys mostly from Venezuela and Mexico. In fact, as cat and other insurance risks become more transparent and familiar to more investors, there will be little need for dedicated cat event bonds. Corporations will be able to add cat event clauses to their standard debt issues and get competitive pricing on the combined credit and cat risks. This kind of development will further reduce the costs of issuing cat-linked notes while increasing the amount of risk transfer.

The basic conclusion here is that the vision of a world that switches wholesale from insurance to cat bonds is a *reductio ad absurdum*. Cat risk will be transferred more efficiently as we go forward. The insurance cycle will, for all intents and purposes, be gone. But the transfer will occur in many ways—some obvious, some creative. And the cat bond will be only one of many ways to skin the cat.

NOTES

1. Figure 1 actually overstates the fraction of losses covered, since it averages across only those insurers that purchase some amount of reinsurance. If insurers that purchase no reinsurance were included, the fraction shown in Figure 1 would decline.

2. A cat event that generates a loss of $8 billion (1996 dollars) is not extremely unlikely, with a probability of exceedence of approximately 15 percent.

3. Of course, to the extent that the firm has insufficient capital/surplus to sustain a loss, equity holders share the risk with other claimants of the firm: bondholders, trade creditors, and policy holders.

4. For discussion regarding the lack of correlation of cat risks with traditional asset classes, see Kenneth A. Froot, Brian Murphy, Aaron Stern, Steven Usher, "The Emerging Asset Class: Insurance Risk," Guy Carpenter & Co., Special Report, July 1995.

5. Rate-on-Line is the ratio of premium to limit (i.e., maximum possible loss under the contract), averaged across contracts. Data has been compiled by Guy Carpenter & Company, Inc. using a sample of reinsurance contracts it brokered.

6. We thank David Mordecai of Fitch/IBCA for providing this figure and the underlying analysis.

7. Figure for 1996 from Standard & Poor's.

8. This section draws on Kenneth A. Froot and Mark Seasholes, "USAA: Catastrophe Risk Financing" Harvard Business School, case no. N9-278-007, July 1997.

9. The reinsurance contract was 80% of the layer of losses in the range of $500 million in excess of $1 billion, deriving from a single hurricane. The structure of the Residential Re reinsurance contract is similar to that of standard reinsurance contracts. The main differences are that only one cat-event loss can be claimed and that there are no reinstatement features.

10. To compare these percentages with actuarial losses, the risk of USAA sustaining losses in excess of $1 billion is somewhat less than 100 basis points.

11. In addition to credit risk issues, derivative contracts such as swaps and forwards run the risk of being classified as "insurance" contracts by insurance commissioners. "Insurance" contacts are highly regulated and are not considered appropriate for investors.

12. See the discussion below for more details on these indexes.

13. Bond ratings are promulgated by firms such as Moody's, Standard and Poor's, Fitch, etc.

14. The options which appear to have the lowest prices remain relatively illiquid, and the returns which appear on the chart are reduced by transaction costs. Transaction costs are not included in the returns for cat bonds or reinsurance. Furthermore, the options are based on indexes of catastrophe losses, rather than net losses of individual insurers or reinsurers.

15. The implications of moral hazard can be clearly seen in a recent cat-bond transaction. The protection was intended to cover several lines of business and types of events. As a result, there was a concern that the cedent would have an incentive to grow those lines of business that were less attractive from investors' point of view. To limit the scope for moral hazard, the cedent agreed to a complicated set of restrictions—taking up some 80 pages in the offering memorandum. Moral hazard was reduced, but at the cost of considerable complexity and opacity.

16. When there is more than one trigger, contracts normally require both conditions are met before the cedent is entitled to obtain a recovery.

17. Contracts linked to the PCS index are traded on the Chicago Board of Trade.

18. Contracts linked to the GCCI index are traded on the Bermuda Commodities Exchange. See Kenneth A. Froot and Markus F. Mullarkey, "Mid Ocean Limited—Trading Catastrophe Index Options," Harvard Business School, case no. 9-298-073, April 1998, and *The Guy Carpenter Catastrophe Index*, January 1998, published by IndexCo (www.indexco.com).

19. Under U.S. law, it is the existence of the insurance/reinsurance operations that allows the assets to qualify for tax-advantaged status.

6. INDUSTRIAL RISK MANAGEMENT WITH WEATHER DERIVATIVES

RICHARD JEFFERIS

OBJECTIVES

These notes address the role of weather derivatives in managing volumetric exposure induced by variation in the weather. My objective is to demonstrate that weather risk management problems are meaningful, in that the risk faced by the afflicted parties is compelling, and also to demonstrate that weather derivatives are an effective means of dealing with this risk. I present examples from fuels transport, agriculture, and power generation that illustrate the role of weather derivatives in managing profit fluctuations. I also discuss the role of market makers in the weather derivatives market, and contrast this with the service provided by intermediaries in other, more conventional derivative markets.

INSTRUMENTS AND MARKET STRUCTURE

Over the counter trading of weather derivatives commenced in the autumn of 1997. Most claims traded to date have been linked to temperature. A few transactions based on precipitation have been executed. The metric for temperature-related trades is heating-degree days in the winter and cooling-degree days in the summer. A heating-degree day is defined by

$$HDD = Max[65 - T, 0]$$

where T is the daily average temperature at a particular location. Heating-degree days (HDDs) are an increasing function of cold. The analogous expression for a cooling-degree day is

$$CDD = Max[T - 65, 0]$$

Cooling-degree days (CDDs) are an increasing function of warmth.

Winter season claims typically price over the period beginning November 1 and ending March 31. The summer season runs from May 1 through September 30. The index used to settle most trades is the sum of cooling-degree days or heating-degree days, over a period as short as a month and as long as a season. Swaps and options are the instruments of choice. Most active participants in the weather derivatives market to date have been engaged in the production, consumption or transportation of energy. We have also observed participation by firms engaged in agriculture and weather-sensitive retail operations.

The weather derivatives market is distinguished from commodity derivative markets by the fact that weather risk tends to be local, while commodity price risk is typically global. Variations in the price of commodities across locations are bounded by transport costs. As a result, a single index, like the price of Brent crude delivered at Sullum Voe, can serve as a marker for the worldwide market in crude oil. The global nature of commodity price risk enhances the utility of a single, well-defined index like the price of Brent crude as a hedging instrument. The universal appeal of a single hedging instrument contributes in turn to market liquidity.

The structure of the weather market is fundamentally different. The fact that weather is a physical phenomenon means that we cannot rely upon market forces like arbitrage to limit variation in the weather across locations. Variation in the price of weather across locations is bounded by the spatial continuity of temperature variation, which can be large over periods of time as long as a month. As a result, there is no universal marker for temperature risk, even within North America. An attempt to introduce exchange-traded contracts appears doomed to failure. Although some locations (major urban hubs) do exhibit more liquidity than other locations where weather derivatives trade, the market is fundamentally an OTC market, and likely to remain so. This is attributable to the nature of weather risk, and not merely a sign of an immature market.

The nature of weather risk is reflected in the role of market markers. In markets like crude oil or natural gas, the existence of a liquid index for price risk allows a market maker to shed, at minimal cost, the risk associated with serving a client. Market makers operating in the weather business must manage a portfolio of trades that settle across a wide variety of locations without access to a liquid marker. The absence of a liquid index for shedding market risk increases the barrier that a market maker must surmount in order to compete effectively in the weather business. Changing the position of one's book from long to short will typically require a number of transactions at a variety of locations. Understanding and managing a book effectively involves a fairly deep appreciation of correlation risk. The market making side of the weather derivatives business is not friendly to dabblers.

WEATHER AND VOLUME RISK

Weather derivatives are useful instruments for managing risk in situations where an agent is exposed to weather induced fluctuations in profit that are not highly correlated with price. Volume risk linked to weather commands attention when the P&L is volume dependent, volume is sensitive to weather, and the feature of the weather that drives volume fluctuations is volatile. The restrictive nature of these statements suggests that weather derivatives will be useful only in specialized situations. The structure of the weather derivatives market is consistent with this hypothesis. The appeal of the market, and its potential for growth derive from the fact that weather risk is often compelling where it is present, rather than some broad universal appeal. I find it difficult to anticipate retail trading of weather derivatives linked to vacation plans.

Natural Gas Transport

My first example of weather risk comes from natural gas transport. This is an appropriate starting point for understanding weather risk, because transportation is a pure volume exposure. The example reveals that price-based instruments are not appropriate tools for managing volume risk. It also affords some insight into the magnitude of weather exposure. The example indicates clearly the role of weather derivatives in managing volume risk.

Figure 1 illustrates the relationship between daily natural gas pipeline throughput during the heating season and daily average temperature in the market to which the gas is delivered. The figure is a conditioning plot. The four boxes within the plot are distinguished by the price of natural gas. The box at the lower left corner of the graph is associated with the quartile of observations where natural gas is cheapest. The box at the upper right corner of the graph is associated with the quartile of observations where natural gas is most expensive. As we move across a row, the price of natural gas increases. The relationship between throughput and temperature is plotted within each box.

One prominent feature of the plots that appear in each of the four boxes is that delivery volumes are sensitive to temperature at all observed prices. The variation in temperatures described in each box is due mostly to seasonal variation in climate. (Temperatures decline steadily from November through January, then rise through the end of March.) For this reason, the graphs do not describe weather risk, which consists of variation in temperature *relative* to the normal seasonal cycle. The locus of points within each box indicates a tight relationship between volume and weather, the slope of which defines the sensitivity of throughput to temperature.

A second feature of the relationship between price and temperature that is revealed by the plots in figure 1 is the fact that the relationship between throughput and temperature is not very sensitive to price. Prices associated with the data in figure 1 vary by a factor of 3, from a low of less than $2 per mmbtu (million British Thermal Units) to a high of more than $6 per mmbtu. The graph of

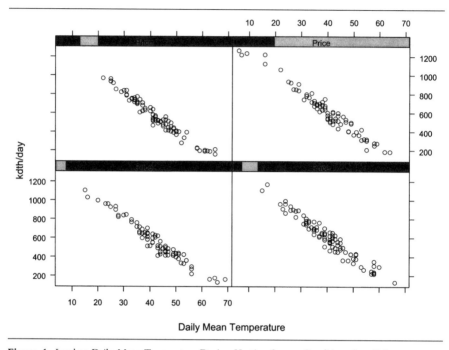

Figure 1. Load vs Daily Mean Temperature During Heating Season Conditioned on Price

temperature vs throughput is roughly constant across the 4 subplots in figure 1. This feature of the graph suggests that price-based instruments are not effective tools for addressing risks associated with temperature fluctuations.

Figure 2 provides some additional evidence on the efficacy of price-based hedges. In the figure, I plot the weekly average natural gas price at Henry Hub against an index of weekly heating demand for natural gas. I have fitted a robust loess to the data. The loess represents our best guess about the relationship between price and temperature. The scatter of the data about the line indicates that a throughput hedge based on the price of natural gas at Henry Hub would carry with it a great deal of risk.[1] The contrast between the price vs weather relationship in figure 2 and the volume vs weather relationship in figure 1 is stark. A weather-based hedge is clearly a superior hedging instrument for volume risk.

Figure 3 speaks to the magnitude of the weather exposure that faces a pipeline operator who generates revenue by collecting fees that are linked to throughput. I present boxplots for the period Nov 1–Mar 31, and Nov 1–Apr 30. In both cases, the maximum and minimum values of the temperature distribution represent a demand variation of approximately 13 percent vs the median, implying a range of throughput that is roughly 25 percent of the median.

This risk is economically meaningful to the owner of a pipeline, or a utility. The fuels transportation business is capital intensive. In the absence of weather risk, demand

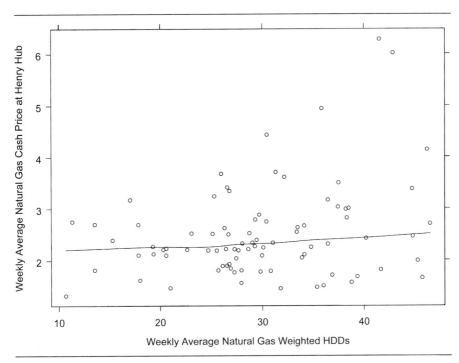

Figure 2. Natural Gas Price vs Heating Demand During Heating Season Jan 95–March ••

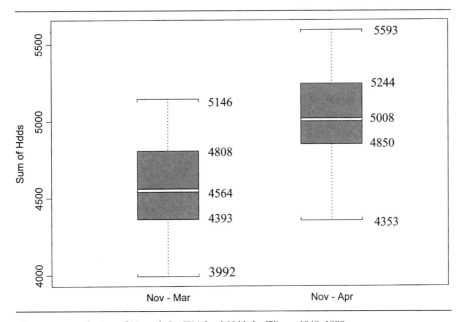

Figure 3. Distribution of Natural Gas Weighted Hdds by Winter 1948–1998

is fairly stable, making a high degree of leverage a reasonable financial strategy. Year to year fluctuations in throughput of 25 percent, as we observed between the winters of 1994–1995 and 1995–1996, can generate large swings in profitability. A warming trend in winter temperatures may have a significant impact on asset value.

Weather derivatives are a simple, effective tool for dealing with the risk described above. The R^2 from the regression of price on temperature is 0.88. Let Δ denote the slope coefficient from this regression, and F denote the fee per unit of throughput that is the revenue source of the pipeline. A weather derivative settled against heating-degree days for the consuming market, with a tick size of $\Delta * F$, may be used to manage the weather exposure of the pipeline.

A November–March swap struck at 4,564 HDDs, which pays the pipeline $\Delta * F$ per HDD in the event that HDDs are below normal, locks in throughput revenue at its median value. The pipeline is short the HDD swap, makes payments in the event that the weather is colder than normal, and receives payments in the event that the weather is warmer than normal. An HDD put option, struck at 4,393 HDDs, which pays the pipeline $\Delta * F$ per HDD, insulates the pipeline from throughput demand that is more than 25 percent below normal. Both types of trades are common in the weather market.

Power Generation

The natural gas transport example illustrates the most basic use of a weather derivative. The example is clean, because the financial risk faced by the pipeline owner is purely volume-based, and the relationship between throughput and temperature is linear. My second example involves a firm that faces price risk as well as volume risk. The hedging problem has some significant non-linear features. The correlation between price and volume is an important aspect of the hedging decision.

Figure 4 describes the relationship between daily average temperature and power demand for a merchant generator. The demand for power is described by a pair of parabolas, one for weekends and one for weekdays. The right-hand leg of each parabola represents cooling demand. The left-hand leg represents heating demand. The weekend load is roughly 70 percent of the weekday load.[2] It is apparent from the figure that load is more sensitive to cooling demand than it is to heating demand. This characteristic of the load is location dependent; in some parts of North America, load is more sensitive to heating demand than cooling demand.

The steep slope of load with respect to cooling demand is economically meaningful. Power generation, like pipeline transport, is capital intensive. A change of 20 degrees in the daily average temperature, from 60 degrees to 80 degrees, swings the consumption of power by nearly 40 percent, from 3,000 MW to 5,000 MW. A protracted period of below normal temperatures can leave an expensive piece of capital sitting idle. The problem is especially acute when the generation facility has been installed to meet peaking demand, as is often the case with turbines fired by natural gas.

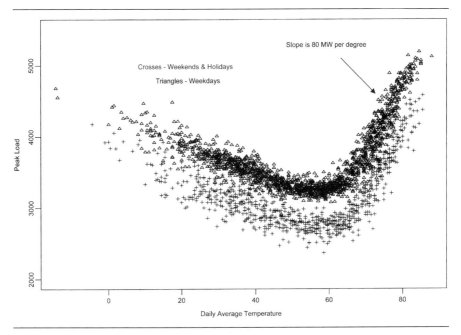

Figure 4. Peak Load vs Average Daily Temperature 5,000 MW Generator

Figure 5 provides some insight into the magnitude of this exposure. In figure 5, I have taken the load generation function that is described in figure 4, and used 50 years of temperature data to bootstrap the distribution of daily peak utilization rates for the generation facility. Consider the distribution that describes utilization during the month of July, which is the central box plot in figure 5. The bootstrapped utilization rate distribution indicates that there exists a day in the historical record that would effect a utilization rate of 100 percent for the generator who owns the assets described in figure 4. If the generator is legally bound to service his customer base, as is often the case in a market that is not fully deregulated, the generator cannot sell capacity forward and be confident of meeting his commitments to deliver power.[3] The implication of the figure for a generator bound by this type of con-tractual obligation is that all generation capacity must be held in reserve against the possibility of hot weather.

The financial consequences of such an obligation, absent any consideration of price, are apparent from the rest of the utilization rate distribution. The median daily utilization rate implied by the historical temperature data is 67 percent. (This is the horizontal bar in the middle of the box plot.) In other words, the temperature record implies that there is a fifty percent chance that the daily utilization rate during the month of July will be less than 2/3.[4]

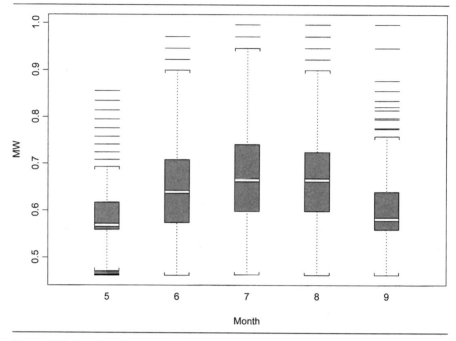

Figure 5. Peaking Plant Capacity Utilization Rate at Peak Implied by 50 Years of Temperature Records

A weather hedge that mitigates the utilization risk of a power generator who sells his load at a fixed price, using inputs purchased at fixed cost, is both easy to calculate and a useful starting point for analysis. Let F denote the revenue realized through the generation of 1 MW of power. If we approximate the right-hand limb of the generation parabola with a straight line, a weather hedge that creates a floor on revenue is a CDD put with a tick size of

$$(dLoad/dCDD) * F$$

The strike on the CDD put determines the level of protection purchased by the generator.

This hedge is imperfect, even though we have assumed away the interaction between price risk and volume risk, which is a significant feature of the hedging problem faced by merchant generators. The linear approximation of parabolic risk is one deficiency in the hedge. A second shortcoming is our failure to distinguish between weekday temperatures and weekend temperatures. (The graph of load vs temperature described in figure 4 indicates that the timing of temperature risk is important.) In practice, the range of available weather claims is coarse compared to the structure of the risk problem faced by generators. We deal with these problems by either ignoring them, or making crude adjustments to the hedge, like switching from a single put with a fixed tick size to a strip of puts with different tick sizes. Our rough hedges typically offset something like 80 percent of actual volume risk, but do not eliminate it altogether.

If we relax the assumption that prices are fixed, and consider the hedging problem that is faced by the typical merchant generator, we introduce another source of non-linearity in the hedging objective function. One point worth making about power prices is that price and volume are highly correlated in many, but not all situations. When generation capacity is constrained, as in the midwest during the summer of 1998 and 1999, and California during the winter of 2000–2001, prices track volume very closely. Price and volume are linked much more weakly when the market is not capacity constrained. The relationship between price and volume is generally quite complicated, since it depends on the structure of the transmission grid, as well as the demand for power across locations.

We manage the risk of a merchant generator who faces fluctuating power prices with static hedges constructed from plain vanilla weather claims and power claims. These hedges mitigate, but do not eliminate the risk associated with price and volume.

Agriculture

My third example of weather risk comes from agriculture. Figure 6 describes the annual corn yield for McLean county, IL between 1972 and 1996. U.S. corn production has an annual value of $20–30 bn. McLean county is a major production center, with a weather exposure that is representative of the corn belt in general.

The salient feature of figure 6 from a risk perspective is the set of low corn yields that occur in one of five years. 1988 stands out in the data. There are a number of years where yields fall by more than 20 percent below trend.

Figure 7 describes the relationship between production risk and weather using a conditioning plot. The four panels of the plot are distinguished by the amount of rain that falls in the month of June. The lower left panel is associated with drought. The upper right panel is associated with excessive rainfall. Rainfall increases as we move from left to right in each row.

The detrended corn yield is plotted against the July average temperature in each of the panels. Hot weather in July impedes the pollination process, and can have a major impact on yields. The sensitivity of yields to temperature exhibits a strong dependence on rainfall.

Figure 8 describes the relationship between actual yields and fitted yields from a two-factor non-linear model based on figure 7. The fitted relationship is quite good, except for 1995. The poor fit in 1995 is attributable to the failure of a particular genetic hybrid in that year.

The simple weather model summarized by figure 6, figure 7 and figure 8 illustrates the reality of corn production risk. It is clear from these figures that weather claims are effective tools for managing this risk. The efficient method of distribut-

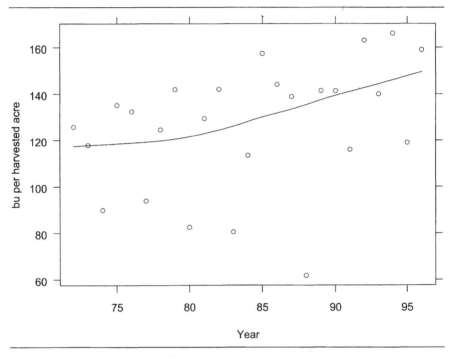

Figure 6. McLean County Corn Yield 1972–1996

ing weather claims to those who face the risk is somewhat roundabout. Grain production is affected by factors apart from weather. Producers purchase insurance to cover their production exposure. Insurers who seek to manage the risk associated with offering this coverage may trade weather claims to mitigate the exposure in their own portfolios.

THE WEATHER MARKET AND RISK PREMIA

Derivatives afford lower cost protection than pure insurance in situations where one party benefits from a phenomenon that damages another. In these circumstances, the development of a derivatives market facilitates risk transfer, making it unnecessary to compensate an insurer for the absorption of risk. The development of a derivatives market reduces the cost of risk management by reducing or eliminating a risk premium.

The three examples presented above illustrate the fact that weather risk has a material impact on a number of industries. The examples also suggest that many weather risks are correlated. To be explicit, the same temperature and rainfall phenomena that affect corn yields also affect construction companies, power generators and power consumers.

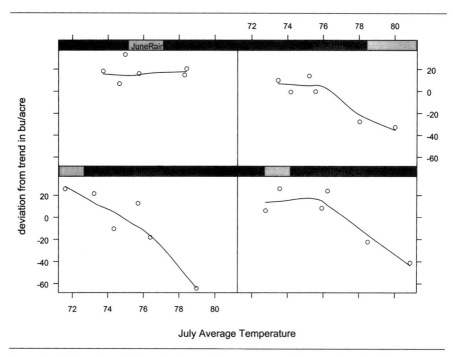

Figure 7. McLean Corn Yield vs July Average Temperature Conditioned on June Rainfall: 1972–1996

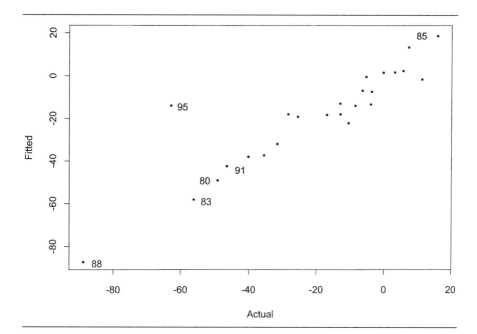

Figure 8. McLean County Corn Yields Actual and Fitted Deviation from Trend Yield

Weather derivative market makers are able to offer risk protection at a lower cost than pure insurance either because the market maker is able to find counterparties who have offsetting exposures to the same risk (which is rare) or because the market maker is able to manage risk across locations by understanding correlation. The feature of the weather market that distinguishes it from other derivative markets is the magnitude of this correlation risk.

NOTES

1. It is possible to obtain a tighter fit between price and weather by looking at variations in local market prices for natural gas. But I have not found a price-temperature relationship that is a viable substitute for a weather trade.

2. Failure to address the difference between weekdays and weekends/holidays leads to some obvious problems in interpreting the load data.

3. I am assuming that the generator cannot be assured of access to a spot market for power in the event that he is unable to meet his generation commitments by using his own assets. Events in North American power markets over the last several summers suggest that this assumption is realistic in the current environment.

4. Temperature is a mean reverting process. The variability of the mean utilization rate over time is a decreasing function of the time horizon over which the mean is computed. The utilization risk illustrated in figure 5 therefore represents an upper bound on the utilization risk actually faced by the generator, if the revenue function depends on average throughput, as would be the case for a generator who has sold his capacity forward at a fixed price. For the location depicted here, monthly or seasonal temperature risk as measured by standard deviation is roughly 1/3 of daily temperature risk.

7. DESIGNING AND PRICING NEW INSTRUMENTS FOR INSURANCE AND WEATHER RISKS

JOSEPH B. COLE

I view weather risk as a subset of the insurance risk securitization that has been ongoing for the last six or seven years. Insurance risk securitization should also continue, especially with the Glass–Steagall repeal potentially encouraging insurance company buyouts. The resulting consolidation of large aggregate risk positions, such as Florida wind and California quake, may need to be "topped-off" and transferred to financial intermediaries other than insurers and reinsurers in the form of swaps and private placement securities. However, I believe this trend will continue and grow and I am happy to offer my observations on this exciting area.

I'll begin my remarks with an overview of insurance risk securitization using a couple of examples. Another idea I'd like to discuss, since several of our customers have been either hedge funds or high yield bond funds, is the similarity of securitized insurance and high yield bonds in terms of their risk characteristics and how they're priced and viewed. Finally, I'll conclude with a description of insurance risk monetization and discuss the different types of catastrophic risk (or cat) bonds that we've seen in the market to this point.

Now at the risk of boring you, I'll tell you also that insurance securitization is not exactly a brand new idea. I've worked with Richard Sandor developing new financial products for almost 15 years. When Richard was at Berkely in 1968 he co-authored a paper about trading a futures contract for insurance. Now why does a futures contract take so long to develop for a market like insurance? There are quite a few impediments and the characteristics that you find for successful futures trading have followed a normal progression for commodity type trading.

R.M. Levich and S. Figlewski (eds.). RISK MANAGEMENT. Copyright © 2001. Kluwer Academic Publishers. Boston. All rights reserved.

Modern futures trading started in grains and progressed to metals, red meats and currencies. In the process, trading was moving from storable commodities to non-storable commodities like live cattle and hogs and more recently to financial instruments, such as equities and indexes. Insurance risk is essentially an indexed product. For indexation to be successful, we've found, sometimes through trial-and-error, that there is a set of five common attributes for the indexed commodity that will make it acceptable for trading by the market.

Number one is that the underlying product should be standardized and uniform. Standardization is a large part of the commoditization process. So we want to have uniform prices and we don't want the index to be constantly changing over time. Secondly, the pricing formula for the index should be well understood and verifiable, such as the S&P500 or Dow Jones indices. And even though S&P adds and subtracts stocks to the index, the market still accepts it as a benchmark because the changes and formula are well understood.

A third characteristic is that the underlying prices should be widely and frequently disseminated. That is a factor that reduces the success potential for insurance risk indexation since the underlying risks do not change that much from day to day. The risk today for a hurricane next autumn is the same as it will be tomorrow and is the same as it was last week. While there is a risk that you might have a lot more people suddenly moving to Florida, demographics don't change that rapidly. The same is true for earthquakes, as the underlying risks tend to be somewhat constant. Weather risks also do not change rapidly from year to year. In these markets, the speculators may get bored with stable risks. Fourth, index inputs should be competitively determined, with no manipulation occurring in the processing of the index. And finally, the index should accurately reflect value.

The Chicago Board of Trade started trading insurance risk in December 1992. The initial contract based on loss ratios was later replaced by the current Property Claim Services (PCS) contract. The PCS Index represents losses for reporting insurance companies in the United States and for various regions. Not only can you trade the U.S. insurance losses for the entire country, you can also trade Northeast exposure of East Coast exposure or Florida-only or Texas-only, or Midwest and California perils. When we first started trading the contract we went from zero to maybe 25,000 contracts open interest. I think now we're probably down back below a 1,000 contracts.

If you recall a paper by Telser and Higinbotham (1977), they describe the trade-offs of the costs and benefits on an organized exchange that influence the listing a commodity-type contract and it's potential acceptability for the trading of a particular contract. Part of the lack of trading, I think, in PCS options at the Chicago Board of Trade is that the risk lacked ex post volatility. We've just had another fairly quiescent hurricane season, even though we had several small storm hits none were in the $2 to $5 billion range. And although we've had Northridge, California hit the earthquake contract, we've been very fortunate overall in that regard. Now, there have been time periods in the Midwest contract which have allowed "reinsurance" to be recovered by those long the contract while the people who were short the contract, and are essentially "synthetic London names" trading through the Board of Trade, had to pay. There still will be buyers and sellers of insurance risk but I think more trading is gravitating to the over the counter market because the cost and benefits tradeoff ratio may not necessarily be favorable for futures. We could, however, see a resurrection in this contract once a series of catastrophes hits the United States again.

Dealer acceptance of standardization and value is especially important for the trading of commodity-type risk. In any contract, you must have acceptance in the dealer market. Where is the dealer market for insurance risks? When you buy insurance from a primary insurer and they aggregate the risk on their books, they diversify that risk both geographically and through product diversification. But the simple fact is, during the last 30 to 40 years, more and more people live in California, Florida, Texas and the East Coast than at any point in time. Housing values have increased to such an extent while at the same time consolidation has occurred in the insurance industry, implying that insurance companies need to move this risk off their balance sheets. Generally, they've been managing their risk through reinsurance, which is like a swap contract between insurance companies. But the reinsurers also needed to manage their risks through an essentially dealer, broker-dealer type telephone market. Hence the dealer market for insurance risk is the reinsurance community either in Bermuda, the United States or London.

What types of reinsurers are out there that actually trade this risk and what investors own reinsurance companies? Actually, there is a very notable list of investors in companies that trade reinsurance risk: Warren Buffet, Kohlberg Kravis Roberts (KKR), Saul Steinberg, Carl Lindner, the Bass Brothers, Richard Rainwater, Steven Gluckstern, the Pritzker Family . . . all well-heeled investors. Generally, the people who own the reinsurance companies are considered to be very savvy investors. And to trade this risk, you have to understand the risk and look at it a little bit differently than in other markets to appreciate the opportunities.

Let me provide an overview of a transaction three or four years ago that spurred Wall Street's interest in insurance securitization. The specifications of the deal that Warren Buffet did through his National Indemnity subsidiary essentially committed $1.5 billion dollars to the California Earthquake Authority (CEA) in the event an earthquake in California resulted in more than $7 billion of homeowners' insurance losses over a four-year period. In exchange, Buffet received upfront a premium of $590 million. That premium turns out to be a rate-on-line (ROL) of close to 10% per annum. The estimated probability of occurrence for an earthquake exceeding $7 billion of homeowners' losses for the CEA is about 1.27%. Thus the risk–reward ratio for this deal is about five-to-one, and is estimated by dividing the ROL of 10% by, let's say an error-adjusted probability of loss of 2%. Buffet's firm gets ten percentage points upfront while the annual risk is maybe 2%. I'd do that trade any day. What's the most Mr. Buffet's company stands to lose on this trade? Well, its $1.5

billion less the upfront premium of close to $600 million. The $600 million dollars could have been invested internally and earned 20% to 25% during the duration of the reinsurance. So it shouldn't take too long to cover the remaining $900 million dollars of exposure to loss.

One way to characterize the risk transference that's happening in the insurance industry is to go back to the capital asset pricing model. Most of you realize, of course, the beta encompasses systemic risks and could even be expanded to a multifactor model of interest rate, equity market, real estate and commodity risks. But it's the firm-specific risks that are in the alpha and here is where the trading of property catastrophe risks, auto liability, general liability, inland marine, aviation, errors and omissions, directors' liability and other risks resides. From my perspective, these are new types of asset classes that are being securitized and traded in the form of indexed swaps or cat bonds with the sophisticated investors that understand these risks. In essence, by trading in these new instruments hedge funds are attempting to fulfill their promise of providing "alpha return" that is uncorrelated with systemic risks. In other words, hedge funds are trying to beat their financing rate by assembling a portfolio of alpha, and being opposite the market in general or making the right trades at the right time. The more securitized risk that hedge funds can aggregate and bring into their portfolio, the better diversified their attempts at positive alpha will be.

There are many similarities but yet a difference in language between insurance risk analysis and what we would typically define on Wall Street. It's an advantage in some sense for the people to understand both markets. To be able to look and trade and view these risks as securitizable, I think is beneficial to an overall understanding of risk. A comparison of analogous terms used by the financial and insurance markets is quite interesting. For example, in insurance markets we talk about "burning cost." Burning cost is really just the forward value of an option at maturity. In finance we really don't talk about burning cost or how much you expect to make or lose on a particular transaction at maturity. We usually just discount the ending value back to present and call that quantity "the option premium." In the insurance market, the burning cost is often an average over 20 to 30 years of the losses that would occur on a particular program. Also, in the insurance market we refer to the "rate-on-line" as the market rate for the particular risk. So the rate-on-line is what we would refer to in the financial markets as option premium divided by risk.

Let me give you an example, say, using IBM now trading (as of January 13, 2000) around $120 per share. If you sold a call spread on IBM, and were short the 120 call option and long the 130 call, you could probably take in about 4 points on February options with a month to run. The amount of risk that you're exposed to is 10 points. The amount of premium that you brought in is 4 points. The rate-on-line in insurance terms is 40%, that's 4 divided by 10. The "attachment point," another insurance term, in the IBM example is the lower strike or what we might also call Trigger 1 in a swap contract. The exhaustion point is the upper strike or Trigger 2. An "excess of loss" contract utilized frequently in reinsurance is in fact a call spread. If I do an excess of loss contract on an insurance risk, I am essentially creating a bear call spread, taking a premium upfront for the amount of indemnities I've agreed to pay.

As another example, a financial guarantee contract can be thought of as analogous to a put spread. Similarly, primary layer coverage is what financial markets would call in-the-money options. A working layer coverage in the insurance markets is what we in the financial market would call at-the-money. A catastrophic layer is an out-of-the-money spread. And there are reinsurance policies referred to as "super Cat coverage" where the premium you receive might only be one or two points rate-on-line for taking that risk. Generally, the ROL on catastrophic coverage tends to be anywhere from 10–20%, the working layer 15–20%, and the primary layer is about 50% which is what you would expect for something that's in the money or at the money.

Now let me attempt a cat bond pricing example for you using East Coast wind or Florida wind. Generally, the underlying risk is distributed Poisson where you have a large number of small events and a small number of very costly events. And you can do an East Coast wind right now with what I would call "5 billion excess 10". That's an excess of loss contract that has a lower attachment point of $10 billion, an exhaustion point of $15 billion. So the risk would be $5 billion on an industry loss basis. The probability for the $10 billion attachment is perhaps 1 in maybe 25 years or 4%, and a 1 in 50 year or 2% probability for the upper attachment. So, the probability of expected loss is about 1 in 33 years, or 3%. If an insurance company has a market share of 10% for the industry, they would go and issue a cat bond for $500 million dollars of loss. Their reinsurance could be indexed to the Property Claim Services index as a proxy the whole industry. Therefore a $5 billion dollar industry event would cost them $500 million given that the 10% market share comes in without any basis risk. This is how a cat bond can be traded and looked at in terms of the odds, in terms of insurance terminology, and in terms of pricing.

There are many ways an insurance company can lay this risk off. They can do reinsurance, they can do industry loss warranties, and they can do cat bonds, cat options at the Chicago Board of Trade, or over the counter or cat index swaps, a private placement, or Rule 144a cat bonds. As it turns out in terms of pricing, the cat bond has to be equal to what they would normally pay as traditional insurance, plus a credit swap, plus some sort of liquidity premium.

Now I'll say this (but many people don't understand this in insurance markets yet), but insurance companies are not doing anything all that fantastic by issuing cat bonds. If I went to a consortium of Bermuda reinsurers, I could ask them to guarantee my payment demands using a bank guarantee. That guarantee may cost about three-eights or half a percentage point, more or less, depending on the credit quality. Thus, we've added a credit swap to the traditional reinsurance that they would normally provide. The reason cat bonds are fully guaranteed is that the money is actually placed through a Special Purpose Vehicle and segregated offshore somewhere with trustee oversight, so the credit quality is "triple A". In order to entice new investors to this market, cat bond issuers have also been adding in a liquidity premium.

Investors should like the insurance risk market. The Sharpe ratio for cat-related exposures during the last 20 to 30 years tends to dominate most other tradable securities. This risk-reward ratio tells you why Buffet, Rainwater, Bass Brothers, or many other savvy investors have been in this market. These numbers have been verified by a study that Bob Litzenberger did at Goldman Sachs and by other studies by Banker's Trust and Guy Carpenter. It does entice investors when they understand what the risk-reward characteristics represent.

High yield bond investors will typically look at what the default rate would be for a particular issue. In the earlier example, the initial attachment point had 4% odds. The upper exhaustion point was 2% with an expected value of 3%. That credit quality falls right in between the default rate for high yield bonds over time, which for a "Ba" or a "B" rated issue is somewhere between 1% and 7%, and is where the 3% odds for the cat bond would lie. Thus, by analogy the numbers are telling you if you overlay these the markets for insurance risk and high yield debt they are very similar in terms of credit assumptions.

Fundamentally, when high yield bond issuers look at a particular piece of paper, they often go through a set of five criteria. They'll look at the industry that the issuer is in, they'll do financial analysis on the credit, they'll do a covenant review, they'll look at senior management and they'll look at trading factors in the market in order to price a high yield bond issue. If you look at most high yield bond pricing literature and you try to assemble either a spread model or pricing model, you're lucky to explain 50% of the variance. Which means half the time you can't explain the pricing of high yield bonds with the assumed underlying factors. What I talk to high yield bond investors. I tell them that more certainty probably exists for the pricing of earthquakes and hurricanes than that for high yield bonds. There is probably less modeling risk in cat bonds than what there is in high yields. The analysis that we would go through when looking at cat bond creditworthiness starts first with the type of peril. We look at the demographic recasting and risk adjustments. We examine the "Treaty" structures and payout triggers. We analyze the peril and come up with our burning cost, looking at ratios of the rate-on-line with burning cost. We talk to senior management and we compare other types of transactions that have been done recently. So analogously again, the analytics are comparable in the high yield and cat bond market.

Finally, the types of cash-flow monetization that exist in the cat bond market are either indemnity-based, index-based or parametric-based. An indemnity-based type of investment would be the USAA Residential Re deal that came out about 3 years ago at $500 million and was linked to USAA, a very large insurance company that tends to be concentrated around military bases such as Norfolk, Virginia, Florida and elsewhere. The cat bond is set up so that the losses are geared to the actual indemnities paid by USAA. An index-based type of issue would be against the industry as a whole using a PCS index or Sigma index or some other type of index that financial engineers can dream up. A parametric-based deal may have a structure where the entire payoff of the bond is determined statistically. For example, an issue that came out about 3 or 4 months ago that is parametric-based is Namazu Re, structured by AON and Goldman Sachs. This issue utilized a Special Purpose Vehicle for Gerling Re with the underlying peril being earthquake risk in several specifically identified prefectures surrounding Tokyo.

The term *Namazu* comes from Japanese mythology concerning a very large turtle that causes earthquakes in Japan whenever it swims offshore. This issue was for $100 million over a five-year term. What is notable about this issue is that the indemnification is entirely determined by a statistical model of earthquakes with inputs from a pre-determined set of around 400 shake monitors. Whenever there is an earthquake in these prefectures, the data from the earthquake sensors is inputted into the statistical model and the resulting output of the model entirely determines how much the bond will pay or not pay the holders. The issue was priced at a 4% rate-on-line and has a 1% statistical probability of loss for a four-to-one risk-reward ratio. This 4% premium can be added to five year LIBOR for price comparison purposes.

To provide closure for my talk, let me remind you that we began by describing the changing nature of risk trading, moving from storable commodities like grain to indexed commodities like the S&P500 index and insurance risk. To me, the type of index embedded in the Namazu Re deal is just incredible and quite innovative. In essence, the buyers and sellers of Japanese quake risk have agreed to reduce their monitoring costs and basis risks by utilizing an index constructed entirely by statistical methodology and mechanical input, not unlike a giant slot machine but hopefully without the "vigorish" or "house take". If this bond can trade successfully, I believe we will see additional parametric-based issues for the securitization of insurance risk in the future.

REFERENCE

Telser, Lester G. and Harlow N. Higinbotham. "Organized Futures Markets: Costs and Benefits," *Journal of Political Economy*, Vol. 85, No. 5. (Oct., 1977), pp. 969–1000.

8. MEASURING CREDIT RISK: THE CREDIT MIGRATION APPROACH EXTENDED FOR CREDIT DERIVATIVES

MICHEL CROUHY, JOHN IM AND GREG NUDELMAN

Canadian Imperial Bank of Commerce (CIBC)[1]

I. INTRODUCTION

Over the last few years, three approaches to measure credit risk in a portfolio context have emerged in the banking industry. The "credit migration approach", as initially proposed by JP Morgan with CreditMetrics, is based on the analysis of credit migration, i.e., the probability of moving from one credit quality to another, including default, within a given time horizon (often arbitrarily taken to be one year). The first generation of credit migration models derive the forward distribution of the values of a credit portfolio, say one year forward, where the changes in value are related to credit migration only; interest rates are assumed to evolve in a deterministic fashion. The credit value-at-risk (CVaR) of a portfolio is then derived in a similar fashion as for market risk. It is the distance from the mean of the percentile of the forward distribution, at the desired confidence level. (This definition of CVaR applies to all credit models, and is independent of the underlying theoretical framework.)

KMV Corporation, a firm specialized in credit risk analysis, has developed a "structural approach" to credit risk measurement, based on the asset value model originally proposed by Merton (1974). The structural approach relies upon the "expected default frequency", or EDF, for each issuer, rather than upon the average transition frequencies for each rating class. The EDF is firm specific and varies continuously with the asset value, the asset volatility and the capital structure of the firm.

R.M. Levich and S. Figlewski (eds.). RISK MANAGEMENT. Copyright © 2001. Kluwer Academic Publishers. Boston. All rights reserved.

Finally, Credit Suisse Financial Products (CSFP) proposed an approach, Credit Risk+, based on actuarial science. CreditRisk+ focuses on default rather than credit migration. It assumes that the dynamics of default for individual bonds, or loans, follows a Poisson process.[2]

All these first generation models apply well to portfolios of straightforward bonds and loans without option features. However, all the models assume deterministic interest rates. These models are less suited for measuring the credit risk of swaps, credit derivatives, and other derivative-like products such as loan commitments. The major challenge in extending any of these credit measurement frameworks to credit derivatives is that risk distributions are derived using "natural" migration and default probabilities, while pricing of complex securities, such as credit derivatives, is based on "risk neutral" probabilities. The question, then, is: how can we derive the risk neutral probabilities from the natural ones, and vice versa?

At CIBC we have implemented a proprietary model, CreditVaR, based on the credit migration framework. We have extended the basic framework to allow for stochastic interest rates and for the pricing of credit derivatives in a multi-period setting. We prefer the credit migration framework to the other approaches because it is versatile, and it is consistent with our internal credit process. The credit approval process at CIBC has relied for the last 9 years on an internal rating system that applied to both private and public firms. The structural approach works well for public firms whose equity is traded. But, more than 60% of the loan portfolios of the major banks are composed of private names. Our rating process at CIBC passed the backtesting tests and we strongly believe that it is as forward looking as any other alternative. The transition probabilities in CIBC's CreditVaR model are derived from internal data accumulated over the last few years. This data set allows us to differentiate between different markets such as "large corporates" and "middle market".

This chapter focuses on the extension of the credit migration framework to allow for the inclusion of credit derivatives in a loan portfolio. The issue we address here is, given the natural transition probabilities, how to derive the corresponding risk neutral probabilities needed to price credit derivatives? In this chapter we derive the theoretical relationship between both the natural and risk neutral probabilities to migrate from one credit class to another, including the probabilities of default. But, we also discuss how to implement in practice this approach given that only limited data is available, and data sources for natural probabilities (historical data for migrations and defaults) and risk neutral probabilities (credit spreads) are somewhat inconsistent. As is true for the other approaches, such as KMV, some compromises with the original theoretical framework are necessary. Credit risk measurement still requires a blend of fundamental theory and art.

The credit migration approach assumes that an obligor's credit migration process is driven by its asset value. Equity returns that are directly observable are used as a proxy for asset returns. Correlations between equity returns are used to compute the joint probability distribution of obligors' credit migrations, default being a special case of migration. Each obligor's standardized equity return is decomposed into an idiosyncratic component and a weighted average of returns of market indices (multi-factor model), where the weights are specified to appropriately reflect the obligor's participation in the corresponding countries/industries.[3]

The credit migration model is implemented as a Monte Carlo simulation. It calculates the distribution of the portfolio values and its percentiles at given confidence levels (99%, 99.5%, etc). The simulation engine generates scenarios based on the "real world" or "natural" probability distribution (P) of the risk factors. The distribution of the risk factors is assumed to be lognormal with parameters computed from historical time series data. For each generated scenario the portfolio value is computed under the martingale, or "risk neutral" probability measure (Q). The relationship between these two probability measures follows from the assumptions about the stochastic processes for the index and stock returns.

In the credit migration framework it is assumed that the credit migration process forms a discrete Markov chain with fixed time instants $\mathbf{T} = \{t_0 < t_1 < \ldots < t_l < \ldots\}$, $t_0 \geq 0$. In sections 1–5 of this chapter we discuss the mathematical model of the migration process, and define probabilities under P and Q measures to migrate from one credit class at time t_l to another credit class at time t_{l+1}. The results of sections 1–5 are further applied in sections 6–8 to compute P and Q transition probabilities by combining market credit spreads and credit migration historical data.

1. Stochastic Processes for Market Index and Stock Returns under the P Measure

Let $B = (B^1, B^2, \ldots, B^D)$ denotes a standard D-dimensional Brownian motion on a probability space $(\Omega, \mathbf{F}, P)$ $(B^1, B^2, \ldots, B^D$ are independent), where $\mathbf{F} = \{F_t, t \geq 0\}$ is a standard filtration of B.

Let $\mathbf{I} = \{I^1, I^2, \ldots, I^M\}$ be the set of all country/industry indices. It is assumed that I_t^m, the value of index m at time t, $t \geq 0$, satisfies the following stochastic differential equation (SDE):

$$dI_t^m = I_t^m \left(\mu_t^m dt + \theta_{t,1}^m dB_t^1 + \theta_{t,2}^m dB_t^2 + \ldots + \theta_{t,D}^m dB_t^D \right), \quad t \geq 0$$

$$I_0^m = i^m, \qquad m = 1, 2, \ldots, M, \tag{1.1}$$

where $\mu_t^m, \theta_{t,i}^m$ are piecewise continuous deterministic functions of t, $i = 1, 2, \ldots, D$.

For $t \in [t_l, t_{l+1})$ denote $x_t^m = \ln(I_t^m) - \ln(I_{t_l}^m)$ the index I^m log-return for the time interval $[t_l, t]$. Then, from (1.1), it follows that:

$$x_t^m = \int_{t_l}^{t} \left[\mu_s^m - \frac{1}{2}\left(\left(\theta_{s,1}^m\right)^2 + \left(\theta_{s,2}^m\right)^2 + \ldots + \left(\theta_{s,D}^m\right)^2 \right) \right] ds$$

$$+ \int_{t_l}^{t} \theta_{s,1}^m dB_s^1 + \theta_{s,2}^m dB_s^2 + \ldots + \theta_{s,D}^m dB_s^D \tag{1.2}$$

with the initial condition $x_{t_l}^m = 0$.[4] Expression (1.2) can be written in a matrix form as:

$$x_t = a_t + \int_{t_l}^{t} \theta_s dB_s, \, x_{t_l} = 0, \, t \in [t_l, t_{l+1})$$ (1.3)

where

$$x_t = \left(x_t^1, \ldots, x_t^M \right)^T,$$

$$a_t = \left(a_t^1, \ldots, a_t^M \right)^T$$

$$= \left(\int_{t_l}^{t} \left[\mu_s^1 - \frac{1}{2} \left(\left(\theta_{s,1}^1 \right)^2 + \left(\theta_{s,2}^1 \right)^2 + \ldots + \left(\theta_{s,D}^1 \right)^2 \right) \right] ds, \ldots, \right.$$

$$\left. \int_{t_l}^{t} \left[\mu_s^M - \frac{1}{2} \left(\left(\theta_{s,1}^M \right)^2 + \left(\theta_{s,2}^M \right)^2 + \ldots + \left(\theta_{s,D}^M \right)^2 \right) \right] ds \right)^T,$$

$$\theta_t = \left\| \theta_{t,i}^m \right\|_{M \times D},$$

$$dB_s = \left(dB_s^1, \ldots, dB_s^D \right)^T.$$

Assume that the portfolio is composed of facilities issued by N obligors, $O = \{O^1, O^2, \ldots, O^N\}$, and let S_t^n be the stock price of obligor O^n at time t. We assume that S_t^n satisfies the following SDE:

$$dS_t^n = S_t^n \left(\alpha_t^n dt + \sigma_{t,1}^n dB_t^1 + \sigma_{t,2}^n dB_t^2 + \ldots + \sigma_{t,D}^n dB_t^D \right), \quad t \geq 0,$$

$$S_0^n = s^n, \qquad n = 1, 2, \ldots, N,$$ (1.4)

where $\alpha_t^n, \sigma_{t,i}^n$ are deterministic functions of time, $i = 1, 2, \ldots, D$. Then, the stock log-returns $y_t^n = \ln(S_t^n) - \ln(S_{t_l}^n)$ satisfy:

$$y_t = b_t + \int_{t_l}^{t} \sigma_s dB_s, \, y_{t_l} = 0, \, t \in [t_l, t_{l+1}),$$ (1.5)

where

$$y_t = \left(y_t^1, \ldots, y_t^N \right)^T,$$

$$b_t = \left(b_t^1, \ldots, b_t^N \right)^T$$

$$= \left(\int_{t_l}^{t} \left[\alpha_s^1 - \frac{1}{2} \left(\left(\sigma_{s,1}^1 \right)^2 + \left(\sigma_{s,2}^1 \right)^2 + \ldots + \left(\sigma_{s,D}^1 \right)^2 \right) \right] ds, \ldots, \right.$$

$$\left. \int_{t_l}^{t} \left[\alpha_s^N - \frac{1}{2} \left(\left(\sigma_{s,1}^N \right)^2 + \left(\sigma_{s,2}^N \right)^2 + \ldots + \left(\sigma_{s,D}^N \right)^2 \right) \right] ds \right)^T,$$

$$\sigma_t = \left\| \sigma_{t,i}^n \right\|_{N \times D}.$$

2. Multi-Factor Equity Return Model

The credit migration approach derives equity return correlations from a multi-factor model that links correlations to fundamental country/industry factors. By imposing a structure on the return correlations, sampling errors inherent in simple historical correlations are avoided, and a better accuracy in forecasting correlations is achieved.

It is assumed that the firm's equity returns are generated by a set of common, or systematic, risk factors and idiosyncratic factors. The idiosyncratic factors are either firm specific, or country or industry specific, and do not contribute to equity return correlations since they are not correlated with each other, and not correlated with the common factors. Equity return correlations between two firms can be explained only in terms of the factors common to all firms.

In the following we assume that the equity return generating process for all M obligors is:

$$y_t^n = \beta_t^{n,0} + \beta_t^{n,1} x_t^1 + \beta_t^{n,2} x_t^2 + \ldots + \beta_t^{n,M} x_t^M + \varepsilon_t^n, \, t \in [t_l, t_{l+1})$$ (2.1)

with $n = 1, 2, \ldots, N$, $m = 1, 2, \ldots, M$ and where ε_t^n and x_t^m are uncorrelated: $\mathrm{cov}(\varepsilon_t^n, x_t^m) = 0$, and $E(\varepsilon_t^n) = 0$. Expression (2.1) can be rewritten in matrix form as:

$$y_t = \beta_t^0 + \beta_t x_t + \varepsilon_t,$$ (2.2)

where $\beta_t^0 = (\beta_t^{1,0}, \ldots, \beta_t^{N,0})^T$, $\beta_t = \|\beta_t^{n,m}\|_{N \times M}$ is the matrix of stock "betas", $\varepsilon_t = (\varepsilon_t^1, \ldots, \varepsilon_t^N)^T$ is a vector of idiosyncratic components which are uncorrelated with index returns and among themselves.

$$\mathrm{cov}(\varepsilon_t, x_t) = \|\mathrm{cov}(\varepsilon_t^n, x_t^m)\|_{N \times M} = 0,$$

$$\mathrm{cov}(\varepsilon_t, \varepsilon_t) = J_N,$$

where J_N is the $(N \times N)$ identity matrix. It is assumed that $\mathrm{rank}(\theta_t) = M \leq D$ for all t, in which case it is easy to derive the relationship between (2.1) and the index return and stock return processes (1.3) and (1.5):

$$\beta_t = \left(\int_{t_l}^{t} \sigma_s \theta_s^T \, ds \right) \left(\int_{t_l}^{t} \theta_s \theta_s^T \, ds \right)^{-1}.$$ (2.3)

Indeed, from (1.3) and (1.5) it follows that:

$$\mathrm{cov}(x_t, x_t) = \int_{t_l}^{t} \theta_s \theta_s^T \, ds,$$ (2.4)

$$\mathrm{cov}(y_t, x_t) = \int_{t_l}^{t} \sigma_s \theta_s^T \, ds,$$ (2.5)

Then, combining (2.2) and (2.4) we obtain:

$$\mathrm{cov}(y_t, x_t) = \mathrm{cov}(\beta_t^0 + \beta_t x_t + \varepsilon_t, x_t) = \beta_t \, \mathrm{cov}(x_t, x_t) = \beta_t \int_{t_l}^{t} \theta_s \theta_s^T \, ds.$$

Therefore,

$$\int_{t_l}^{t} \sigma_s \theta_s^T ds = \beta_t \int_{t_l}^{t} \theta_s \theta_s^T ds$$

and, as a result, (2.3) holds true.

3. Credit Migration Model under "Natural" Probability Measure P

It is assumed that at any time t each obligor belongs to one of the K credit classes $\mathbf{R} = \{R_1, \ldots, R_K\}$, where R_K corresponds to default. Suppose that the credit migration process forms a Markov chain on $\mathbf{R}$, with discrete times $\mathbf{T}$ and an absorbing state R_K. Denote by R_t^n the credit class of obligor O^n at time t. Suppose that $R_{t_l}^n = R_i$ and denote $p_{i,j}^n(t_l \rightarrow t_{l+1})$ the probability of O^n to migrate from credit class R_i at time t_l to credit class R_j at time t_{l+1}:

$$p_{i,j}^n(t_l \rightarrow t_{l+1}) = P(R_{t_{l+1}}^n = R_j | R_{t_l}^n = R_i). \tag{3.1}$$

Denote by

$$T_n^P(t_l \rightarrow t_{l+1}) = \left\| p_{i,j}^n(t_l \rightarrow t_{l+1}) \right\|_{K \times K} \tag{3.2}$$

the transition matrix of O^n for the time interval $[t_l, t_{l+1})$. Then,

$$\begin{cases} \sum_{j=1}^{K} p_{i,j}^n(t_l \rightarrow t_{l+1}) = 1, i = 1, \ldots, K \\ p_{K,j}^n(t_l \rightarrow t_{l+1}) = 0, \quad j = 1, \ldots, K-1. \\ p_{K,K}^n(t_l \rightarrow t_{l+1}) = 1 \end{cases} \tag{3.3}$$

The last two conditions of (3.3) characterize R_K as an absorbing state; once an obligor is in default it stays in default and cannot recover from default.

Note that in the standard implementation of the credit migration approach the transition probabilities are not firm specific. They are assumed to be the same for all obligors. This is because, in practice, these probabilities are calibrated from historical data associated with a given rating system, such as Moody's, S&Ps or any internal rating system. Therefore, in the following we will assume that the transition matrix under P for all obligors, over the time interval $[t_l, t_{l+1})$, is:

$$T^P(t_l \rightarrow t_{l+1}) = \left\| p_{i,j}(t_l \rightarrow t_{l+1}) \right\|_{K \times K} \tag{3.4}$$

with

$$p_{i,j}(t_l \rightarrow t_{l+1}) = P(R_{t_{l+1}} = R_j | R_{t_l} = R_i)$$

$$\begin{cases} \sum_{j=1}^{K} p_{i,j}(t_l \rightarrow t_{l+1}) = 1, i = 1, \ldots, K \\ p_{K,j}(t_l \rightarrow t_{l+1}) = 0, \quad j = 1, \ldots, K-1 \\ p_{K,K}(t_l \rightarrow t_{l+1}) = 1 \end{cases} \tag{3.5}$$

where R_i, for $i = 1, \ldots, K$, are prespecified credit classes that are the same for all obligors.

For each non-default state R_i and migration probabilities $p_{i,j}(t_l \to t_{l+1}), j = 1, \ldots,$ K we define the thresholds $h_{i,j}(t_l \to t_{l+1}), j = 1, \ldots, K - 1,$ for the standard normal distribution, as follows:

$$p_{i,1}(t_l \to t_{l+1}) = 1 - N(h_{i,1}(t_l, t_{l+1}))$$

$$p_{i,2}(t_l \to t_{l+1}) = N(h_{i,1}(t_l, t_{l+1})) - N(h_{i,2}(t_l, t_{l+1}))$$

$$\ldots$$

$$p_{i,K-1}(t_l \to t_{l+1}) = N(h_{i,K-2}(t_l, t_{l+1})) - N(h_{i,K-1}(t_l, t_{l+1}))$$

$$p_{i,K}(t_l \to t_{l+1}) = N(h_{i,K-1}(t_l, t_{l+1})) \tag{3.6}$$

where $N(.)$ denotes the standard normal cumulative density function. In other words, we "slice" the horizontal axis defining the standardized returns into buckets $(-\infty, h_{i,K-1}], \ldots, (h_{i,j}, h_{i,j-1}], \ldots, (h_{i,1}, +\infty)$, for $i = 1, \ldots, K - 1$, that correspond to the rating categories $R_K, \ldots, R_j, \ldots, R_1$, respectively, and the corresponding migration probabilities (3.5).

Let $w_t = Z_{y,t}^{-1}(y_t - E(y_t)), t \in [t_l, t_{l+1})$, be a vector of standardized stock returns with the correlation matrix given by:

$$\text{cor}(w_t, w_t) = Z_{y,t}^{-1}\text{cov}(y_t, y_t)Z_{y,t}^{-1} = Z_{y,t}^{-1}\left(\int_{t_l}^{t}\sigma_s\sigma_s^T\,ds\right)Z_{y,t}^{-1}, \tag{3.7}$$

where $Z_{y,t}$ is the $(N \times N)$ diagonal matrix of stock returns standard deviations:

$$Z_{y,t} = \begin{pmatrix} \sqrt{\text{var}(y_t^1)} & 0 & \cdots & 0 \\ 0 & \sqrt{\text{var}(y_t^2)} & \cdots & 0 \\ \vdots & \vdots & \ddots & \vdots \\ 0 & 0 & \cdots & \sqrt{\text{var}(y_t^N)} \end{pmatrix} \tag{3.8}$$

where $\text{var}(.)$ denotes the variance under the P measure, conditional on F_{t_l}.[5]

The credit migration model is based on the assumption that the credit class of obligor O^n at time t_{l+1} is uniquely defined by the value of its normalized stock return w_t^n relative to the thresholds $h_{i,j}(t_l, t_{l+1})$:

Assumption 1: Given $R_{t_l}^n = R_i$, then $R_{t_{l+1}}^n = R_j$ if and only if $w_{t_{l+1}}^n \in (h_{i,j}(t_l, t_{l+1}), h_{i,j-1}(t_1, t_{l+1})]$, $i, j = 1, 2, \ldots, K$, $h_{i,0}(t_l, t_{l+1}) = \infty$, $h_{i,K}(t_l, t_{l+1}) = -\infty$.

From this assumption it follows that the joint migration process for the N obligors can be defined in terms of the joint probability distribution of their normalized stock returns. The bucket in which the obligor's normalized return falls into defines unambiguously its rating at the end of the period $[t_l, t_{l+1})$. Suppose that $R_{t_l}^n = R_{i_n}$ for obligor n, $n = 1, \ldots, N$. The normalized obligors' stock returns are distributed as a N-dimensional normal distribution with zero means, unit standard deviations and correlations matrix (3.7). Denote by $f_N(x_1, x_2, \ldots, x_N)$ the joint density function. Then, the joint probability that, at time t_1, obligors 1 to N will be in credit classes $R_{j_1}, R_{j_2}, \ldots, R_{j_N}$, respectively, is:

$$P\left(R^1_{tl+1} = R_{j_1}, \ldots, R^N_{tl+1} = R_{j_N} \middle| R^1_{tl} = R_{i_1}, \ldots, R^N_{tl} = R_{i_N}\right)$$

$$= \int_{h_{i1,j1}(t_l,t_{l+1})}^{h_{i1,j1-1}(t_l,t_{l+1})} \int_{h_{i2,j2}(t_l,t_{l+1})}^{h_{i2,j2-1}(t_l,t_{l+1})} \cdots \int_{h_{iN,jN}(t_l,t_{l+1})}^{h_{iN,jN-1}(t_l,t_{l+1})} f_N(x_1, x_2, \ldots, x_N) dx_1 dx_2 \ldots dx_N. \tag{3.9}$$

4. Stochastic Processes for the Index and Stock Returns under the "Risk Neutral" Q Measure

In this section we derive the stochastic differential equations for the index and stock returns under the martingale, or risk neutral, probability measure Q.

Let r_t be the instantaneous risk-free interest rate at time t. We assume that r_t is a deterministic positive function of t. Then, the index values I^m_t, $m = 1, 2, \ldots, M$, and stock prices S^n_t, $n = 1, 2, \ldots, N$, for non-dividend-paying stocks[6] satisfy the following conditions under risk neutral probability measure Q:

$$dI^m_t = I^m_t\left(r_t dt + \theta^m_{t,1} d\hat{B}^1_t + \theta^m_{t,2} d\hat{B}^2_t + \ldots + \theta^m_{t,D} d\hat{B}^D_t\right), \quad t \geq 0,$$

$$I^m_0 = i^m, \quad m = 1, 2, \ldots, M, \tag{4.1}$$

$$dS^n_t = S^n_t\left(r_t dt + \sigma^n_{t,1} d\hat{B}^1_t + \sigma^n_{t,2} d\hat{B}^2_t + \ldots + \sigma^n_{t,D} d\hat{B}^D_t\right), \quad t \geq 0,$$

$$S^n_0 = s^n, \quad n = 1, 2, \ldots, N, \tag{4.2}$$

where $\hat{B}^d_t$, $d = 1, \ldots, D$, are Brownian motions under Q.

We can now derive the index and stock log-returns from (4.1) and (4.2) over the time interval $[t_l, t]$, $t \in [t_l, t_{l+1})$:

$$x_t = \hat{a}_t + \int_{t_l}^t \theta_s d\hat{B}_s, \, , \, x_{t_l} = 0 \tag{4.3}$$

$$y_t = \hat{b}_t + \int_{t_l}^t \sigma_s d\hat{B}_s, \, , \, y_{t_l} = 0 \tag{4.4}$$

where

$$\hat{a}_t = \left(\hat{a}^1_t, \ldots, \hat{a}^M_t\right)^T$$

$$= \left(\int_{t_l}^t \left[r_s - \frac{1}{2}\left(\left(\theta^1_{s,1}\right)^2 + \left(\theta^1_{s,2}\right)^2 + \ldots + \left(\theta^1_{s,D}\right)^2\right)\right] ds, \ldots,\right.$$

$$\left.\int_{t_l}^t \left[r_s - \frac{1}{2}\left(\left(\theta^M_{s,1}\right)^2 + \left(\theta^M_{s,2}\right)^2 + \ldots + \left(\theta^M_{s,D}\right)^2\right)\right] ds\right)^T,$$

$$\hat{b}_t = \left(\hat{b}_t^1, \ldots, \hat{b}_t^N\right)^T$$

$$= \left(\int_{tl}^{t}\left[r_s - \frac{1}{2}\left((\sigma_{s,1}^1)^2 + (\sigma_{s,2}^1)^2 + \ldots + (\sigma_{s,D}^1)^2\right)\right]ds, \ldots,\right.$$

$$\left.\int_{tl}^{t}\left[r_s - \frac{1}{2}\left((\sigma_{s,1}^N)^2 + (\sigma_{s,2}^N)^2 + \ldots + (\sigma_{s,D}^N)^2\right)\right]ds\right)^T,$$

$$d\hat{B}_s = \left(d\hat{B}_s^1, \ldots, d\hat{B}_s^D\right)^T.$$

Let $E^Q(.)$ and $\mathrm{cov}^Q(.,.)$ denote the expected value and covariance matrix under the probability measure Q, conditional on F_{tl}. Then, from (4.3) and (4.4) it follows that:

$$E^Q(x_t) = \hat{a}, \tag{4.5}$$

$$E^Q(y_t) = \hat{b}, \tag{4.6}$$

$$\mathrm{cov}^Q(x_t, x_t) = \mathrm{cov}(x_t, x_t) = \int_{tl}^{t} \theta_s \theta_s^T ds, \tag{4.7}$$

$$\mathrm{cov}^Q(y_t, x_t) = \mathrm{cov}(y_t, x_t) = \int_{tl}^{t} \sigma_s \theta_s^T ds, \tag{4.8}$$

$$\mathrm{cov}^Q(y_t, y_t) = \mathrm{cov}(y_t, y_t) = \int_{tl}^{t} \sigma_s \sigma_s^T ds. \tag{4.9}$$

In particular,

$$\mathrm{var}^Q(y_t^n) = \mathrm{var}(y_t^n) \tag{4.10}$$

for all $n = 1, 2, \ldots, N$. Moreover,

$$\mathrm{cov}^Q(\varepsilon_t, x_t) = \mathrm{cov}(\varepsilon_t, x_t) = 0 \tag{4.11}$$

$$\mathrm{cov}^Q(\varepsilon_t, \varepsilon_t) = \mathrm{cov}(\varepsilon_t, \varepsilon_t), \tag{4.12}$$

In other words the variances and correlations are the same under the two probability measures P and Q.

5. Credit Migration Model under the "Risk Neutral" Q Measure

In section 3 we defined the relationship between credit migration events and movements of the normalized stock returns. It allows the derivation of the probabilities of credit migration for different credit classes under the P measure. We can also derive the corresponding migration probabilities under the Q measure.

Assume that obligor S^n is in credit class $R^n_{t_l} = R_i$ at time t_l. According to Assumption 1 in Section 3, its credit rating at time t_{l+1} will be $R^n_{t_{l+1}} = R_j$ if and only if $w^n_{t_{l+1}}$ $\in (h_{i,j}(t_l, t_{l+1}), h_{i,j-1}(t_l, t_{l+1})], j = 1, 2, \ldots, K$, where the thresholds $h_{i,j}(t_l, t_{l+1})$ are derived from the standard normal distribution according to (3.6). Then, the probability under the Q measure for obligors $O^1, O^2, \ldots, O^N$ to migrate from the credit classes $R^1_{t_l}$ $= R_{i_1}, \ldots, R^N_{t_l} = R_{i_N}$ at time t_l, to the credit classes $R^1_{t_{l+1}} = R_{j_1}, \ldots, R^N_{t_{l+1}} = R_{j_N}$ at time t_{l+1}, respectively, is:

$$Q(R^1_{t_{l+1}} = R_{j_1}, \ldots, R^N_{t_l} = R_{j_N} | R^1_{t_{l+1}} = R_{i_1}, \ldots, R^N_{t_l} = R_{i_N})$$
$$= Q(w^n_{t_{l+1}} \in (h_{i_1,j_1}(t_l, t_{l+1}), h_{i_1,j_1-1}(t_l, t_{l+1})], \ldots, w^n_{t_{l+1}} \in (h_{i_N,j_N}(t_l, t_{l+1}), h_{i_N,j_N-1}(t_l, t_{l+1})]) \quad (5.1)$$

From the definition of $w_t = (w^1_t, \ldots, w^N_t)^T$ and (4.10) it follows that:

$$w^n_t = \frac{1}{\sqrt{\text{var}(y^n_t)}}(y^n_t - E(y^n_t))$$
$$= \frac{1}{\sqrt{\text{var}^Q(y^n_t)}}(y^n_t - E^Q(y^n_t)) + \frac{1}{\sqrt{\text{var}(y^n_t)}}(E^Q(y^n_t) - E(y^n_t))$$
$$= \hat{w}^n_t + C^n_0(t_0, t)$$

where

$$\hat{w}^n_t = \frac{1}{\sqrt{\text{var}^Q(y^n_t)}}(y^n_t - E^Q(y^n_t)) \quad (5.2)$$

and $C^n_0(t_0, t)$ is a constant that is obligor specific and does not depend on its rating:

$$C^n_0(t_l, t) = \frac{1}{\sqrt{\text{var}(y^n_t)}}(E^Q(y^n_t) - E(y^n_t))$$
$$= \frac{1}{\sqrt{\text{var}(y^n_t)}} \int_{t_l}^{t}(r_s - \alpha^n_s)ds$$
$$= \frac{\int_{t_l}^{t}(r_s - \alpha^n_s)ds}{\left(\int_{t_l}^{t}\left((\sigma^n_{s,1})^2 + (\sigma^n_{s,2})^2 + \ldots + (\sigma^n_{s,D})^2\right)ds\right)^{\frac{1}{2}}} \quad (5.3)$$

Then, for the vector $\hat{w}_t = (\hat{w}^1_t, \ldots, \hat{w}^N_t)^T$ using (3.7), (4.4) and (4.10) we obtain:

$$\text{cov}^Q(\hat{w}_t, \hat{w}_t) = \text{cov}^Q(w_t, w_t)$$
$$= E^Q\left(Z^{-1}_{y,t}(y_t - E(y_t))(y_t - E(y_t))^T Z^{-1}_{y,t}\right)$$
$$= Z^{-1}_{y,t}\text{cov}^Q(y_t, y_t)Z^{-1}_{y,t}$$
$$= Z^{-1}_{y,t}\text{cov}(y_t, y_t)Z^{-1}_{y,t}$$
$$= \text{cov}(w_t, w_t) \quad (5.4)$$

From equations (4.4), (5.2) and (5.4) it follows that the random vector $\hat{w}_t = (\hat{w}_t^1, \ldots, \hat{w}_t^N)^T$ has a normal distribution under the probability measure Q with zero means and a covariance matrix $\mathrm{cov}^Q(w_t, w_t) = \mathrm{cov}(w_t, w_t)$. Then $\hat{w}_t^n$ is a standard normal variable under the Q measure for each obligor O^n, $n = 1, \ldots, N$, and the risk neutral probabilities are:

$$
\begin{aligned}
q_{i,j}^n(t_l \to t_{l+1}) &= Q(w_{t_{l+1}}^n \in (h_{i,j}(t_l, t_{l+1}), h_{i,j-1}(t_l, t_{l+1})]) \\
&= Q(\hat{w}_{t_{l+1}}^n + C_0^n(t_l, t_{l+1}) \in (h_{i,j}(t_l, t_{l+1}), h_{i,j-1}(t_l, t_{l+1})]) \\
&= Q(\hat{w}_{t_{l+1}}^n \in (h_{i,j}(t_l, t_{l+1}) - C_0^n(t_l, t_{l+1}), h_{i,j-1}(t_l, t_{l+1}) - C_0^n(t_l, t_{l+1})]) \\
&= N(h_{i,j-1}(t_l, t_{l+1}) - C_0^n(t_l, t_{l+1})) - N(h_{i,j}(t_l, t_{l+1}) - C_0^n(t_l, t_{l+1})).
\end{aligned}
\tag{5.5}
$$

Therefore, the transition probabilities $q_{i,j}^n(t_l \to t_{l+1})$ under the martingale measure Q are defined in a similar fashion as the transition probabilities $p_{i,j}(t_l \to t_{l+1})$ under the P measure, but the transition probabilities $q_{i,j}^n(t_l \to t_{l+1})$ depend on n and are different for each obligor. Indeed, the threshold factors $g_{i,j}^n(t_l, t_{l+1})$ under the Q measure are now obligor specific and equal to those derived under the P measure shifted, for each obligor, by the obligor specific "shift factor" $C_0^n(t_l \to t_{l+1})$ as defined in (5.3). Under the Q measure the thresholds that define migration are:

$$
g_{i,j}^n(t_l \to t_{l+1}) = h_{i,j}(t_l \to t_{l+1}) - \frac{\displaystyle\int_{t_l}^{t_{l+1}} (r_s - \alpha^n)\,ds}{\left(\displaystyle\int_{t_l}^{t_{l+1}} \left((\sigma_{s,1}^n)^2 + (\sigma_{s,2}^n)^2 + \ldots + (\sigma_{s,D}^n)^2\right)ds\right)^{\frac{1}{2}}}.
\tag{5.6}
$$

Conditions (5.5) and (5.6) show the relationship that exists between the transition matrices $T_n^P(t_l \to t_{l+1}) = \|p_{i,j}(t_l \to t_{l+1})\|$ and $T_n^Q(t_l \to t_{l+1}) = \|q_{i,j}^n(t_l \to t_{l+1})\|$ derived under the P and Q measures, respectively.

The Q probability of joint migrations is:

$$
\begin{aligned}
Q(R_{t_{l+1}}^1 &= R_{j1} \ldots, R_{t_{l+1}}^N = R_{jN} | R_{t_l}^1 = R_{i1} \ldots, R_{t_l}^N = R_{iN}) \\
&= Q(w_{t_{l+1}}^{i_1} \in (h_{i_1,j_1}(t_l, t_{l+1}), h_{i_1,j_1-1}(t_l, t_{l+1})], \ldots, w_{t_{l+1}}^{i_N} \in (h_{i_N,j_N}(t_l, t_{l+1}), h_{i_N,j_N-1}(t_l, t_{l+1})]) \\
&= Q(\hat{w}_{t_{l+1}}^1 \in (g_{i_1,j_1}^1(t_l, t_{l+1}), g_{i_1,j_1-1}^1(t_l, t_{l+1})], \ldots, \hat{w}_{t_{l+1}}^n \in (g_{i_N,j_N}^N(t_l, t_{l+1}), g_{i_N,j_N-1}^N(t_l, t_{l+1})]) \\
&= \int_{g_{i_1,j_1}^1(t_l,t_{l+1})}^{g_{i_1,j_1-1}^1(t_l,t_{l+1})} \cdots \int_{g_{i_N,j_N}^N(t_l,t_{l+1})}^{g_{i_N,j_N-1}^N(t_l,t_{l+1})} f_N(x_1, x_2, \ldots, x_N)\,dx_1 dx_2 \ldots dx_N.
\end{aligned}
\tag{5.7}
$$

6. Construction of the Transition Matrix under the Q-Measure over the First Period $[t_0, t_1)$

There is no straightforward direct implementation of the model since it is practically impossible to compute the obligor specific shift factors (5.3) and the corresponding risk neutral probabilities (5.5). We propose a practical approach that requires the independent estimation of:

(i) the P-transition matrix based on historical data of migrations and defaults by credit rating, and
(ii) the risk neutral default probabilities based on the "reduced form" analysis of credit spreads as proposed by Duffie and Singleton (1997), Lando (1997) and Jarrow and Turnbull (1995).

Denote by $T^P(t_0, t_1) = \|p_{i,j}(t_0, t_1)\|$ the P-transition matrix for the period $[t_0, t_1)$, and

$$\mathbf{q}(t_0 \rightarrow t_1) = \begin{pmatrix} q_1(t_0 \rightarrow t_1) \\ q_2(t_0 \rightarrow t_1) \\ \vdots \\ q_\kappa(t_0 \rightarrow t_1) \end{pmatrix}, \tag{6.1}$$

with $\kappa = K - 1$, is a vector of Q default probabilities, for the period $[t_0, t_1)$, that have been calibrated for each credit rating,[7] i.e.

$$q_i(t_0 \rightarrow t_1) = Q(R_{t_1} = R_K | R_{t_0} = R_i), \quad i = 1, 2, \ldots, \kappa$$

The proposed approach proceeds in three steps.

1. Derivation of the "shift factor" $C_0 = C_0^n(t_0 \rightarrow t_1)$ which, in our implementation, is obligor independent.[8]
    First, we compute the thresholds corresponding to the P and Q probabilities of default (see 3.6):

$$h_{i,\kappa} = N^{-1}(p_{i,K}),$$

$$g_{i,\kappa} = N^{-1}(q_i)$$

and then take the simple average of their differences:

$$C_0 = \frac{1}{\kappa} \sum_{i=1}^{\kappa} (h_{i,\kappa} - g_{i,\kappa}). \tag{6.2}$$

where κ is the number of non–default states.[9]

2. Recalibration of a new transition matrix $\overline{T}^P(t_0, t_1) = \|\overline{p}_{i,j}(t_0, t_1)\|$ by

$$\overline{p}_{i,j}(t_0, t_1) = \begin{cases} N(g_{i,\kappa} + C_0), & j = K \\ v_i p_{i,j}, & j < K \end{cases} \quad (i \neq K) \tag{6.3}$$

where υ_i is a scaling factor that ensures that the sum of the probabilities for each rating class is one: $\upsilon_i = \dfrac{1 - N(g_{i,\kappa} + C_0)}{1 - p_{i,K}}$. Default being an absorbing state we have $\bar{p}_{K,j}(t_0, t_1) = 0$ if $j < K$ and $\bar{p}_{K,K}(t_0, t_1) = 1$.

Therefore, the last column of the given matrix $T^P(t_0, t_1)$ is adjusted in such a way that the new P default thresholds satisfy $N^{-1}(\bar{p}_{i,K}(t_0, t_1)) = g_{i,\kappa} + C_0$, i.e., they differ from the Q default thresholds $g_{i,\kappa}$ by the constant C_0, independent of i. The probabilities of migration into non-default states are then adjusted while maintaining, for each row, the same relative weights with respect to the survival probability, i.e.,

$$\frac{p_{i,j}(t_0, t_1)}{1 - p_{i,K}(t_0, t_1)} = \frac{\bar{p}_{i,j}(t_0, t_1)}{1 - \bar{p}_{i,K}(t_0, t_1)} \quad \text{for all } i, j < K. \tag{6.4}$$

There is some good economic logic in the proposed adjustment of the original transition matrix. Indeed, the Q-default probabilities are derived from current credit spreads that are forward looking. P-transition and default probabilities are historical averages that may not be consistent with the Q-probabilities. If migration probabilities are relatively stable over time, it is less the case of default probabilities that vary with the credit cycle. The adjustment makes the P and Q default probabilities consistent with one another.

3. Derivation of the risk neutral transition matrix $T^Q(t_0, t_1) = \|q_{i,j}(t_0, t_1)\|$.

From the adjusted P-transition matrix $\bar{T}^P(t_0, t_1) = \|\bar{p}_{i,j}(t_0, t_1)\|$ we can obtain the desired Q-transition matrix over the period $[t_0, t_1)$. Let $\bar{h}_{i,j}(t_0, t_1)$, $i, j < K$, be the thresholds of $\bar{T}^P(t_0, t_1)$ computed from (3.6). In particular, we have:

$$\bar{h}_{i,\kappa}(t_0, t_1) = N^{-1}(\bar{p}_{i,\kappa}(t_0, t_1)) = g_{i,\kappa} + C_0. \tag{6.5}$$

According to (5.5) and (5.6) the (i, j)-th entry of $T^Q(t_0, t_1) = \|q_{i,j}(t_0, t_1)\|$ is defined by:

$$q_{i,j}(t_0, t_1) = N(g_{i,j-1}(t_0, t_1)) - N(g_{i,j}(t_0, t_1)), \quad i, j = 1, 2, \ldots, K \tag{6.6}$$

where $g_{i,j}(t_0, t_1) = \bar{h}_{i,j}(t_0, t_1) - C_0(t_0, t_1)$. Using (6.5), (6.6) and $N^{-1}(-\infty) = 0$, we have

$$q_{i,\kappa}(t_0, t_1) = N(\bar{h}_{i,\kappa}(t_0, t_1) - C_0) - N(-\infty) = N(g_{i,\kappa}) = q_i(t_0 \to t_1)$$

for each $i = 1, 2, \ldots, \kappa$. Thus, by construction, the last column of $T^Q(t_0, t_1)$ fits exactly the given default probabilities under Q over the period $[t_0, t_1)$:

$$\begin{pmatrix} q_{1,K}(t_0, t_1) \\ q_{2,K}(t_0, t_1) \\ \vdots \\ q_{\kappa,K}(t_0, t_1) \\ 1 \end{pmatrix} = \begin{pmatrix} q_1(t_0 \to t_1) \\ q_2(t_0 \to t_1) \\ \vdots \\ q_\kappa(t_0 \to t_1) \\ 1 \end{pmatrix} = \begin{pmatrix} \mathbf{q}(t_0 \to t_1) \\ 1 \end{pmatrix} \tag{6.7}$$

In summary, a suitable adjustment is made to the given P-transition matrix such that its last column is consistent with the given Q-default probabilities. For each row, the remaining entries in the P-transition matrix are also adjusted by retaining the same relative weights with respect to the survival probability. The constant C_0 is then subtracted from other non-default thresholds of the modified P-matrix to obtain the corresponding thresholds, and therefore the entries, of the desire Q-matrix.

7. Forward Transition Matrices under Q

In this section, we propose an algorithm to generate a series of Q-forward transition matrices matching the *given* term structure of Q-default probabilities across various maturities.[10] We assume that the Q-default probabilities satisfy:[11]

$$0 \le \mathbf{q}(t_0 \rightarrow t_1) \le \mathbf{q}(t_0 \rightarrow t_2) \le \ldots \le \mathbf{q}(t_0 \rightarrow t_L) < \mathbf{e} \tag{7.1}$$

where

$$\mathbf{q}(t_0 \rightarrow t_1) = \begin{pmatrix} q_1(t_0 \rightarrow t_l) \\ q_2(t_0 \rightarrow t_l) \\ \vdots \\ q_\kappa(t_0 \rightarrow t_l) \end{pmatrix},$$

$l = 1, \ldots, L$ and $\mathbf{e}$ is the κ-dimensional vector whose components are all equal to 1 ($\kappa = K - 1$).

We are also given a series of spot P-transition matrices constructed from historical data:

$$T^P(t_0, t_1), \; T^P(t_0, t_2), \; \ldots, \; T^P(t_0, t_L) \tag{7.2}$$

Applying the procedure described in Section 6 we derive the Q-transition matrix $T^Q(t_0, t_1)$ for the first time interval $[t_0, t_1)$ and $\overline{T}^P(t_0, t_1)$.

The issue we address here is, given this information, i.e. the term structure of risk neutral default probabilities for all rating classes and the P-transition matrices, how can we derive the Q-forward transition matrices:

$$T^Q(t_1, t_2), \; T^Q(t_2, t_3), \; \ldots, \; T^Q(t_{L-1}, t_L) \tag{7.3}$$

over the consecutive time intervals

$$[t_1, t_2), [t_2, t_3), \ldots, [t_{L-1}, t_L) \tag{7.4}$$

that are used in the risk neutral valuation of credit derivatives discussed in the next section.

To motivate our approach, let us consider the case of two time intervals $[\theta_0, \theta_1)$ and $[\theta_1, \theta_2)$. Let M, M_1, M_2 be the transition matrices (all under the same probability measure) corresponding to the intervals $[\theta_0, \theta_2)$, $[\theta_0, \theta_1)$ and $[\theta_1, \theta_2)$, respectively. Assuming that the credit migration process is Markovian, we have:

$$M = M_1 M_2. \tag{7.5}$$

From this relation we can derive the relationship between the probabilities of default over the time intervals $[\theta_0, \theta_2)$ and $[\theta_1, \theta_2)$. Let

$$\begin{pmatrix} \mathbf{m}(\theta_0 \to \theta_2) \\ 1 \end{pmatrix} \quad \text{and} \quad \begin{pmatrix} \mathbf{m}^2(\theta_1 \to \theta_2) \\ 1 \end{pmatrix},$$

be the last columns of M and M_2, respectively, where

$$\mathbf{m}(\theta_0 \to \theta_2) = \begin{pmatrix} m_1(\theta_0 \to \theta_2) \\ m_2(\theta_0 \to \theta_2) \\ \vdots \\ m_\kappa(\theta_0 \to \theta_2) \end{pmatrix} \qquad \mathbf{m}^2(\theta_1 \to \theta_2) = \begin{pmatrix} m_1^2(\theta_1 \to \theta_2) \\ m_2^2(\theta_1 \to \theta_2) \\ \vdots \\ m_\kappa^2(\theta_1 \to \theta_2) \end{pmatrix}.$$

denote the corresponding default probabilities. Then, from (7.5) it follows that:

$$\begin{pmatrix} \mathbf{m}(\theta_0 \to \theta_2) \\ 1 \end{pmatrix} = M_1 \begin{pmatrix} \mathbf{m}^2(\theta_1 \to \theta_2) \\ 1 \end{pmatrix}$$

and, if M_1 is invertible, we have:

$$\begin{pmatrix} \mathbf{m}^2(\theta_1 \to \theta_2) \\ 1 \end{pmatrix} = M_1^{-1} \begin{pmatrix} \mathbf{m}(\theta_0 \to \theta_2) \\ 1 \end{pmatrix} \tag{7.6}$$

Equation (7.6) allows us to compute the forward probabilities of default over the time interval $[\theta_1, \theta_2)$ from the probabilities of default on the time interval $[\theta_0, \theta_2)$, and the transition matrix M_1. This is the key relationship we use in the iterative procedure described below for computing the Q-forward transition matrices (7.3).

First, we apply (7.6) with $[\theta_0, \theta_1) = [t_0, t_1)$ and $M_1 = T^Q(t_0, t_1)$ to compute the forward default probabilities over the time intervals $[t_1, t_2), [t_1, t_3), \ldots, [t_1, t_L)$ ($\theta_2 = t_2, t_3, \ldots, t_L$). Relation (7.6) only applies if $T^Q(t_0, t_1)$ is invertible. If it is not the case, then we suggest to apply a minor transformation of $T^Q(t_0, t_1)$ that keeps intact its last column (default probabilities), but affects only the migration frequencies, so that the modified transition matrix, $Z^Q(t_0, t_1; \alpha)$, becomes invertible and, moreover, the implied forward default probabilities are non-negative and monotonically increasing.[12]

Let

$$Z^Q(t_0, t_1; \ \alpha) = \alpha X(t_0, t_1) + (1 - \alpha) T^Q(t_0, t_1), \quad 0 \le \alpha \le 1 \tag{7.7}$$

where $X(t_0, t_1)$ is the following invertible matrix:

$$X(t_0, t_1) = \begin{pmatrix} (1-q_1) & \cdots & 0 & q_1 \\ \vdots & \ddots & \vdots & \vdots \\ 0 & \cdots & (1-q_\kappa) & q_\kappa \\ 0 & \cdots & 0 & 1 \end{pmatrix} \tag{7.8}$$

with $q_i = q_i(t_0 \rightarrow t_1) < 1$ for $i = 1, 2, \ldots, \kappa$. The matrices $Z^Q(t_0, t_1; \alpha)$ and $T^Q(t_0, t_1)$ have the same last column, i.e. $\begin{pmatrix} q(t_0 \rightarrow t_1) \\ 1 \end{pmatrix}$ with $q(t_0 \rightarrow t_1) = (q_1, \ldots, q_\kappa)^T$. We choose the "smallest" α, denoted $\overline{\alpha}_1$, in (7.7) such that:[13]

1. $Z^Q(t_0, t_1; \overline{\alpha}_1)$ is invertible,
2. The vectors of Q-forward default probabilities $\mathbf{q}(t_1 \rightarrow t_l)$, $l = 2, \ldots, L$, defined by

$$\begin{pmatrix} \mathbf{q}(t_1 \rightarrow t_l) \\ 1 \end{pmatrix} = Z^Q(t_0, t_1; \overline{\alpha}_1)^{-1} \begin{pmatrix} \mathbf{q}(t_0 \rightarrow t_l) \\ 1 \end{pmatrix}$$

satisfy

$$0 \leq \mathbf{q}(t_1 \rightarrow t_2) \leq \mathbf{q}(t_1 \rightarrow t_3) \leq \ldots \leq \mathbf{q}(t_1 \rightarrow t_L) < \mathbf{e}. \tag{7.9}$$

Such $\overline{\alpha}_1$ exists since, for $\overline{\alpha}_1 = 1$, the condition is satisfied. In practice we find that $\overline{\alpha}_1$ stays very small. Then, we define $T^Q(t_0, t_1) = Z^Q(t_0, t_1; \overline{\alpha}_1)$.

If this procedure changes the Q-transition matrix $T^Q(t_0, t_1)$ derived in section 6, then the corresponding adjustment should be made to the P-transition matrix $\overline{T}^P(t_0, t_1)$. We thus obtain a new set of transition matrices $\overline{T}^P(t_0, t_1)$ and $T^Q(t_0, t_1)$ which preserve the original Q-default probabilities over the first interval (see Figure 1).

We can now iterate the same procedure for the period $[t_1, t_2)$ with condition (7.9) playing the role of (7.1) in the previous phase. In order to construct the transition matrix $T^Q(t_1, t_2)$ we need to know the vector $q(t_1 \rightarrow t_2)$ of forward default probabilities, and the P-transition matrix $T^P(t_0, t_1)$. The vector $q(t_1 \rightarrow t_2)$ is given by (7.9). $T^P(t_1, t_2)$ can be derived using the empirical information given by (7.2):

$$T^P(t_1, t_2) = T^P(t_0, t_1)^{-1} T^P(t_0, t_2) \tag{7.10}$$

adjusting, if necessary, the matrix $T^P(t_0, t_1)$ to make it invertible and to guarantee that all elements of $T^P(t_1, t_2)$ are nonnegative. This can be achieved by applying the technique (7.7) applied to $T^Q(t_0, t_1)$ to make it invertible.

Once we have derived $T^P(t_1, t_2)$ we can apply the procedure developed in Section 6 to derive $T^Q(t_1, t_2)$ (see Figure 2).

Finally, for subsequent periods $[t_l, t_{l+1})$, $l \geq 1$, we proceed recursively to construct invertible transition matrices $T^Q(t_2, t_3), \ldots, T^Q(t_{L-1}, t_L)$, ensuring, at each

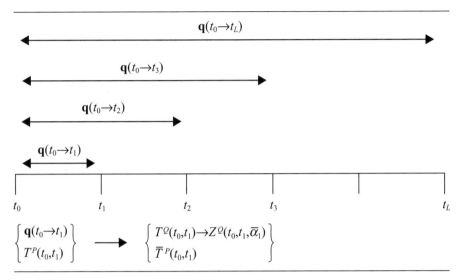

Figure 1. Iterative process to derive the Q-forward transition matrices (phase 1)

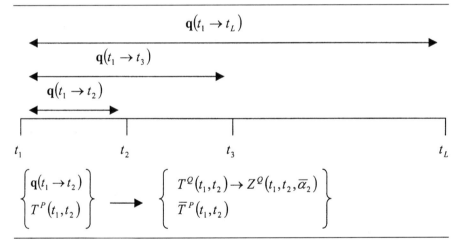

Figure 2. Iterative process to derive the Q-forward transition matrices (phase 2)

stage of the process, the non–negativity and monotonicity of the forward default probabilities.

8. Example: Pricing of a Default Swap on a Bond

A default swap on a bond provides protection to the holder of the reference bond against the loss of its value when the bond issuer defaults. The buyer of the contract makes a series of premium payments at scheduled times to the seller of the protection, provided that the issuer of the underlying bond has not defaulted and the contract is still alive.

In this example, we choose the scheduled dates for the premium payments as observation times $\mathbf{T}$,[14] and assume that we are given the Q-transition matrices over the consecutive payment dates. Let C be the counterparty on the default swap, i.e. the seller of the default swap, and B the issuer of the underlying facility to the contract. The fixed premium payments can be made either in arrears or in advance from the buyer to the seller. We shall consider in the following the case when the payments are made in advance.

Let t_0 be the current time at which the contract is evaluated, and T be the expiration date of the credit swap. Let $t_0 < t_1 < t_2 < \ldots < t_L = T$ be a partition of the interval $[t_0, T]$ that includes all remaining premium payment times. Let $x_0, x_1, \ldots, x_{L-1}, x_L$ be the respective payments to be made by the buyer at these times (note that $x_L = 0$ since payments are made in advance).

Let τ_B be the random default time of the underlying facility and τ_C the random default time of the counterparty. To represent the different default status of B and C on the interval $(t_{l-1}, t_l]$, for $l = 1, \ldots, L$, we introduce the following set of events (Fig. 3):

These events are all conditional on the initial credit ratings $I_0 = (R^B_{t_0}, R^C_{t_0}) = (R_{i_0}, R_{j_0})$ of (B, C) at time t_0. Let E_l describe the event where B defaults during $(t_{l-1}, t_l]$ while C remains alive during the same period, and vice versa for set $\hat{E}_l$; let F_l represent the event that both parties default in the same period $(t_{l-1}, t_l]$; finally, G_l denotes the situation where both obligors remain alive beyond t_l.

For each such event, we describe the corresponding stream of cashflows from the viewpoint of the buyer of the default swap. For this, let N be the notional amount

$$E_l = \{t_{l-1} < \tau_B \le t_l, \tau_C > t_l\},$$
$$\hat{E}_l = \{t_{l-1} < \tau_C \le t_l, \tau_B > t_l\},$$
$$F_l = \{t_{l-1} < \tau_B \le t_l, t_{l-1} < \tau_C \le t_l\},$$
$$G_l = \{\tau_B > t_l, \tau_C > t_l\}.$$

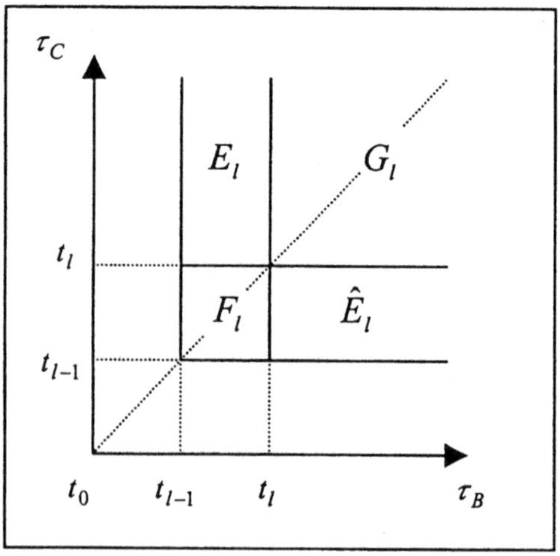

Figure 3. Joint default events

and $z_B(t_l)$ the value of the bond's obligations had it not defaulted as at time t_l. When default of the bond occurs in $(t_{l-1}, t_l]$, we assume that its defaulted, or recovery value is $R_B z_B(t_l)$ which is less than the notional amount N, where R_B denoted the recovery rate on the defaulted bond. When the counterparty C defaults, the recovery rate on C's obligation is R_C.

- E_l: The buyer pays premiums $x_1, \ldots, x_{l-1}$ at times $t_0, t_1, \ldots, t_{l-1}$, respectively, and upon default of the underlying bond in $(t_{l-1}, t_l]$, receives cash amount N at time t_l while delivering the defaulted bond of value $R_B z_B(t_l)$.
- F_l: The buyer pays premiums $x_1, \ldots, x_{l-1}$ at times $t_0, t_1, \ldots, t_{l-1}$, respectively, and upon default of both the underlying bond and the counterparty in interval $(t_{l-1}, t_l]$, receives the contingent cash amount net of the defaulted bond: $R_C(N - R_B z_B(t_l))$ at t_l.
- $\hat{E}_l$: The buyer pays premiums $x_1, \ldots, x_{l-1}$ at times $t_0, t_1, \ldots, t_{l-1}$, respectively, and when the counterparty defaults in $(t_{l-1}, t_l]$, the contract terminates by time t_l.
- G_L: The credit swap expires at t_L as scheduled with both the underlying bond and the counterparty surviving until that time; the buyer pays all premiums $x_1, \ldots, x_{L-1}$ at times $t_0, t_1, \ldots, t_{L-1}$, respectively.

Now, note that $G_0 = \{\tau_B > t_0, \tau_C > t_0\}$ describes all possible future events from time t_0, so that its probability is $Q(G_0) = 1$. It can further be decomposed into a union of mutually disjoint events:

$$G_0 = \left(\bigcup_{l=1}^{L} (E_l \cup \hat{E}_l \cup F_l) \right) \cup G_L$$

and, for each time interval:

$$Q(E_L) + Q(F_l) + Q(\hat{E}_l) + Q(G_l) = Q(G_{l-1}).$$

From this and the above description of the cash-flow streams, it follows that the value of the credit swap for the buyer of the credit protection is:

$$\text{price} = \sum_{l=1}^{L} d_l (N - R_B z_B(t_l))(Q(E_l) + R_C Q(F_l)) - \sum_{l=1}^{L} d_{l-1} x_{l-1} Q(G_{l-1}) \tag{8.1}$$

where Q is the risk-neutral pricing measure and d_l is the discounting factor from t_l to t_0 based on the risk-free rate. Recall that the probabilities $Q(E_l)$, $Q(F_l)$, etc., in (8.1) are conditional on the initial credit ratings I_0 of B and C.

To derive the price (8.1), note that the first sum expression comes from the contingent payments in the events E_l and F_l, with cashflows discounted appropriately. The second sum comes from the premium payments, as their present value equals

$$\sum_{l=1}^{L}\left(\sum_{i=1}^{l}d_{i-1}x_{i-1}\right)(Q(E_l)+Q(F_l)+Q(\hat{E}_l))+\left(\sum_{i=1}^{L}d_{i-1}x_{i-1}\right)Q(G_L)$$

$$=\sum_{i=1}^{L}\sum_{l=i}^{L}d_{i-1}x_{i-1}(Q(G_{l-1})-Q(G_l))+\sum_{i=1}^{L}d_{i-1}x_{i-1}Q(G_L)$$

$$=\sum_{i=1}^{L}d_{i-1}x_{i-1}\left(\sum_{l=1}^{L}(Q(G_{l-1})-Q(G_l))+Q(G_L)\right)$$

$$=\sum_{i=1}^{L}d_{i-1}x_{i-1}Q(G_{i-1})$$

To evaluate (8.1) we need to evaluate the Q-probabilities of the events E_l, F_l and G_l. In fact, they can be explicitly computed in terms of the entries in the appropriate Q-forward transition matrices. To this end, let T^l denote the Q transition matrix over period $[t_{l-1}, t_l)$ for both obligors B and C, U^l the corresponding Q transition matrix for their joint process (B, C), and let $\hat{T}^l = T^1 T^2 \ldots T^l$ and $\hat{U}^l = U^1 U^2 \ldots U^l$ be their cumulative transition matrices. Here, U^l is a matrix of size $K^2 \times K^2$ and its rows and columns are indexed by $\eta_{ij} = (i-1)K + j$ corresponding to rating class state (R_i, R_j) for the joint process (B, C). By definition, its $(\eta_{ij}, \eta_{i'j'})$-entry is the probability of B and C co-migrating to state $(R_{i'}, R_{j'})$ by time t_l, given that they were in state (R_i, R_j) at time t_{l-1}. More precisely, let $R^B_{t_{l-1}}$ and $R^B_{t_l}$ be the rating of B at time t_{l-1} and t_l, respectively, and similarly, $R^C_{t_{l-1}}$ and $R^C_{t_l}$ for C. By (5.7), with $N = 2$, the $(\eta_{ij}, \eta_{i'j'})$-entry over the time interval $[t_{l-1}, t_l)$ can be explicitly computed by the following double integral:

$$U^l(\eta_{ij}, \eta_{i'j'}) = Q(R^B_{t_l} = R_{i'}, R^C_{t_l} = R_{j'} | R^B_{t_{l-1}} = R_i, R^C_{t_{l-1}} = R_j)$$

$$= \int_{g^B_{i,i'}}^{g^B_{i,i'-1}} \int_{g^C_{j,j'}}^{g^C_{j,j'-1}} f(x,y)\,dy\,dx \tag{8.2}$$

where $g^B_{i,i'}$, $g^B_{i,i'-1}$, $g^C_{j,j'}$ and $g^C_{j,j'-1}$ are the thresholds determined from the transition matrix T^l, and f is the joint density which, in this case, is the standard bivariate normal density function with correlation parameter equal to the asset returns correlation of B and C. Recall that this correlation is the same under both the P and Q measures, as observed in (5.4). This gives a complete realization of the joint matrix U^l; the entries of the cumulative transition matrix $\hat{U}^l$ are easily read off from the product $U^1 U^2 \ldots U^l$.

To continue with evaluation of Q-probability terms appearing in (8.1), consider for example the event E_l. Its probability can be written as a difference

$$Q(E_l) = Q(\tau_B > t_{l-1}, \tau_C > t_l) - Q(\tau_B > t_l, \tau_C > t_l),$$

and the two joint probabilities can be expanded:

$$Q(\tau_B > t_{l-1}, \tau_C > t_l) = Q(R^B_{t_{l-1}} \neq R_K, R^C_{t_l} \neq R_K)$$

$$= 1 - Q(R^B_{t_{l-1}} = R_K) - Q(R^C_{t_l} = R_K) + Q(R^B_{t_{l-1}} = R_K, R^C_{t_l} = R_K)$$

$$Q(\tau_B > t_l, \tau_C > t_l) = Q(R^B_{t_l} \neq R_K, R^C_{t_l} \neq R_K)$$

$$= 1 - Q(R^B_{t_l} = R_K) - Q(R^C_{t_l} = R_K) + Q(R^B_{t_l} = R_K, R^C_{t_l} = R_K)$$

where R_K denotes the default state. It then follows that $Q(E_l)$ is equal to

$$Q(R^B_{t_l} = R_K) - Q(R^B_{t_{l-1}} = R_K) + Q(R^B_{t_{l-1}} = R_K, R^C_{t_l} = R_K) - Q(R^B_{t_l} = R_K, R^C_{t_l} = R_K) \qquad (8.3)$$

The first two terms can be read directly from T^l. The last term is the joint risk neutral probability of default and can be computed from (5.7). The third term of (8.3) can be written as:

$$Q(R^B_{t_{l-1}} = R_K, R^C_{t_l} = R_K) = \sum_{j=1}^{K} Q(R^B_{t_{l-1}} = R_K, R^C_{t_{l-1}} = R_j, R^C_{t_l} = R_K)$$

$$= \sum_{j=1}^{K} Q(R^C_{t_l} = R_K | R^B_{t_{l-1}} = R_K, R^C_{t_{l-1}} = R_j) Q(R^B_{t_{l-1}} = R_K, R^C_{t_{l-1}} = R_j)$$

$$= \sum_{j=1}^{K} Q(R^C_{t_l} = R_K | R^C_{t_{l-1}} = R_j) Q(R^B_{t_{l-1}} = R_K, R^C_{t_{l-1}} = R_j)$$

where we have used the Markov property for both the joint and single migration processes. For the last equality, we observe more generally that

$$Q(R^C_{t_l} = R_{j'} | R^B_{t_{l-1}} = R_i, R^C_{t_{l-1}} = R_j) = Q(R^C_{t_l} = R_{j'} | R^C_{t_{l-1}} = R_j); \qquad (8.4)$$

This is valid since the left hand side of (8.4) equals

$$\sum_{i'=1}^{K} Q(R^B_{t_l} = R_{i'}, R^C_{t_l} = R_{j'} | R^B_{t_{l-1}} = R_i, R^C_{t_{l-1}} = R_j)$$

$$= \sum_{i'=1}^{K} \int_{g^B_{i,i'}}^{g^B_{i,i'-1}} \int_{g^C_{j,j'}}^{g^C_{j,j'-1}} f(x, y) dy \, dx = \int_{g^C_{j,j'}}^{g^C_{j,j'-1}} \int_{-\infty}^{\infty} f(x, y) dx \, dy = \int_{g^C_{j,j'}}^{g^C_{j,j'-1}} f_C(y) dy \qquad (8.5)$$

using (5.7), with marginal density function $f_C(y)$ for $\hat{w}^C_t$, and the appropriate thresholds g under Q as in (8.2). The last integral in (8.5) is simply the probability on the right side of (8.4). (QED.)

Combining the above equations in (8.3), we obtain the following expression for $Q(E_l)$ in terms of indicated entries in cumulative or single period transition matrices:

$$Q(E_l) = \hat{T}^l(i_0, K) - \hat{T}^{l-1}(i_0, K) + \sum_{j=1}^{K} \hat{U}^{l-1}(\eta_{i_0 j_0}, \eta_{Kj}) T^l(j, K) - \hat{U}^l(\eta_{i_0 j_0}, \eta_{KK})$$

Similar expressions, involving entries of such matrices, can be obtained for $Q(F_l)$ and $Q(G_{l-1})$.

Numerical Example

An underlying bond has a maturity of 7 years and pays an annual coupon of 7.5% on a notional of $10,000. The bond issuer has a Ba-rating and the bond has a mean recovery rate of 40%. A 3-year default swap is sold by a Aaa-rated obligor for a series of annual premium payments of 2.25% to be made in advance; the credit

Table 1. Forward default swap valuation at horizon net of premium paid

Credit rating of counterparty		Aaa	Aa	A	Baa	Ba	B	Caa
Credit Rating of Bond's Issuer	Aaa	−427.53	−427.45	−427.19	−422.15	−419.22	−417.13	−404.42
	Aa	−418.04	−418.06	−418.16	−414.16	−411.67	−409.85	−398.10
	A	−353.89	−354.27	−356.22	−357.18	−357.28	−357.02	−351.01
	Baa	−108.14	−109.17	−114.50	−128.66	−135.54	−139.55	−151.37
	Ba	28.14	26.91	20.24	0.56	−9.62	−15.78	−36.76
	B	94.94	93.67	86.58	64.78	53.21	46.12	20.95
	Caa	441.90	440.41	431.85	400.40	383.14	372.20	327.98

swap has a mean recovery rate of 60%. The correlation between the asset returns of the two obligors is 0.465.

From the above pricing formula (8.1) it follows that the current value (at time $t = 0$) of the default swap is $13.91.[15]

Table 1 provides forward values of the default swap under various migration scenarios at the end of 1-year risk horizon. (We assume that both the counterparty and the bond have survived in the first year. The first payment of $225 made in advance at the beginning of the risk horizon is not part of these figures; however, the remaining premium payments do contribute to its future price.)

In 1-year from now both the counterparty and the bond's obligor can migrate to different rating classes (or individually default). For example, assume that the counterparty remains Aaa at the end of 1-year, and the bond's obligor downgrades to Caa, then the forward value of the default swap is $441.90, while if the obligor upgrades to Aaa its value is −$427.53. These values are reasonable since, in the first case, when the bond issuer is downgraded to Caa the future probability of default is high, and the protection is worth more. In the case where the bond issuer is upgraded to Aaa, it is very unlikely that the bond will default in the remaining years of protection. Then, the protection is not worth much, and the negative value of − $427.53 reflects mostly the two remaining premium payments. We also observe that the lower the credit rating of the bond's obligor the more sensitive is the price with respect to the seller's credit rating, depending on their correlation.

It is also interesting to compare the risk of the bond and of the combination of the bond and the default swap. At the 99.5 percent confidence level and a risk horizon of 1-year, the credit value-at-risk of the bond only is $4,456, whereas the portfolio consisting of the bond and the default swap has a CVaR reduced significantly to $738. (Here, the scenarios of migrations at the end of the risk horizon are to be generated under P-measure, while the valuations are done under the Q-measure.)

NOTES

1. The three authors belong to the Risk and Capital Management group in Risk Management at CIBC. The authors are very appreciative for the constructive comments and help of Robert Mark, Chief Risk Officer at CIBC, and their colleague Alex Tchernitser.

2. For a detailed presentation of these credit measurement approaches, see Crouhy, Galai and Mark (2001).

3. We assume that the reader is already familiar with the basic principles of the credit migration framework. Those who need a tutorial should consult J.P. Morgan (1997) or Crouhy et al. (2001).

4. Note that $[t_l, t_{l+1})$, the interval over which a transition matrix is derived, is assumed to be an open on the right interval. This technical condition is required since we reset the rate of return to zero at the beginning of each interval.

5. We also define $w_{t_{l+1}} = Z_{\gamma, t_{l+1}}^{-1}(\bar{y}_{t_{l+1}} - E(\bar{y}_{t_{l+1}}))$ over the time interval $[t_l, t_{l+1})$ by setting $t = t_{l+1}$ in (1.5) and $\bar{y}_{t_{l+1}} = \lim_{t \to t_{l+1}-0} y_t$, whereas $y_{t_{l+1}}$ is set to zero according to the initial assumption in (1.5). See also footnote 4.

6. This assumption is easily relaxed and is made only for the sake of simplicity in the exposition.

7. The Q-default probabilities can be derived for each individual obligor when there is enough reliable bond and loan price data available for each specific borrower. When it is not the case, the alternative approach consists of calibrating the risk neutral default probabilities by credit rating. Another possibility is to implement a blend of the two approaches. For the sake of simplicity we assume in the following that the risk neutral default probabilities are estimated by credit rating, i.e. are the same for each obligor in the same credit class.

8. Note that it is also credit rating independent (see Section 5).

9. In certain cases, it may be necessary to consider the average over a *subset* of non-default rating classes for which the given default probabilities are deemed 'reliable'. This is because a small sampling noise in default probability can cause a large discrepancy in the corresponding threshold.

10. As a reminder, we assume that the term structure of risk neutral default probabilities is derived from credit spread data using the "reduced form" approach. See Section 6.

11. Interpolations may be required if the risk horizons and the terms of the term structure of the risk neutral default probabilities are different. If default probabilities, $\bar{q} = q_i(t_0 \to u)$ and $\bar{\bar{q}} = q_i(t_0 \to v)$, are given for $u < v$ and $s \in (u, v)$, then the default probability $q = q_i(t_0 \to s)$ can be defined by linearly interpolating the logarithms of their survival probabilities, $(1 - \bar{q})$ and $(1 - \bar{\bar{q}})$, i.e., $\log(1 - q) = (1 - \alpha(s))\log(1 - \bar{q}) + \alpha(s)\log(1 - \bar{\bar{q}})$ where $\alpha(s) = (s - u)/(v - u)$. This is equivalent to assuming that the hazard rate is constant over the period (u, v). Let h_0 be a constant hazard rate over (u, v). Then, the survival probabilities for (u, v) and (u, s) are respectively $\lambda_{[u,v]} = e^{-h_0(v-u)}$ and $\lambda_{[u,s]} = e^{-h_0(s-u)} = \lambda_{[u,v]}^{\alpha(s)}$. Since $(1 - \bar{q})\lambda_{[u,v]} = (1 - \bar{\bar{q}})$, we then have

$$1 - q = (1 - \bar{q})\lambda_{[u,s]} = (1 - \bar{q})\lambda_{[u,v]}^{\alpha(s)} = (1 - \bar{q})^{1-\alpha(s)}(1 - \bar{\bar{q}})^{\alpha(s)}.$$

12. The monotonicity condition is necessary to iterate this process and compute the forward default probabilities over the time intervals $[t_2, t_3), [t_3, t_4), [t_{L-1}, t_L)$.

13. In practice, we fix a positive integer $l > 1$ from beginning, and restrict values of α in the set $A(l) = \{0, 1/l, 2/l, \ldots, (l - 1)/l, 1\}$. Then α_1 is chosen to be the smallest α in $A(l)$ for which condition (7.8) holds.

14. For this, if a payment date s is in between two observation times u, v and M is a transition matrix for period $[u, v]$ then we can interpolate for a transition matrix over the subinterval $[u, s]$ by taking the fractional power M^α, with $\alpha = \dfrac{s - u}{v - u}$, provided by the Taylor's expansion around the identity I:

$$M^a = I + a(M - I) + \frac{\alpha(\alpha - 1)}{2}(M - I)^2 + \frac{\alpha(\alpha - 1)(\alpha - 2)}{6}(M - I)^3 + \frac{\alpha(\alpha - 1)(\alpha - 2)(\alpha - 3)}{24}(M - I)^4 + \ldots$$

This approximation works well, especially when the length $v - u$ of interval is not too long so that the matrix M is near I. In practice, this expansion method may give rise to some small negative entries and may require slight smoothing adjustment.

15. Of course, the price will depend on the relevant series of transition matrices and the zero curves given as input.

REFERENCES

Crouhy, M., D. Galai, and R. Mark, *Risk Management*, New York: McGraw-Hill, 2001.

Duffie, D., and K. Singleton, "Modelling Term Structures of Defaultable Bonds," *Review of Financial Studies* 12(4) (1999), pp. 687–720.

J.P. Morgan, *CreditMetrics, Technical Document*, 1997.

Jarrow, R.A., and S.M. Turnbull, "Pricing Derivatives on Financial Securities Subject to Credit Risk." *Journal of Finance* 50(1) (1995), pp. 53–85.

Lando, D., "Modelling Bonds and Derivatives with Default Risk." In *Mathematics of Derivatives Securities*, eds. M. Dempster and S. Pliska. Cambridge University Press, 1997.

Merton, R.C., "On the Pricing of Corporate Debt: The Risk Structure of Interest Rates." *Journal of Finance* 28(1974), pp. 449–70.

9. THE Y2K ENIGMA

MENACHEM BRENNER

Stern School of Business, New York University

MICHEL CROUHY

Risk Management Division, Canadian Imperial Bank of Commerce (CIBC)

DAN GALAI

School of Business Administration, The Hebrew University and Sigma P.C.M. Investment Ltd.

1. INTRODUCTION

One of the major challenges faced by society in the past few years has been the Y2K computer problem. Briefly, the Y2K problem was created in the early days of computers when programmers used two digits to represent the full four-digit year, e.g., "72" rather than" 1972". A few years ago it was realized that this abbreviation is ambiguous as we enter the new millennium. "00" for 2000 could also mean "00" for 1900. The two digit 'years" code may cause many disruptions and severe miscalculations. For example, a bond maturing in 2001 may be registered as if it already expired in 1901.

The problem can also affect computerized production processes. The fear is that the "bug" may be hiding in embedded computer chips and computerized systems and can affect, in unexpected ways, the production process. Banks and financial institutions that operate many computerized systems, developed by many vendors over an extended period of time, are potentially vulnerable to the "bug" problem.

In response to the problem, banks, industrial corporations, utilities, government agencies, and many other organizations had to check all their computerized systems, and invest substantial amounts of money to diagnose the problem and replace suspected faulty systems.

In the latest issue of *Banking Strategies* (July/August 1999) it is estimated that the U.S. financial industry will spend about 9 billion dollars to prepare for the Y2K computer problem. The estimates of the costs to fix the potential problem range widely, from the initial one provided by the Gartner Group (a consultancy in Connecticut) who put the number at $600 billion worldwide, to more recent estimates of $80–100 billion in the U.S. alone and approximately $200 billion worldwide (see Merrill Lynch, July 13, 1999). These estimates are rather problematic since it is practically impossible to isolate the costs associated with the "remediation" of the system from the routine investment in upgrading computer systems.

Most Western European countries seem to be prepared at some level while other countries in Asia, Latin America, and Eastern Europe seem to be at much lower levels of preparedness. Federal examiners in the USA have been satisfied by the level of preparation and so are the institutions themselves. Similar statements cannot be made with regard to the financial institutions in other countries. The level of uncertainty about the functioning of the system varies across countries and industries.

The basic fear regarding the functioning of the system has, in the US, given way to the fear of the human factor. This uncertainty nevertheless is on the minds of many financial institutions: How would the public behave as we approach the end of the millennium? Would they sell stocks and withdraw deposits from banks and hoard the cash?

It is therefore interesting to examine market information which is forward looking to see what are the public's expectations. If there is a fear that at the turn of the millennium there will be a "shortage" of funds in the system and people may hoard cash[1] then, for example, we should find that the December Eurodollar futures contract reflects a higher rate of interest than the September 1999 futures and the March 2000 futures. In fact, this was the case in April 1999. Recently, however, the Federal Reserve has announced that it ordered $70 billion of cash such that households could get extra cash from ATMs. Such an announcement should have reduced the uncertainty and, therefore, the observed interest rate differential should have declined. Another interesting market that can provide such information is the credit risk market. Have spreads between corporate bonds and comparable government bonds increased since last January? An article in the *Economist* (Sept. 27, 1999) shows that interest rate spreads have widened lately, probably reflecting the expectations of investors' behavior toward the end of the millennium.

In this note we would like to focus on yet a third market, the equities market. If there is a lot of uncertainty regarding the effect of Y2K on corporations and financial institutions we should find an increase in expected volatility. We can observe the market's perception regarding the uncertainty from prices of options as we approach the end of the millennium. In the analysis that follows we will examine the anticipated uncertainty as measured by implied volatility from the options market. Can we learn from these numbers what the markets think about how well prepared are the various corporations, banks and the economy as a whole? We have information on the market as a whole, in the U.S. and other countries around the globe. We also have information on specific companies and financial institutions.

In the next section we present the hypotheses and the methodology that we use to examine these hypotheses. In Section 3 we present some evidence on volatilities implied in index options. Future research will analyze more detailed data on index as well as equity options, including the resolution of uncertainty as we approach the end of the millennium.

2. THE HYPOTHESES AND METHODOLOGY

The Y2K problem, whether it is a real problem or mostly a psychological one, introduces uncertainty. The uncertainty is primarily about the extent to which the system will fail, disrupting economic activities and operations of financial markets. But even if computerized systems will turn out to be fully reliable, there is the risk of people's panic reactions to the uncertainty concerning computerized systems. Actually, as surveyed in the above section, it seems that the human problem may be more serious than the machine problem. For example, it is expected that many investors may sell their financial assets and turn them into cash in order to maintain liquidity, and avoid any potential bookkeeping errors of banks or brokers, or any disruption to the computerized payment system.

The hypotheses, therefore, pertain mainly to the reflection of uncertainty in financial instruments. The question is to what extent uncertainty exhibits a trend that can be related to the end of the millennium.

The tool to measure expected volatility is the implied standard deviation (ISD),[2] derived from options prices. It has a few features making it very suitable for our purposes. First, the volatility estimates are forward-looking, since the price of an option reflects the volatility of the underlying instrument over the life of the option. Second, since options on the same underlying instruments are available for different maturities, we can derive estimates of ISD for different expiration dates and hence look at the term structure of volatilities. Third, since options are traded on different underlying instruments, including country stock indices, we can also compare the results across countries.[3]

The null hypothesis is that the markets are not concerned with the Y2K problems, which would be manifested by an (annualized) implied volatility that is constant over different maturities. Let us denote by $\sigma_{i,t,K}$ the implied volatility on day t for options on asset i maturing at date K. The null hypothesis is therefore

$$H_0: \quad \sigma_{i,t,K} = \sigma_{i,t,L}$$

where $L \neq K$ are different maturity days for options on the underlying asset i with the same striking price, E.

Two alternative sets of hypotheses should be explored. One possibility is that as we come closer to the end of the year, the fear related to the Y2K problem increases and uncertainty is also expected to remain high beyond January 1, 2000. So if markets expect real disruption in the year 2000, we should observed increased uncertainty before and after year 2000:

$$H_{1,a}: \quad \sigma_{i,t,K} < \sigma_{i,t,L} \quad \text{for } L > K$$

where both L and K are maturities before Jan. 1, 2000, and also

$$\sigma_{i,t,K} < \sigma_{i,t,L} \quad \text{for } L > K$$

where both L and K are maturities after Jan. 1, 2000.

Alternatively, potential Y2K disruption is perceived as short lived, not having long lasting real consequences, and therefore uncertainties beyond Jan. 1, 2000 are expected to level off:

$$H_{1,b}: \quad \sigma_{i,t,K} < \sigma_{i,t,L} \quad \text{for } L > K$$

where both L and K are maturities before Jan. 1, 2000, and also

$$\sigma_{i,t,K} > \sigma_{i,t,L} \quad \text{for } L > K$$

where both L and K are maturities after Jan. 1, 2000.

Another set of hypotheses is related to the degree a country, or a company in a certain country, is prepared for the Y2K problem. If country A (company) is less prepared than country (company) B we would expect the term structure of the implied volatilities in the former to be much steeper than in the latter.

$$H_2: \quad \sigma_{A,t,L} - \sigma_{A,t,K} > \sigma_{B,t,L} - \sigma_{B,t,K}$$

where $L > K$. This hypothesis should be tested against the null hypothesis that the differences are equal. One can claim that H_2 exists not due to Y2K, but because of other basic structural issues in comparing country (company) A to B, and the steepness of the term structure of volatilities should be tested against the relative slopes in previous years. Therefore, the dynamics of the slope of the two term structures should also be investigated.

The dynamics of the term structure of implied volatilities are also interesting in finding how uncertainty due to Y2K is resolved (or enhanced) as we approach the end of the millennium. If information arrives which shows that financial institutions, utilities and major industrial companies are well prepared and are taking necessary steps to face any potential problems, such as liquidity problems or potential shortages of essential goods and commodities, we may expect the uncertainty to decline as we approach the turn of the year. If, however, news will indicate that some major systems may fail and that some countries are not well prepared, the uncertainty in the markets may increase.

We can write the hypothesis that uncertainty will decline as we approach 1.1.2000 as follows:

$$H_{3,a}: \quad \sigma_{i,t_1,K} - \sigma_{i,t_2,K} > 0$$

for $t_2 > t_1$. And, the alternative hypothesis that uncertainty will increase, is:

$$H_{3,b}: \quad \sigma_{i,t_1,K} - \sigma_{i,t_2,K} < 0$$

3. THE EVIDENCE

In this note we rely on information on implied volatilities on seven country indices compiled by Goldman Sachs in their monthly "Index and Derivatives Perspectives". The implied volatilities used in the graphs are trader estimates collected weekly, based on Monday's closing prices.

Figure 1 provides the term structure of volatilities measured in August 1999 (published in the September issue) for seven country indices. The term structure depicts the implied volatilities for options with different maturities up to twelve months (i.e. up to August 2000). For each index additional information is supplied: the term structure of implied volatilities in the previous month (i.e. July 1999), and the average term structure of the last 12 months. Also the confidence interval for the average term structure, of ± one standard deviation is depicted.

The general conclusions from looking at the estimated term structures of volatilities in August 1999 is that in all countries for which data are available, there is some evidence of increasing uncertainty in the markets as we approach the end of the millennium and beyond. There is a slight positive spread between the short maturities and the longer ones. The implied volatilities from options on the S&P 500 index show more of an upward sloping curve, which turns flat for maturities of 6 months and more. The difference between the shortest term (~22%) and the 6-month maturity (~24%) is 2%. This observation should be contrasted with the pattern observed in previous years when the slope of the term structure of volatility was declining. It should be noted that the August term structure lies below the July term structure, and both are below the 12-month average, indicating a general decrease in uncertainty.

The graph for the Japanese Nikkei 225 is almost flat (between 23% and 24% for the whole range of maturities) and substantially below the 12-month average. The Hang Seng index, of the Hong Kong stock exchange, shows a positive slope up to six months but then it turns to be virtually flat. The August term structure is substantially below the July term structure which indicates a general decrease in uncertainty, and both are much below the 12-month average. The decrease is especially noticeable for the short maturities.

The European term structure based on the Euro Stoxx 50, the British FTSE 100, the German DAX, the French CAC, were generally flat in July, but decreased in August especially in the short end, and therefore, became somewhat upward sloping. All are below the 12-month average. It is interesting to note that the June term structure (not in the graph) showed a steeper slope than July, but had generally lower volatilities. August and June term structures look similar, and July is the exception with volatilities increasing and the term structures being flat.

These results can be interpreted as follows: while general uncertainty in the markets increased between June to July, due, for example, to fears of interest rates hikes, this risk subsided in August. The uncertainty that can be attributed to the Y2K problem reappeared in August, but it was rather modest. With the exception of Japan we see an increase in uncertainty as we approach December 1999.

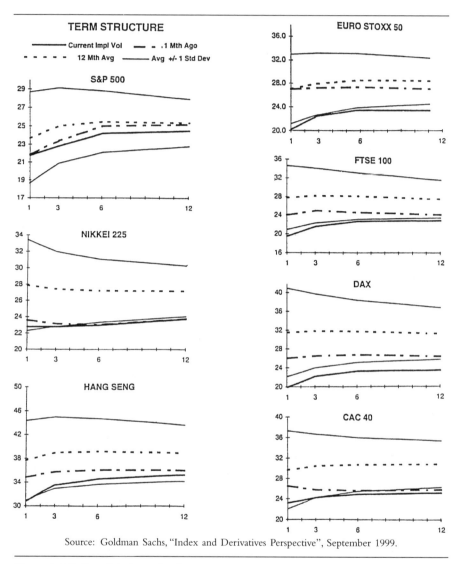

Source: Goldman Sachs, "Index and Derivatives Perspective", September 1999.

Figure 1. Volatility of Options of Different Terms (Aug. 1999) for 7 Country Indices

Nevertheless, there is no evidence to support $H_{1,a}$, that more volatility was expected beyond December, 1999.

The resolution of uncertainty is depicted in Figure 2 which presents the monthly changes that took place in the level and slope of the term structure of implied volatilities of the S&P 500 over the period April to August 1999. Each monthly

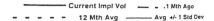

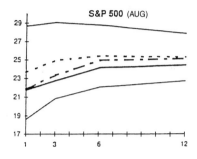

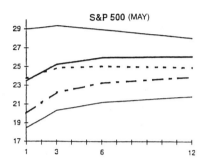

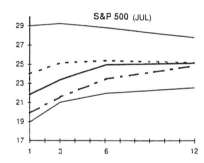

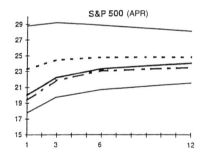

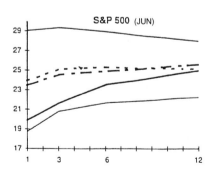

Source: Goldman Sachs, "Index and Derivatives Perspective", May–Sept. 1999.

Figure 2. Volatility of Options of Different Terms for S&P 500 for Apr.–Aug. 1999

frame includes also the term structure in the previous month as well as the 12-month average implied volatility (with an exception that April's graph contains the 3-month average).

For the six months[4] data in Figure 2 we find that implied volatilities were not stable. The highest level of implied volatilities was experienced in May 1999, and it was close to the 12-month average curve (which includes the high volatility period of August–October 1998). While the volatility level for May was relatively high, the term structure was rather flat with approximately 1% difference between the 6-month and the 1-month volatilities.

The June–August period shows a reduction in volatilities, especially so for the short maturities. As a result, the slope increased to 2–3% difference between the 6-month and the 1-month maturities. The reduction in the general level of volatility may reflect decreased fears of major interest rate hikes, or also decreased uncertainty to market disruption due to the Y2K problem (i.e. confirmation of $H_{3,a}$). The increased slope, however, may still reflect some fears of flight to liquidity, and flight from stocks as we approach the end of the millennium. But, then the reduction in the slope from June to August can reflect the reduced uncertainty due to Y2K with the information arriving continuously regarding the state of preparation of major banking institutions, industrial companies and government agencies. If this information has an impact on the market, we should expect the slope to further decline as we approach December 1999.

4. CONCLUSIONS

Three main observations emerge as we examine the implied volatilities of various markets. First, the uncertainty regarding the end of the millennium shows up in an increasing term structure of implied volatilities in the U.S. and other major countries. It is a different pattern that we observed over many years of a declining term structure but similar to the pattern since August 1998 (as is also reflected in the 12-month average). Is this associated with the Y2K issue, or, is this a permanent shift that will stay with us for a long time beyond year 2000? Second, the term structure of the Japanese market exhibits an indifference to the Y2K issue. Is this because the Japanese are better prepared or is it due to the much less active longer term options contracts in the Japanese market? Third, the general level of volatility seems to be declining since it peaked in May 1999. It can be a reflection of the additional information on the level of preparation toward the Y2K problem.

NOTES

1. This is known as "flight to liquidity" or "flight to safety".
2. The ISD was first suggested by Latane and Rendleman (1976). See also Brenner and Galai (1984) and Galai (1991) for a survey of the literature.
3. We concentrate here on uncertainty exhibited in the stock market. We intend to contrast it with information obtained from the bond market.

4. Since April's graph contains also the March term structure, we have a full description of the curves for March–August 1999.

REFERENCES

Best, E., "YK2 and the End of the Great Bull Market," *The International Economy*, September/October 1998.

Brenner M. and Galai D., "On Measuring the Risk of Common Stocks Implied by Option Prices: A Note," *Journal of Financial and Quantitative Analysis*, Vol. 14, No. 4, pp. 403–412 (1984).

Galai, D., "Inferring Volatility from Options Prices," *Finance*, Vol. 12, No. 1, pp. 45–64 (1991).

"Get Ready for 'Doom 2000' ". YK2 Survey, *The Banker*, April 1999.

Goldman Sachs, "Index and Derivatives Perspectives," a monthly publication of the Equity Derivatives Research, May–September 1999 issues.

Latane, H.A. and Rendleman, R.J., "Standard Deviation of Stock Price Ratios Implied in Option Prices," *Journal of Finance*, Vol. 31 (May 1976), pp. 369–381.

"Nothing to Fear But Fear Itself," *The Economist*, 9–2729, Editorial.

Swift, C., "Challenge," *Banking Strategies*, July/August 1999.

Terrile, J.G., "YK2: Ready or Not?" < Merril Lynch & Co., Global Securities Research & Economics Group.

II. MANAGING RISK IN FINANCIAL INSTITUTIONS

10. PAYMENT AND SETTLEMENT RISKS IN INTERNATIONAL FINANCIAL MARKETS

DARRYLL HENDRICKS*

Federal Reserve Bank of New York

Wholesale payment and settlement systems are the core infrastructure for today's modern financial markets. They consist of the systems that are used to settle commercial and financial transactions including foreign exchange trades, securities transactions—both the stock market and the corporate bond market—as well as derivative transactions. Most of the transactions that flow through what we call wholesale payment and settlement systems are high-value, meaning at least in the millions of dollars, and in some cases the tens and occasionally even the hundreds of millions or billions of dollars per transaction. The volume of this activity is extremely large on a daily basis through the two major payment systems in the United States: the Fedwire system which the Federal Reserve operates, and the Clearing House Interbank Payments System (CHIPS), which is a private system operated by the New York Clearing House Association. Over three trillion dollars a day goes through those systems, so the amounts involved are quite significant.

The key parts of the overall international payment and settlement infrastructure can be divided into a few key categories. First, there are payment systems, which generally are of two types. Let me apologize for all of the acronyms that are used in discussing payment systems. RTGS stands for Real Time Gross Settlement, which means a system where each payment is sent through on an individual basis in real time. Thus, when bank A makes a payment to bank B over an RTGS system, it's

* The views expressed here are those of the author and not necessarily those of the Federal Reserve Bank of New York or the Federal Reserve System.

essentially final at the time that it is recorded on the system itself. The other major type of payment system is a net settlement system, where the system will record debits and credits throughout the day and final settlement will occur on a net basis after summing up all the debits and credits at the end of the day.

In addition to payment systems, there are systems for the settlement of securities and here things become more complicated. There are generally national depositories in each country where the ultimate settlement of securities takes place. In the United States, the Depository Trust Company (DTC) is the ultimate depository for stocks, corporate bonds, municipal bonds, commercial paper and other kinds of securities. The Federal Reserve is the depository U.S. Treasury securities, as well as Federal National Mortgage Association (FNMA) and Federal Home Loan Mortgage Corporation (FHLMC) securities. International securities depositories also are very important to global financial markets. Euroclear and Cedel—now known as Clearstream—are two entities that provide the infrastructure for the ultimate settlement of eurobonds and also many national securities in the European countries and some other countries as well. Additionally, there are securities clearinghouses or clearing corporations. For example, the National Securities Clearing Corporation (NSCC) and the Government Securities Clearing Corporation (GSCC) are clearinghouses for U.S. stocks and government securities, respectively. While not that many people are familiar with these organizations, they operate in New York and perform a very important function in guaranteeing trades, taking on quite a bit of risk from their members on a daily basis.

S.W.I.F.T. (the Society for Worldwide Interbank Financial Transfers) is an organization that was formed in 1973 and provides a secure global messaging service for banks and other financial firms around the world. SWIFT has become a very central part of the overall infrastructure not only for payments and foreign exchange but increasingly for securities and derivatives as well.

Finally, although I will not talk about them as much, are futures and options clearinghouses. These include the clearinghouses associated with the Chicago Board of Trade and the Chicago Mercantile Exchange.

Now let me turn to the risks that are involved in payment and settlement systems. It is fair to say that this is not rocket science. First, consider those transactions that have two components to them, such as securities transactions where there is a securities leg and a cash leg, or foreign exchange trades where for example there is a dollar leg and a yen leg. Since there are two sides, one of the key risks is that one side will pay but the other side will not pay, for example because of a sudden default or otherwise there is a refusal to pay. This risk is referred to as principal risk, and for these sorts of transactions, increasingly efforts have been made aiming to eliminate this risk. In addition, many wholesale systems require significant amount of credit or liquidity in order to function effectively and smoothly during the day. Part of the reason for this is that there are many back-to-back transactions in the marketplace where a financial firm is buying a security from somebody and selling it somebody else in the same day. So for settlement purposes it's helpful for the system to provide liquidity as one of the transactions hits the system but before the other one has hit the system. Depending upon the way the system works, that credit can be more implicit or in some cases very explicit. The credit or liquidity risks involved may arise between the participants or may arise directly from the system's extension of credit.

Finally, there is replacement cost risk, which arises because of the time lag between the execution of a trade and settlement. If the other side of a transaction fails at the time of settlement, then even if there is no principal risk, there will still be a need to go out and replace the transaction. This is one reason why there is a continuing effort to move to shorter settlement cycles. We moved from five days after trade date (T + 5) to T + 3 several years ago in the U.S. equity market and now there is much talk about moving to T + 1 in the next few years.

I will now move on to a discussion of some of the recent efforts to reduce payment and settlement risks. In the United States, the Fedwire system provides unsecured intra-day credit to many banks operating on the system. The risks associated with these overdrafts have been the focus of considerable efforts by the Federal Reserve in recent years. For example, we have initiated a number of efforts including pricing of those overdrafts to reduce them. Similarly, CHIPS has undertaken a number of efforts to reduce its own settlement risks. Securities settlement systems have taken steps to provide greater assurance that each side of the transaction will settle if and only if the other side also settles (Delivery vs. Payment). Internationally, these risk-reduction efforts have been spurred on by organizations seeking to remind market participants of the externalities associated with these kinds of systems and of their importance to the daily functioning of the market. The Group of Thirty—a non-profit group with both public and private-sector membership—issued a very influential report on securities settlement in the late 1980s. In the 1990s, the ball has been picked up by the G-10 central banks, who have developed a number of reports and analyses seeking to induce major financial institutions to focus on ways to reduce payment and settlement risks.

One of the first of these efforts was a report that was highly influential in the world of payment systems, known as the Lamfalussy report and issued in 1990. This report encouraged net settlement systems, such as CHIPS, to improve their risk management practices. In particular, the report included the standard that such systems be able to withstand, at a minimum, the default of their single largest participant without collapsing. It is worth noting that since that time, CHIPS has moved well beyond that standard and can today withstand the default of its two largest participants and soon will be moving to an even safer mode of operation.

I want to spend some time talking about foreign exchange settlement risk because that issue has been the focus of a lot of attention in the payment and settlement world for a number of years. This relates to the payment vs. payment principle, since both sides of the transaction typically do not settle at the same time. Because the Japanese and other Asian markets are open early in the global day, U.S. markets are open late, and European markets are open in the middle, it is not really possible to settle them at the same time. So these is an inevitable lag. The most serious and famous case of foreign exchange settlement risk was the failure of the Herstatt bank in 1974, and many people have since referred to this risk as Herstatt risk. The bank's failure took place in such a way that many of its trading counterparties had already paid out European currencies to Herstatt, but subsequently did not receive the corresponding U.S. dollars associated with those trades. This event caused very serious disruption in the payment systems and financial markets at that time.

The volumes in foreign exchange markets are now so large such that several years ago central bankers began to wonder whether there was not some way of tackling this risk once and for all. Further examination of the issue revealed that foreign exchange settlement risk is not simply an intra-day phenomenon since bank practices typically involve making irrevocable payment instructions quite early in the process. Amounts at risk to even single counterparties were found to be very large, in some cases even exceeding a bank's capital. These findings convinced the G-10 central banks that the current arrangements for settling foreign exchange trades needed considerable improvement.

Along these lines, it is worth noting that every time a financial firm gets into trouble and there are worries about its continued operations in the market, the issue of its foreign exchange settlement arrangements comes up. There have been some real losses since Herstatt. Banks do not like to talk about them but they are there. I think there is a legitimate concern that a large unexpected failure, admittedly a very rare event, would be extremely disruptive. Thus, the size of the foreign exchange market today suggests that it may be worth a significant amount of money to invest to try to prevent such an event.

The G-10 central banks invested considerable effort in trying to get the private sector to respond to these concerns. Let me then move on to the major response to that effort, which is the development of a special purpose bank. The Continuous Linked Settlement (CLS) Bank, which will be chartered here in New York, is a project that now has joint ownership from around 60 of the largest foreign exchange market participants in the world. The CLS Bank is designed to provide a payment vs. payment settlement alternative for foreign exchange transactions. The goal is to get this up and running sometime in the next few years. When it is effective, it will certainly change the way that people settle these transactions and will probably support other changes in the foreign exchange markets, possibly including a shorter settlement cycle than the existing T + 2.

The CLS bank will work as follows. There will be core set of institutions that will be settlement members in the bank, meaning they will have an account on the books of the CLS bank. This account will be subdivided into sub-accounts, one for each currency that the CLS bank settles. The CLS bank itself will maintain accounts at the relevant central banks around the world meaning they will have remote access to a number of those central bank payment facilities. CLS will start with seven major currencies: the U.S. dollar, the euro, the Japanese yen, the Canadian dollar, the British pound, the Swiss franc, and the Australian dollar.

Although the payment vs. payment principle seems straightforward, implementing it in practice for the foreign exchange market turns out to have required quite a lot of effort. The processing for CLS bank will have three different stages and will occur during a five-hour window, which will be extremely early here in New York, from 1:00 am to 6:00 am in the morning. Both the Fedwire and the CHIPS systems have now been open for about two years at these early hours in the morning. There is not much activity there now but this was done in the anticipation that something like CLS would come along.

The three stages of the CLS processing cycle are (1) pay-in, (2) settlement, and (3) payout. During the pay-in stage the settlement members that owe funds in individual currencies would pay those in over the national payment systems. Thus, the CLS bank accounts at the national central banks would be credited and in turn CLS would credit on its books the accounts of its settlement members. The second stage, which would occur concurrently, entails the actual settlement of the foreign exchange trades. On its own books, the CLS bank will simultaneously post the two sides of the individual foreign exchange transactions so that there is true payment vs. payment settlement. This settlement is final, meaning legally irrevocable and unconditional. The third and final stage of the CLS bank processing cycle involves payout to those settlement members that have long positions in individual currencies. CLS will make payments via the national payment systems over the books of the central banks. There are a number of risk management tests involved in this process that I do not have time to detail, but their aim is to protect the CLS bank from itself being subject to credit and liquidity risk to the maximum extent possible.

In terms of the benefits that we see from the central bank perspective—and I think this is shared by foreign exchange participants—there is obviously the reduction in settlement risk, particularly principal risk. We are hoping that the benefits will get shared widely in the market through broad participation in the system and through a growing range of currencies being brought into it over time. The CLS bank of course is something that the Federal Reserve will be looking at quite closely to see that it prudently manages its own risk and serves as a source of stability in stressful market conditions.

In conclusion, I have tried to convey that there are important risks in wholesale payment and settlement arrangements and that these arrangements are a very important part of the international financial system. While they do not typically make the front page of the newspaper, there have been quite a lot of efforts to focus on reducing risks in these systems over the last several years. Particularly in foreign exchange settlement risk area, there is an important ongoing initiative seeking to reduce the substantial remaining risks.

11. RISK, REGIMES, AND OVERCONFIDENCE

MARK KRITZMAN

Mark Kritzman is a managing partner at Windham Capital Management Boston in Cambridge, MA.

KENNETH LOWRY

Kenneth Lowry is vice president of State Street Bank in Boston, MA.

ANNE-SOPHIE VAN ROYEN

Anne-Sophie Van Royen is director of research at Windham Capital Management Boston and is senior quantitative strategist for State Street Associates in Cambridge, MA.

Investors typically think of risk as the uncertainty of wealth at the end of their investment horizon. By focusing on the dispersion of ending wealth, investors ignore the effect of interim losses, no matter how severe. Investors also measure risk as though returns come from a single regime, which may understate the likelihood and severity of interim losses.

The authors argue that the perception of risk as fully represented by the distribution of terminal wealth, together with the assumption of a single regime, leads to overconfidence. They apply first-passage probabilities to compare the risk of loss during an investment period with the risk of loss at the end of a horizon. Application of a methodology to measure risk based on quiet or turbulent regimes shows the extent to which the traditional measurement of risk understates exposure to loss.

The authors present a forecasting procedure to assess the relative likelihood of quiet and turbulent regimes, and show how to use this information to structure portfolios that are regime-sensitive.

When investors think of risk as the uncertainty of wealth at the end of their investment horizon, they implicitly ignore the effect of interim losses, no matter how severe. Investors also measure risk as though returns come from a single regime characterized by a lognormal distribution.[1] If, instead, returns are generated by two regimes, one quiet and the other turbulent, severe interim underperformance may be more likely to occur than is implied by the full-sample covariance matrix.

R.M. Levich and S. Figlewski (eds.). RISK MANAGEMENT. Copyright © 2001. Kluwer Academic Publishers. Boston. All rights reserved.

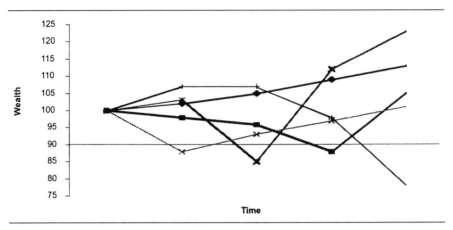

Exhibit 1. Risk of Loss: Ending Wealth versus Interim Wealth

We argue that the perception of risk as depending only on the distribution of terminal wealth, together with the assumption of a single regime, leads to overconfidence. We propose a methodology for structuring portfolios that are regime-sensitive.

The methodology, which identifies multivariate outliers according to work by Chow, Jacquier, Kritzman, and Lowry [1999], is better than an approach that stratifies returns solely on the basis of volatility. We present evidence that belies the assumption of a single lognormal distribution, and we measure the extent to which this assumption, together with emphasis on ending wealth, understates interim risk. Regime-sensitive portfolios may be structured using a model for forecasting the relative probability of quiet and turbulent regimes.

I. RISK OF LOSS

In Exhibit 1 we compare the distinction between the risk of loss if we focus on ending wealth instead of on interim wealth. Each line represents the path of a hypothetical investment through four periods. The horizontal line represents a loss threshold, which in this example equals 10%. Only one of the five paths breaches the loss threshold as of the end of the horizon; hence we might conclude that the likelihood of a 10% loss equals 20%.

Four of the five paths breach the loss threshold at some point during or at the end of the investment period, however, although three of the four paths subsequently recover. If we care about the investment's performance along the way to the end of our horizon, we should conclude that the likelihood of a 10% loss equals 80%.

This example illustrates the distinction between the riskiness of ending wealth and interim wealth. To quantify this distinction, we use a statistic called first-passage time probability.[2] For a lognormal diffusion with an initial value of S at time 0, the

Expected Return		10%	
Standard Deviation		20%	
	1 Year	5 Years	10 Years
End of Investment Horizon	15.33%	10.72%	5.81%
During Investment Horizon	41.81%	56.49%	58.85%

Exhibit 2. Likelihood of a 10% Loss

probability that it will first reach a given critical value C at or before date T is given by:

$$N[(\ln(C/S) - \mu T)/(\sigma\sqrt{T})] + (C/S)^{2\mu/\sigma2} \times N[(\ln(C/S) + \mu T)/(\sigma\sqrt{T})] \tag{1}$$

where:

$N[\ ]$ = cumulative normal distribution function;
ln = natural logarithm;
μ = continuous return; and
σ = continuous standard deviation.

We use the first-passage time statistic to estimate the probability that an investment will depreciate to a particular value over some horizon if it is monitored continually. Consider, for example, an investment that has an expected return of 10% and a standard deviation of 20%. Exhibit 2 compares the likelihood of a 10% loss over a one-, five-, and ten-year investment horizon if we monitor the investment only at the end instead of continually throughout each period.

There are two interesting points to note from Exhibit 2. First, the likelihood of a 10% loss during an investment horizon is much greater than the likelihood of a 10% loss at the end of the horizon. And second, while the likelihood of loss at the end of a horizon diminishes as the horizon is extended from one to ten years, the likelihood of loss during the horizon rises with its duration.

The critical question, of course, is whether we have the forbearance to weather severe interim losses and to sustain our exposure to risky assets. If not, our expectation for the strategy's long-term performance may be misguided. Moreover, it is often the case that this decision is not ours to make. If we are managing someone else's assets, we must be confident that our client will not force us to abandon the agreed-upon strategy should it experience severe losses along the way.

II. IDENTIFYING OUTLIERS

The common assumption is that returns are generated by a single regime characterized by a lognormal distribution. One of the implications of this assumption is that the correlations we estimate do not change as we sample different returns, as long as the samples are sufficiently large. If, however, returns are generated by different regimes, we must estimate regime-specific correlations if we are to accurately assess the risk of loss during an investment period.

We invoke the methodology of Chow, Jacquier, Kritzman, and Lowry (CJKL) [1999] to partition return samples into ordinary returns and unusual returns. They argue that ordinary returns are more likely to be associated with noise, and thus characteristic of quiet regimes, while unusual returns are more likely to be event-driven and characteristic of turbulent regimes.

CJKL define an unusual return vector as an outlier and measure its unusualness in terms of a multivariate distance from the mean as shown in Equation (2).

$$d_t = (y_t - \mu) \sum^{-1} (y_t - \mu)'$$

(2)

where:

d_t = vector distance from multivariate average (dimension: $1 \times k$);
y_t = return series ($1 \times k$);
μ = mean vector of return series $y_t (1 \times k)$; and
Σ = covariance matrix of return series $y_t (k \times k)$.

CJKL assume the return series y_t is normally distributed with a mean vector μ and a covariance matrix Σ. Thus the distance d_t follows a chi square distribution with k degrees of freedom. The authors choose a confidence level, calculate the corresponding tolerance distance for the chi square distribution, and compare it with each d_t. If the observed distance d_t is greater than the tolerance distance, CJKL define that vector as an outlier, and if the distance is smaller, as an inlier.

For two return series that are uncorrelated and have equal variances, the d_t are the radii of circles that are centered on the average of the return pairs and whose perimeters pass through each return pair. Exhibit 3 illustrates this process for the return pair denoted by the star. The radius of the tolerance circle corresponds to the tolerance distance associated with the chosen confidence level.

CJKL's methodology assumes implicitly that returns are not generated by a single distribution, but rather from separate distributions representing a quiet regime and a turbulent regime. If so, the risk parameters estimated from the full sample of returns may understate a portfolio's exposure to first-passage risk. The risk parameters associated with the quiet and turbulent regimes identified by Equation (2) provide a more accurate description of first-passage risk.

A critical feature of the CJKL methodology is that it takes into account not only unusually volatile returns but also returns that interact in strange ways. If we associate a turbulent regime only with returns that are unusually volatile, we might conclude falsely that there are multiple regimes.[3] An experiment demonstrates this point:[4]

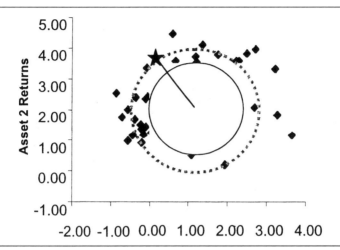

Exhibit 3. Bivariate Outlier for Uncorrelated Return Pairs with Equal Variance

- We draw 30,000 return pairs randomly from a correlated joint-normal distribution. Both assets have a 10% mean and 20% standard deviation. The correlation is equal to 60%.
- We rank the return pairs from highest to lowest on the basis of their average returns.
- We select the 10% highest and 10% lowest return pairs, ranked by their average.
- We select outliers using a 20% cutoff.
- We calculate the correlation of the full sample, the sample of high and low returns, and the sample of outliers.

This experiment produces the results as follows:

Full sample correlation:	60.38%
Correlation of high and low returns:	85.84%
Correlation of outliers:	60.48%

The experiment reveals that the correlation estimated from only the volatile returns is significantly biased upward, simply by virtue of the nature of this calculation. The correlation of multivariate outliers, by comparison, is unbiased.

Therefore, if we observe an increase in the correlation of returns from volatile periods, it does not necessarily follow that the returns come from multiple regimes or have an unusual distribution. The rise in the correlation may be simply an artifact of correlation mathematics.[5] A rise in the correlation of an outlier sample, however, is evidence that the returns come either from more than one regime or from an unusual distribution.

	U.S. Bonds	U.K. Stocks	U.K. Bonds	German Stocks	German Bonds	Japanese Stocks	Japanese Bonds
U.S. Stocks		51%		42%		22%	
U.S. Bonds			27%		36%		21%
U.K. Stocks				48%		39%	
U.K. Bonds					68%		51%
German Stocks						31%	
German Bonds							63%
Japanese Stocks							

Exhibit 4. Cross-Country Correlations Within Asset Classes—Quiet Regime

	U.S. Bonds	U.K. Stocks	U.K. Bonds	German Stocks	German Bonds	Japanese Stocks	Japanese Bonds
U.S. Stocks		78%		48%		40%	
U.S. Bonds			54%		41%		27%
U.K. Stocks				64%		60%	
U.K. Bonds					56%		55%
German Stocks						37%	
German Bonds							62%
Japanese Stocks							

Exhibit 5. Cross-Country Correlations Within Asset Classes—Turbulent Regime (10% Outliers)

III. OVERCONFIDENCE

We apply the CJKL methodology to determine whether global stock and bond returns come from a single regime or from quiet and turbulent regimes. We find that cross-country correlations within asset classes are substantially higher during turbulent regimes than during quiet regimes, and that correlations between asset classes within countries are substantially lower during turbulent regimes than during quiet regimes, which is consistent with the presence of multiple regimes. We also

	U.S.	U.K.	U.K.	German	German	Japanese	Japanese
	Bonds	Stocks	Bonds	Stocks	Bonds	Stocks	Bonds
U.S. Stocks	45%						
U.S. Bonds							
U.K. Stocks			68%				
U.K. Bonds							
German Stocks					46%		
German Bonds							
Japanese Stocks							53%

Exhibit 6. Cross-Asset Class Correlations Within Countries—Quiet Regime

measure the extent to which the assumption of a single regime understates a portfolio's exposure to risk if, in fact, there are multiple regimes.

Our sample includes monthly stock and bond returns in the U.S., U.K., Germany, and Japan from January 1986 through December 1999. This sample is but one pass through history and may not be representative of the future, but it is nonetheless illustrative of the point we wish to make. With this caveat in mind, we choose a cutoff that defines the 10% most unusual periods as outliers.

The cross-country correlations within asset classes are shown in Exhibit 4 for the quiet regime and in Exhibit 5 for the turbulent regime (10% outlier sample). These correlations are from a U.S. dollar perspective. We omit the other correlations in order to focus on the correlations of interest.

Exhibits 6 and 7 show the asset class correlations within countries for the quiet and turbulent regimes. Again, we omit the other correlations in order to focus attention on the correlations of interest.

Exhibit 8 shows the average correlation across countries within asset classes and across asset classes within countries associated with a shift from a quiet regime to a turbulent one. We include results from the perspective of four currencies to show that the results are not caused by exchange rate differences.

Exhibit 8 shows that the average correlation across countries (top right bar) is about 12% higher in turbulent regimes than it is during quiet regimes. The average correlation across asset classes (top left bar) is by contrast nearly 25% lower during turbulent regimes than it is during quiet regimes. There is nearly a 40 percentage point difference between country correlations and asset class correlations, depending on which regime prevails.

Although these results are consistent with the presence of multiple regimes, they are not a sufficient condition. An alternative explanation is that these results are

	U.S.	U.K.	U.K.	German	German	Japanese	Japanese
	Bonds	Stocks	Bonds	Stocks	Bonds	Stocks	Bonds
U.S. Stocks	0%						
U.S. Bonds							
U.K. Stocks			29%				
U.K. Bonds							
German Stocks					19%		
German Bonds							
Japanese Stocks							47%

Exhibit 7. Cross-Asset Class Correlations Within Countries—Turbulent Regime (10% Outliers)

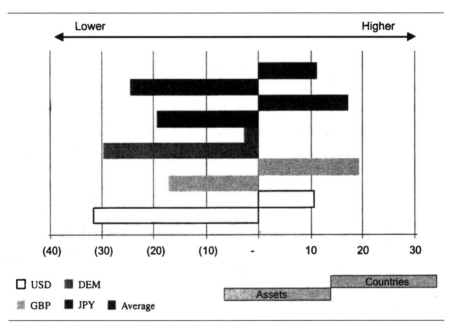

Exhibit 8. Changes in Correlations—Quiet Regime → Turbulent Regime

generated by a single regime with a very unusual distribution. In either case, the consequence is the same: We will underestimate risk if we assume a single and lognormal distribution.

To what extent does the assumption of a single lognormal distribution understate risk when instead returns are generated by a quiet regime or a turbulent regime? To answer this question, we compare the results of a Monte Carlo simulation with the results of a non-parametric bootstrapping simulation.

We begin by estimating the optimal weights of the global stocks and bonds in our sample, based on equilibrium returns, the full-sample covariance matrix, and risk aversion equal to 2.0. We estimate equilibrium returns as those that are proportional to the assets' systematic risk, assuming the full-sample covariance matrix, a 60/40 stock/bond mix equally weighted across countries as the reference portfolio, a riskless return of 4%, and an expected return for the reference portfolio of 10%. The optimal weights are subject to constraints of greater than or equal to 0% and less than or equal to 100%. They are: U.S. stocks 12.5%, U.S. bonds 0.0%, U.K. stocks 20.8%, U.K. bonds 8.9%, German stocks 18.4%, German bonds 9.9%, Japanese stocks 19.3%, and Japanese bonds 10.2%.

Next, we assume investment in this portfolio with monthly rebalancing and calculate its return each month. It has a mean of 1.0626% and a standard deviation of 3.1171%. We then perform the simulations as described below.

Monte Carlo Simulation

- Randomly select monthly returns from a lognormal distribution based on empirical mean and standard deviation. Repeat 30,000 times.
- Calculate monthly cumulative wealth for each return sequence.
- Calculate frequency with which threshold is breached.

Bootstrapping Simulation

- Estimate the density function of the empirical returns.
- Randomly select monthly returns from the empirical distribution, replacing the selected return before each draw. Repeat 30,000 times.
- Calculate monthly cumulative wealth for each return sequence.
- Calculate frequency with which threshold is breached.

The Monte Carlo simulation assumes that returns come from a single regime characterized by a lognormal distribution. The bootstrapping simulation assumes that the returns come from the actual distribution associated with the sample of returns, which could be a blend of multiple regimes.[6]

Exhibit 9 presents the results. It shows how many of the 30,000 simulation paths breach the threshold in at least one of the month-ends during the investment period, depending on whether we assume the theoretical lognormal distribution or the empirical distribution. There are more breaches during the investment horizon

Loss During 1 Year	Theoretical Probability	Empirical Probability	Loss During 2 Years	Theoretical Probability	Empirical Probability
5%	19.9%	23.7%	5%	23.3%	26.7%
10%	4.8%	6.9%	10%	6.5%	9.5%
15%	0.9%	1.8%	15%	1.7%	3.4%
20%	0.1%	0.4%	20%	0.4%	1.0%

Loss During 5 Years	Theoretical Probability	Empirical Probability	Loss During 10 Years	Theoretical Probability	Empirical Probability
5%	23.0%	28.3%	5%	23.1%	28.5%
10%	7.2%	11.2%	10%	7.3%	11.5%
15%	2.1%	4.6%	15%	2.1%	5.0%
20%	0.5%	1.8%	20%	0.5%	2.1%

Exhibit 9. Misestimation of Risk During Investment Horizon

assuming the empirical distribution than there are associated with the theoretical assumption of a single lognormal distribution. These differences measure the extent to which we underestimate exposure to first-passage risk by assuming a single lognormal distribution.

IV. DETECTING REGIME SHIFTS

We have developed an econometric model to forecast the relative likelihood that the next period will be quiet or turbulent. We first investigate the serial dependence of multivariate distances, and find that log differences are serially correlated. Thus we transform the multivariate distances D_t as follows:

$$d_t = \log(D_t) - \log(D_{t-1}) \tag{3}$$

where:

   d_t = log difference of multivariate distance, and
   D_t = multivariate distance.

We assume that the extent to which d_t is correlated from one month to the next depends upon the current state. We model the random process that determines the current state as a two-state Markov chain. Let S_t be a random variable that assumes only two values, 1 or 2, corresponding to state 1 or 2 at time t. The probability that S_t takes on a particular value depends only on last period's state, S_{t-1}:

R^2	=	0.6747	
σ^2	=	0.6527	
Log-Likelihood = -189.3627			

Variable	Coefficient	t-statistic	t-probability
Results for State 1			
Constant c_1	0.935474	5.961824	0.000000
Coefficient ϕ_1	-0.342242	-1.645128	0.101957
Results for State 2			
Constant c_2	-0.264555	-4.407919	0.000019
Coefficient ϕ_2	-0.512586	-6.113402	0.000000

Exhibit 10. Hamilton-Markov Model Estimates

$$P[S_t = i \mid S_{t-1} = j, S_{t-2} = k \ldots] = P[S_t = i \mid S_{t-1} = j]$$

We also assume that the probabilities of switching from one state to another are time-invariant and are collected in a transition matrix P. It is written as follows, with p_{ij} equal to the probability that state i will be followed by state j:

$$P = \begin{bmatrix} p_{11} & p_{21} \\ p_{12} & p_{22} \end{bmatrix} = \begin{bmatrix} p_{11} & 1 - p_{22} \\ 1 - p_{11} & p_{22} \end{bmatrix}$$

Every period there is a probability π_t of entering state 1 ($S_t = 1$) and a $1 - \pi_t$ probability of entering state 2 ($S_t = 2$). The elements of P are conditional probabilities, while π_t and $1 - \pi_t$ are unconditional. The relation between the two is expressed as follows:

$$\begin{bmatrix} \pi_t \\ 1 - \pi_t \end{bmatrix} = \begin{bmatrix} p_{11} & p_{21} \\ p_{12} & p_{22} \end{bmatrix} \times \begin{bmatrix} \pi_{t-1} \\ 1 - \pi_{t-1} \end{bmatrix}$$

The regime-switching model is written:

State 1 (with probability π_t): $\quad d_t = c_1 + \phi_1 d_{t-1} + \varepsilon_t$
State 2 (with probability $1 - \pi_t$): $\quad d_t = c_2 + \phi_2 d_{t-1} + \varepsilon_t$
with ε_t follows $N(0, \sigma^2)$

Estimation of the unknown parameters $p_{11}, p_{22}, p_{12}, c_1, \phi_1, c_2, \phi_2$, and σ^2 is accomplished through maximization of the log-likelihood function, using the EM algorithm.[7] Exhibit 10 reports the results of the two-state model. The dependent variable is the log difference in multivariate distance.

All coefficients are significant at a 10% confidence level. Explanatory power is high ($R^2 = 67.4\%$). A simple autoregressive model that assumes only one state yields by comparison an R^2 equal to 38%.[8] This result suggests that it is more realistic to model returns as generated by two states rather than one state.

The estimated transition matrix equals:

$$P^* = \begin{bmatrix} 17.40\% & 23.23\% \\ 82.60\% & 76.77\% \end{bmatrix}$$

This result shows that state 1 tends to be much more short-lived than state 2. The unconditional probability that we enter state 1 at any given time is equal to 21.9% [$(1 - p_{22})/(2 - p_{11} - p_{22})$] compared to 78.1% for state 2.

The presence of two regimes as defined by CJKL does not require that a forecasting model of these regimes involve two states. Nonetheless, it would be interesting to see if there is a correspondence between the two regimes and the two states of the Markov switching model. In fact, we do find a correspondence between state 1 and the turbulent regime and between state 2 and the quiet regime.

Specifically, when a quiet regime prevails, the probability that the forecast is generated by state 2 exceeds the unconditional probability of 78.1% in 91% of the quiet periods. When a turbulent regime prevails, the probability that the forecast is generated by state 1 exceeds the unconditional probability of 21.9% in 57% of the turbulent periods. These frequencies suggest that state 1 corresponds to the turbulent regime (the outliers), while state 2 corresponds to the quiet regime (the inliers).

We also calculate the correlation between the multivariate distances and the probability that the forecasts are generated by state 1. This correlation equals 58.1%, providing additional evidence of the correspondence between the states of the forecasting model and the regimes.

We use the state-dependent coefficients, the estimated probabilities, and the transition matrix to obtain a forecast of next month's log difference and then add it to the current month's log distance. The exponential of this value provides a forecast of next month's multivariate distance. We assume that multivariate distances follow a chi-square distribution, and we estimate the probability that next month's distance will correspond either to a quiet observation or a turbulent one, as defined by CJKL.[9] For example, given a cutoff of 13.4, a forecasted distance equal to 14.2 based on eight assets implies a 92.5% probability that next month will be an outlier.[10]

Although we lack sufficient data to test our forecasting methodology out-of-sample, we can use a simple test proposed by Merton [1981] to determine whether our methodology adds information relative to an unconditional forecast within-sample. We sum the percentage of periods our methodology forecasts a quiet regime when in fact there was a quiet regime and the percentage of periods in which our methodology forecasts turbulence when there was indeed turbulence. A score of 2.0 would indicate perfect forecasting ability, while a score of 1.0 would indicate a total absence of forecasting ability.

Our forecasting methodology achieves a score of 1.28, which implies with 96.33% confidence that it improves the unconditional forecast.[11]

V. REGIME-SENSITIVE PORTFOLIOS

The results of the Merton test suggest that our regime-forecasting methodology helps to distinguish quiet regimes from turbulent regimes one period ahead. This is but one approach, however, for forecasting the relative likelihood of quiet and turbulent regimes. It might be the case that economic or financial variables can add explanatory power. In any event, to the extent that we can distinguish the relative likelihood of quiet and turbulent regimes, here is how we use such information to structure portfolios that are regime-sensitive. We begin by rewriting expected utility in matrix notation, as shown in Equation (4).

$$EU = w'\mu - \lambda(w'\sum w) \qquad (4)$$

where:

EU = expected utility;
w = vector of asset weights;
μ = mean of expected return vector;
λ = risk aversion; and
Σ = covariance matrix.

In order to differentiate the probabilities we wish to assign to the quiet and turbulent regimes, we replace the full-sample covariance matrix Σ with:

$$p_t \sum_Q + (1 - p_t) \sum_T \qquad (5)$$

where:

p_t = predicted probability of an inlier at time t;
Σ_Q = quiet regime covariance matrix; and
Σ_T = turbulent regime covariance matrix.

Substituting these two covariance matrixes into the standard equation for the expected utility of a portfolio yields:

$$EU = w'\mu - \lambda(p_t w' \sum_Q w + (1 - p_t) w' \sum_T w) \qquad (6)$$

In order to reduce risk of loss during an investment horizon we should reestimate the parameters of Equation (6) each period and adjust the portfolio weights accordingly.

IV. SUMMARY

We argue that investors with ostensibly long horizons may not have the forbearance to withstand severe interim losses, and we show that the likelihood of an interim loss is much greater than the likelihood of an end-of-period loss.

We use a methodology to partition returns into quiet and turbulent regimes on the basis of a sample's covariances as well as variances. There is evidence that this approach is better than one that relies only on volatility to stratify returns.

We present evidence from global stock and bond returns that is consistent with the notion that returns are generated by multiple regimes, rather than a single lognormal distribution. Moreover, we estimate the extent to which the assumption of a single lognormal distribution understates a portfolio's first-passage risk if instead our return sample is generated by multiple regimes.

Finally, we propose a methodology to assess the relative likelihood of a quiet or turbulent regime one month ahead using a switching regression model. This information can be used to structure regime-sensitive portfolios.

APPENDIX

Covariance of Truncated Returns

We consider n random variables X distributed following an $N(O, V)$ multinormal distribution. The CJKL methodology separates the sample into two parts based on both the distance from the multivariate mean and the interaction between returns. Inliers are defined as all observations for which $X'V^{-1}X \leq b$ and outliers as $X'V^{-1}X > b$.[12] The methodology, known as elliptic truncation, differs from other forms of truncation in that it partitions all returns on the basis of their degree of unusualness, not on a given threshold level.[13]

We demonstrate that the covariance matrix of the truncated distribution takes a simple form. It equals the covariance matrix of the full distribution multiplied by a scale factor. This signifies that: 1) the CJKL methodology produces conditional moments, including correlations, that are unaffected by the conditioning bias reported in the literature; and 2) unless extreme and usual events are generated by two different distributions, the truncated correlation should not spuriously indicate different regimes.

We focus on the moment-generating function (MGF) of the distribution of truncated series. The MGF of a random variable with density f corresponds to:

$$M_X(t) = E(e^{tx}) = \int e^{tx} f(x) dx$$

$$= \int \left(1 + tx + \frac{1}{2!} t^2 x + \ldots + \right) f(x) dx$$

$$= 1 + tm_1 + \frac{1}{2!} t^2 m_2 + \ldots +$$

where m_r is the r-th moment of X around 0. Thus the n-th moment around 0 is given by the value of the n-th derivative of M_X with respect to t, taken at 0:

$M'_x(t) = E(xe^{tx})$ and $M''_x(t) = E(x^2e^{tx})$

Therefore:

$$M'_x(0) = E(x), M''_x(0) = E(x^2)$$
and $Var(X) = M''_x(0) - M'_x(0)^2$

Because $X'V^{-1}X$ is distributed following a chi-square distribution with n degrees of freedom, we obtain the expression for the MGF of the truncated outliers:[14]

$$M_{Trunc}(t) = \frac{1}{Pr(\chi_n^2 > b)}(2\pi)^{\frac{-1}{2n}}|V|^{-1}\int_{X'V^{-1}X>b} \exp\left(-\frac{1}{2}X'V^{-1}X + t'X\right)dX$$

We make the transformation:

$Z' = x'H'$ with $H'H = V^{-1}$

Therefore:

$$M_{Trunc}(t) = \frac{1}{Pr(\chi_n^2 > b)}(2\pi)^{\frac{-1}{2n}}\exp\left(\frac{t'Vt}{2}\right)$$

$$\int_{z'z>b} \exp\left[-\frac{1}{2}(Z-Ht)'(Z-Ht)\right]dZ$$

$$= \frac{1}{Pr(\chi_n^2 > b)}(2\pi)^{\frac{-1}{2n}}\exp\left(\frac{t'Vt}{2}\right)Pr(\chi_n^2(t'Vt) > b)$$

$$= \frac{1}{Pr(\chi_n^2 > b)}\sum_{j=0}^{\infty}\frac{\left(\frac{1}{2}t'Vt\right)^j}{j!}Pr\left[(\chi_{n+2}^2 > b)\right]$$

It follows that the covariance matrix of the outliers is simply equal to cV in which

$$c = \frac{Pr(\chi_{n+2}^2 > b)}{Pr(\chi_n^2 > b)}$$

All elements of the covariance matrix of the outliers are multiplied by a scalar. This implies that, if returns come from a single distribution, truncated correlations are left unchanged.

NOTES

The authors thank George Chow, Alan Marcus, Paul O'Connell, André Perold, Krishna Ramaswamy, Bruno Solnik, and Edouard Stirling; and participants at New York University's Risk Management: State of the Art Conference; the Fall Seminar of the Institute for Quantitative Research in Finance; and the Spring Seminar of Inquire Europe for their helpful comments.

1. Lognormality characterizes the distribution of discrete returns and arises from the process of compounding. The continuous counterparts of discrete returns are normally distributed.

2. The first passage probability is described in Karlin and Taylor [1975].

3. For example, Odier and Solnik [1993] find that correlations rise during volatile markets, but they fail to address the issue of whether this rise is due to multiple regimes or to correlation mathematics. The pitfalls of using conditional correlations to detect regimes are now widely documented. Boyer, Gibson, and Loretan [1997], Forbes and Rigobon [1999], Ang and Chen [2000], and Longin and Solnik [2001] note that deviations from the unconditional correlation do not necessarily indicate different regimes.

4. See the appendix for a formal demonstration.

5. See Ang and Chen [2000, p. 3.]

6. We obtain a smooth approximation of the density function of the empirical returns by applying non-parametric kernel smoothing, which involves weighted local averaging of the density function. See Härdle [1990].

7. See Hamilton [1994], Chapter 22.

8. Obtained with a two-lag autoregressive model.

9. Chi-square is a simplifying assumption. We would prefer to consider the empirical distribution of distances but, given the small number of observations in the sample, this would lead to unreliable results.

10. The cutoff corresponds to the 10% most unusual observations.

11. This confidence value is estimated using a normal approximation based upon the mean and variance of a hypergeometric distribution. For a more detailed discussion of this evaluation procedure, see Henriksson and Merton [1981].

12. b corresponds to the inverse of the chi-square distribution for the chosen degree of tolerance and the number of assets.

13. Most studies focus on single partitioning $(X > c)$ or partitioning based on volatility $(|X| > c)$.

14. See Johnson and Kotz [1972], Chapters 28 and 35.

REFERENCES

Ang, A., and J. Chen. "Asymmetric Correlations of Equity Portfolios." Working paper, Columbia University, 2000.

Boyer, M., B. Gibson, and M. Loretan. "Pitfalls in Test for Changes in Correlations." International Finance Discussion Paper 597, Board of Governors of the Federal Reserve System, 1997.

Chow, G., E. Jacquier, M. Kritzman, and K. Lowry. "Optimal Portfolios in Good Times and Bad." *Financial Analysts Journal*, May/June 1999.

Forbes, K., and R. Rigobon. "No Contagion, Only Interdependence: Measuring Stock Market Co-Movements." Working paper 7267, NBER, 1999.

Hamilton, J. *Time Series Analysis*. Princeton: Princeton University Press, 1994.

Härdle, W. *Applied Nonparametric Regression*. Econometric Society Monographs No. 19. Cambridge: Cambridge University Press, 1990.

Henriksson, R., and R. C. Merton. "On Market Timing and Investment Performance: II. Statistical Procedures for Evaluating Forecasting Skills." *Journal of Business*, Vol. 54, No. 4 (1981).

Johnson, N.L., and S. Kotz. *Continuous Multivariate Distributions*. New York: John Wiley, 1972.

Karlin, S., and H. Taylor. *A First Course in Stochastic Processes*, 2nd ed. New York: Academic Press, 1975.

Longin, F., and B. Solnik. "Extreme Correlations of International Equity Markets." Forthcoming, *Journal of Finance*, 2001.

Merton, R. C. "On Market Timing and Investment Performance: I. An Equilibrium Theory of Value for Market Forecasts." *Journal of Business*, Vol. 54, No. 3 (1981).

Odier, P., and B. Solnik. "Lessons for International Asset Allocation." *Financial Analysts Journal*, March/April 1993.

12. THE BI-CURRENCY BALANCE SHEET MODEL OF LATENT CURRENCY RISK

ANTHONY C. MORRIS

1. INTRODUCTION

One of the most notable empirical puzzles in pricing sovereign credit risk concerns the observed differences in credit spreads between emerging market (EM) sovereigns and identically rated G7 corporate borrowers. These differences can be seen on two axes: rating and maturity. For example, holding maturity constant at 5 years, Cantor and Packer (1996), economists at the Federal Reserve Bank of New York, observed that sovereign debt issues from emerging markets with ratings below "A" were priced at consistently higher spreads relative to U.S. Treasuries than identically rated G7 corporate issuers. In contrast, spreads for sovereigns rated above "A" were equal or lower than comparable corporate debt. An example of this general finding is shown in Figure 1.

Holding rating constant and varying maturity, one can see another aspect to the pricing difference for emerging market sovereign debt compared with corporate debt. In many cases, while observed credit spread term structures of the two issuer-types have diverged in the medium to long part of the curve, they have been much closer if not overlapping at the short end of the curve. Figure 2 shows this pattern for Mexico, which is indicative of a similar pattern for many other EM countries.

This article is based on Chapter 1 of my doctoral dissertation, "A Contingent Claim Model of Emerging Market Sovereign Credit Risk," at the Stern School of Business, New York University. I thank my dissertation committee members including Edward Altman, Stephen Figlewski, Kenneth Garbade, Richard Levich, and Ingo Walter for guidance and encouragement. All errors that remain are my own.

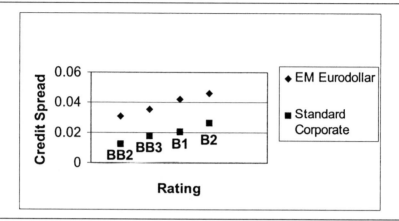

Figure 1. 5-Year Spreads Relative to U.S. Treasuries for Emerging Market Eurodollar Bonds and Standard U.S. Corporate Issuers. Data are as of January 27, 1997. Source: Bloomberg, L.P.

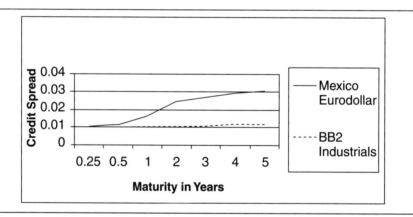

Figure 2. Yield Spreads Relative to U.S. Treasuries for Mexican Eurodollar Bonds and BB2 U.S. Corporate Industrials at Various Maturities. Data as of January 27, 1997. Source: Bloomberg, L.P.

Do these secondary market pricing differences suggest that sovereign risk is misrated or perhaps mispriced? Can this apparent divergence between the credit markets and the rating agencies be explained? Are the markets, or the rating agencies, or both out of line with reality?

In this article, our aim is to provide a richer explanation of these and other empirical regularities in sovereign debt pricing by drawing on principles of contingent claims analysis (CCA). The link between credit risk and contingent claims analysis goes back to the original Black-Scholes (1973) paper. Black and Scholes observed that equity in a leveraged firm could be viewed as a call option on the assets of a borrower struck at the face value of the firm's single outstanding zero-coupon debt instrument. Merton (1974) and Black-Cox (1976), and many others subsequently, have built on this insight. The results of this literature include analysis of what drives a borrower's credit spread term structure and how balance sheet structure can provide option-like incentives to management which conflict with the interests of other corporate constituencies, such as debt-holders.

As such, it seems reasonable to consider what light can be shed on sovereign risk issues by extending the contingent claim framework in this direction. In particular, it would appear that the questions of 1) what drives the distinctions between sovereign and corporate credit curves, and 2) how can we represent the conflicts of interest between sovereign borrowers and international creditors, would lend themselves well to analysis in a contingent claim framework. These questions are closely related to previous work in a corporate setting.

In order to address these questions, we propose a bi-currency balance sheet model of latent currency risk. This model represents an extension of the Merton (1974) model of credit spreads. The model is designed to capture one of the real-life distinctions between EM sovereign and G7 corporate borrowers in the speculative grades: the tendency for EM sovereigns to run mismatched asset-liability foreign exchange exposures to a higher degree.

This article continues with a review of earlier models of emerging market credit risk pricing. In Section 3, we introduce the bi-currency balance sheet model and the notion of latent currency risk. By latent currency risk, we suggest the potential for domestic currency depreciation to jeopardize the credit quality of EM external debt issued in non-domestic currencies, even though such issues bear no explicit currency risk from the perspective of international investors. Section 4 discusses the empirical features of EM debt pricing in the context of the model. Section 5 considers common investment practices in light of the modeling framework. Conclusions are in the final section.

2. PREVIOUS MODELS OF EMERGING MARKET CREDIT RISK PRICING

Earlier studies of sovereign debt valuation in a macroeconomic framework include Edwards (1986) and Boehmer and Megginson (1990). These studies used regression analysis to analyze secondary-market pricing of emerging market (EM) borrowers, specifying credit spread as the dependent variable and economic indicators such as debt-to-output or debt-to-exports ratios as independent variables. Such specifications have shortcomings. Claessens and Pennacchi (1996) point out that debt prices are a concave function of underlying repayment capacity, while regression analysis cannot capture this non-linear relationship. More generally, it could be said that such a regression-based approach is not grounded in a dynamic asset-pricing theory. In addition, term-structure considerations are made problematic. Identification of relevant variables and non-stationarity or statistical relationships also pose dilemmas.

Recent work has advanced the understanding of EM credit risk by viewing debt liabilities with the tools of contingent claims analysis (CCA). CCA, as defined by Jones, Mason and Rosenfeld (1984), is the generalization of option pricing, refined by Merton (1974) and Black and Cox (1976), which views corporate liabilities as combinations of option contracts. A recent example of this literature is Longstaff and Schwartz (1995). The analysis of EM debt in a CCA framework instead of with descriptive regressions parallels the relationship between Jones, Mason and Rosenfeld (1984) and Fisher (1959) in the context of corporate debt. Whereas Fisher (1959) examined corporate debt credit spreads as a dependent variable in a regression specification, Jones, Mason, and Rosenfeld (1984) analyzed spreads as an output of a CCA functional form.

Claessens and Pennacchi (1996) and Cumby and Evans (1995) analyze Brady-debt with an approach related to that of Longstaff and Schwartz (1995) for default-risky debt in general. The innovation of these Brady studies was not the characterization of sovereign debt as having option features. Previous work did this, but had difficulty identifying input parameters to an option pricing model, such as the level and volatility of underlying sovereign asset value. Proxies were estimated from macroeconomic data. Among other innovations, Claessens and Pennacchi (1996) and Cumby and Evans (1995) identified parameters governing a stochastic sovereign credit quality process directly from market information. This allowed a market-based assessment of sovereign credit quality in a more structured framework and with a dynamic asset-pricing model.

3. CONTINGENT CLAIM ANALYSIS AND THE BI-CURRENCY BALANCE SHEET MODEL

A model of emerging market debt pricing could focus on any of a number of factors which distinguish EM debt issuers from standard corporate debt issuers. These include (1) incomplete information disclosure, and (2) uncertain enforcement of contractual provisions. We examine the pricing implications of this second factor in another paper. In this part of the study, we focus on a third factor that is perhaps less obvious: the potential for EM borrowers to have severe asset-liability mismatches in foreign exchange (FX) exposure. Our model is based on the following premise: *emerging market sovereigns or corporates borrowing in non-domestic currencies may have asset-liability mismatches in foreign exchange exposure which are difficult to hedge.*

We posit that the extent of such mismatches is a fundamental difference between emerging-market and standard corporate borrowers. The reasoning is as follows. Speculative-grade U.S. firms, for example, may have few if any FX cash flows. And if they do, U.S. firms have ready access to FX derivatives to match their currency exposures between assets and liabilities. Among other tools, currency swaps facilitate such hedging. Deep and liquid currency swap markets exist for reserve currencies in all maturities. However, hedging exposures to emerging market currencies is difficult. Applicable derivative products have limited liquidity and usually cover only short maturities.[1] Emerging-market sovereign and corporate borrowers with large, foreign-currency liabilities and predominantly local-currency assets are especially exposed to this risk. For this reason, it seems important to consider the contribution of unhedged asset-liability mismatches in FX exposure to the credit risk of debt issued in non-domestic currencies. We do this with a simple bi-currency extension of the Merton model.

The Merton CCA framework is chosen for its relative simplicity, facilitating focus on latent currency risk. The choice to avoid "default-barrier" models adopted by

Black and Cox (1976), Claessens and Pennacchi (1996), Cumby and Evans (1995), and Longstaff and Schwartz (1995) among others is deliberate. One reason is the requisite first-passage-time analysis would add little to expository clarity. A secondary reason is that the safety-covenant provision of standard corporate debt that motivates default-barrier models is less likely to exist or be enforceable in EM debt. It should also be noted that, since sovereigns issue no direct equity shares traded in public markets, it is unclear that the arbitrage-based risk-neutral valuation underlying the Merton framework is appropriate. Again, to focus attention on how latent currency risk might be expected to impact EM debt pricing *ceteris paribus*, it is assumed here that the sovereign's equity is tradable in a liquid and efficient local market, rendering risk-neutral valuation plausible.

The present focus on latent currency risk is not meant to suggest that other factors do not play an equal if not more important role in EM credit pricing. For example, investors may anticipate more problematic reorganization proceedings or lower recovery rates in the event of sovereign as opposed to standard corporate default. These issues are examined in other sections.

The Merton Model

We first briefly review the original Merton (1974) framework, which describes a borrower with a single risky zero-coupon bond outstanding. All the usual Black–Scholes-Merton assumptions apply, among which, the market value of the borrower's assets, V, follows a geometric Brownian motion of the form:

$$\frac{dV}{V} = \mu dt + \sigma dW,$$

where dW is a standard Wiener process. Default occurs if V is less than the face value of the bond, B, at maturity, T. In the event of default, creditors receive recovery rate, V/B. Market value of the bond is F, market value of equity is f, and $V = F + f$. The riskless interest rate is r, such that the value of corresponding riskless debt is Be^{-rT}. These conditions are summarized in the following diagram and specifications.

A. The value of the risky debt can be expressed as $F = V - f$.
B. Since f has payoff $\max(V - B, 0)$ at T, equity is a European call option on V, with strike price B.
C. Using put-call parity and the two previous relations, it can be shown that the risky bond is a portfolio of two component assets: a long position in the corresponding riskless debt and a short position in a European put option, $p(V, T)$, on V with strike price B.

$$F(V, T) = V - f(V, T) = V - p(V, T) + Be^{-rT} - V$$

$$F(V, T) = Be^{-rT} - p(V, T) \tag{1}$$

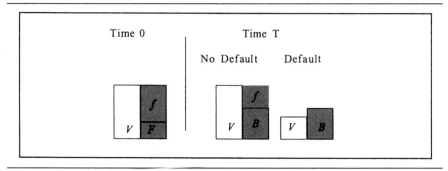

Figure 3. Assets and Liabilities of the Firm at Time 0 and Time T

which can be expressed as:

$$F(V, T) = Be^{-rT}\left\{N[h_2(d, \sigma^2 T)] + \frac{1}{d}N[h_1(d, \sigma^2 T)]\right\},$$

where

$$d = \frac{Be^{-rT}}{V},$$

$$h_1(d, \sigma^2 T) = -\frac{(\sigma^2/2)T - \ln(d)}{\sigma\sqrt{T}},$$

$$h_2(d, \sigma^2 T) = -\frac{(\sigma^2/2)T + \ln(d)}{\sigma\sqrt{T}} \qquad (2)$$

D. Given this functional form for risky debt pricing, the term structure of credit spreads is an increasing function of two inputs:
   1. Leverage (the borrower's ratio of liabilities to assets). Higher leverage leads to higher spreads. Higher leverage means V (the level of the underlying) is lower relative to B (the strike price).
   2. Volatility. When volatility of V is high, the credit spread will be high.

The figures below show the pricing implications of the Merton framework. Figure 4 displays credit spreads associated with varying levels of asset value. Lower levels of asset value (higher leverage) lead to higher spreads. Figure 5 displays credit spreads associated with varying levels of asset volatility. Higher levels of asset volatility lead to higher spreads. Note credit-risk term structures share some the features of the more familiar riskless interest rate term structures. They can be upward sloping, humped, or downward sloping.

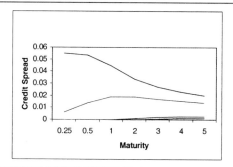

Figure 4. Credit Spreads for Various Levels of V from 2.5, 2.0, 1.5, 1.25, 1.10

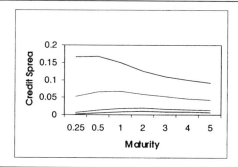

Figure 5. Credit Spreads for Various Volatilities of V from 0.2, 0.25, 0.3, 0.4, 0.6

The Bi-Currency Balance Sheet Model

We now consider a borrower with a simple unhedged bi-currency balance sheet. The setting is identical to Merton (1974) except that the borrower's assets are denominated in one currency and liabilities in another. Let the borrower have non-dollar assets, $V^\star$, but a single dollar-denominated zero-coupon bond outstanding, having face value B. Define $r^\star$ as the non-dollar riskless rate. Let S define the exchange rate (dollar/non-dollar), such that a decline in S represents a depreciation of the non-dollar currency. The dollar value of firm Y's assets, V, is simply the product of S and $V^\star$. Default on the dollar liability occurs if V is less than B at maturity. $V^\star$ and S follow the geometric Brownian motion processes:

$$\frac{dV^\star}{V^\star} = \mu_{V^\star} dt + \sigma_{V^\star} dW_{V^\star},$$

$$\frac{dS}{S} = \mu_S dt + \sigma_S dW_S,$$

$$\rho dt = \text{corr}(dW_{V^\star}, dW_S) \tag{3}$$

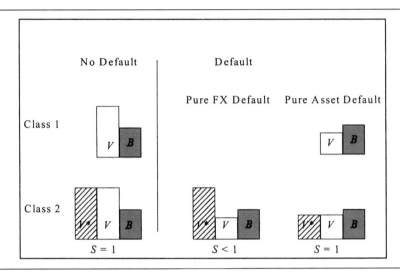

Figure 6. Assets and Liabilities of a Firm with Two Classes of Shareholders at Time 0 and Time T

In the diagram above, Class 1 illustrates the standard Merton framework, in which both assets and liabilities are in the same currency. In this case, default risk is a function of the level and volatility of assets alone. Class 2 illustrates the extended framework with the simple bi-currency balance sheet. When assets and liabilities are in separate currencies, S is a random variable, making default risk a function of the level and volatility of *both $V^\star$ and S* and the correlation between them. As shown, default can occur with no change in S if $V^\star$ declines (Pure Asset Default), or with no change in $V^\star$ if S declines (Pure FX Default). It can also be seen that the standard framework (Class 1) is a special case of the extended framework (Class 2) with S constant and unity, leaving $V^\star = V$ and $\text{Var}(V^\star) = \text{Var}(V)$. In short, there is an additional source of ruin in the bi-currency balance sheet.

Pricing Implications of the Bi-Currency Balance Sheet for Dollar-Debt

The market value, F, of the borrower's risky dollar bond is determined by investor analysis of the borrower's repayment capacity in terms of dollars. As mentioned, the credit spread of the bond, and the entire term structure of credit risk specific to that borrower, is a function of the level and volatility of V, given B. We now examine the determination of these parameters in terms of the bi-currency balance sheet.

The current level of borrower asset value in dollar terms, V, is straightforward to determine. As mentioned, $V = V^\star \times S$. As in the standard Merton framework, valuation of the risky debt claim can be seen as the combined value of corresponding riskless debt and a short put option on the underlying value of the firm, with strike price equal to debt service, B. However, in the bi-currency balance sheet framework this put option, p_{BC} is on an underlying ($V^\star \times S$) which is itself the product of two jointly stochastic assets and must be valued as such. This is done with quanto option pricing results (e.g. Hull (1993), p. 284ff.). $V^\star$ in dollar terms has risk-neutral drift $r^\star - \rho\sigma_S\sigma_{V^\star}$, making the risk neutral process followed by V from the perspective of a dollar-based investor identical to that of a dollar-denominated stock with a continuous dividend yield, $q^\star$, where

$$r - q^\star = r^\star - \rho\sigma_S\sigma_{V^\star},$$

$$q^\star = r - r^\star + \rho\sigma_S\sigma_{V^\star} \tag{4}$$

Thus, the functional form for the risky bond price in the bi-currency balance sheet framework is given by:

$$F(V,T) = Be^{-rT} - p_{BC}(V,T),$$

where

$$p_{BC}(V,T) = Be^{-rT}N(-d_2) - Ve^{-q^\star T}N(-d_1),$$

and

$$d_1 = \frac{\ln(V/B) + (r - q^\star + \sigma^2/2)T}{\sigma\sqrt{T}},$$

$$d_2 = d_1 - \sigma\sqrt{T},$$

$$\sigma = \sqrt{\sigma_S^2 + \sigma_{V^\star}^2 + 2\rho\sigma_{V^\star}\sigma_S} \tag{5}$$

Given the functional form (5) of the risky dollar-denominated debt price, F, we can make the following observations about the dependencies of F:

$$\frac{dF}{d\sigma_{V^\star}} < 0, \frac{dF}{d\sigma_S} < 0, \frac{dF}{d\rho} < 0, \frac{dF}{dV^\star} > 0, \frac{dF}{dS} > 0 \tag{6}$$

As would be expected, dollar debt value is an increasing function of non–dollar asset value and the exchange rate, but a decreasing function of these parameters' volatilities. It is also a decreasing function of the correlation between non–dollar asset value and the exchange rate. This is logical given that investors would be more averse to higher correlation of the two sources of ruin.

Comparison of Credit Risk Term Structures

These dependencies have implications for how the credit risk term structures of Class 2 borrowers should differ from those of Class 1 borrowers. We first examine a simple case. Assume that $S = 1$, $V = V^\star$, $\text{Var}(V^\star) = \text{Var}(V)$ and $\text{Cov}(V^\star, S) = 0$. In other words, assume 1) the classes are identical in all respects except FX exposure, and 2) the two credit risk factors for Class 2 borrowers are independent. Both Class 1 and Class 2 borrowers would have the same credit-spread term structure if asset-induced credit risk were the only factor. However, vulnerable also to FX-

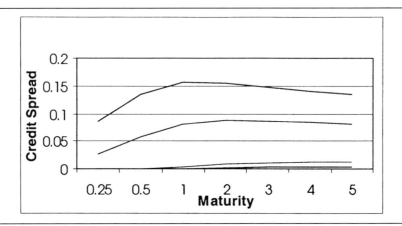

Figure 7. Credit Spread by Maturity for Varying Volatility of S from 0.0, 0.2, 0.4, 0.6, 0.8

induced credit risk, Class 2 borrowers should have a term structure over and above the Class 1 term structure.

Figure 7 illustrates this point. It shows the results of a simulation in which all parameters were held constant except the volatility of the exchange rate, which takes values between 0.00 (representing Class 1) and 0.80. In particular:

$$S = 1, V^\star = 1.75, B = 1, r = r^\star = 0.06, \sigma_{V^\star} = 0.25, \rho = 0, \sigma_S = [0, 0.20, 0.40, 0.60, 0.80]$$

As expected, the credit risk term structures of Class 2 borrowers are higher than those of Class 1 borrowers, which are identical to Class 2 except for having no FX-induced credit risk (represented by the volatility of S). In this simulation, given that the correlation between changes in S and $V^\star$ is zero, a Class 2 borrower can be viewed as having a dollar credit spread term structure which is the sum of two independent term structures, one for each credit risk factor. A characteristic of this property is that the difference in spreads between Class 1 and Class 2 is increasing in maturity.

We now consider the impact of correlation between changes in $V^\star$ and S, with:

$$S = 1, V^\star = 1.75, B = 1, r = r^\star = 0.06, \sigma_{V^\star} = 0.25, \sigma_S = 0.20, \rho = [-1.0, -0.25, 0.00, 0.25, 1.0]$$

While casual observation would suggest local-currency depreciation is likely to be associated with situations in which sovereigns find it difficult to service hard-currency debt, it is much harder to determine if such crises are examples of pure-FX default or some combination of declines in $V^\star$ and S. In the bi-currency balance sheet framework, investor expectations of this correlation between $V^\star$ and S would be reflected in different credit-spread term structures. Figure 8 illustrates a simulation in which all parameters are held constant except correlation, showing

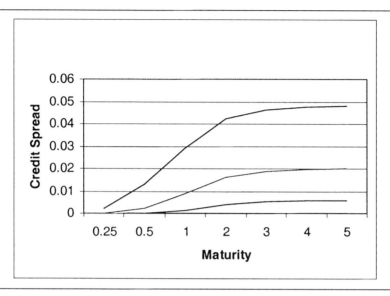

Figure 8. Credit Spread by Maturity for Varying Correlation (Rho) Between V* and S, from −1.0, −0.25, 0.0, 0.25, 1.0

that higher correlations cause higher spreads. It can be seen that negative correlation can be sufficient to reduce credit spreads significantly.

4. EMPIRICAL FEATURES OF EMERGING MARKET DEBT PRICING

Having presented the bi-currency balance sheet model, we now examine the two empirical features of EM external debt pricing. This framework of latent currency risk provides a new perspective on why G-15 debt can trade at discounts to G-7 debt despite similar total-debt-to-GDP ratios. Latent currency risk and the correlation of this risk with asset value in local terms are sufficient reasons for large pricing differences, even without distinctions between the two country classes regarding expected primary surpluses or the trade-off between the value of future business opportunities and default windfalls. In addition, similar factors make it nearly impossible for EM debt *not to* trade at different spreads from identically-rated standard corporate debt at most parts of the term structure.

Pricing differences between G-15 and G-7 debt

Guidotti and Kumar (1991) noted that by the end of 1988, the external debt of the G-15 (i.e. highly-indebted developing) countries traded at discounts of at least 50% in secondary markets, with only a few exceptions. While such pricing no doubt reflected rescheduling-related increases in external-debt ratios and concurrent domestic debt service requirements, it also remained that the average G-15 ratio of total public debt to GDP in 1988 was 54.0% vs. the G-7's 58.5%. Table 1 presents

Table 1. Total public debt as percentage of GDP

	1983	1984	1985	1986	1987	1988
U.S.	44.2	45.2	48.3	51.1	51.6	51.5
Japan	66.9	68.4	69	72.8	75.5	73
Italy	71.9	77.1	84	88.5	92.7	95
G-15	43	47.6	50.5	53.2	53.6	54

Source: Guidotti and Kumar (1991).

ratios in the mid-1980s for the G-15 and three G-7 countries: the U.S. as benchmark, and debt-ridden Japan and Italy.

In a CCA context, leverage alone does not determine spread levels. As such, the implicit sentiment in the question raised by Guidotti and Kumar (1991)—that the ratio of total public debt to GDP *by itself* should explain pricing patterns—does not necessarily hold. Even if this ratio provided a reasonable proxy for leverage in the balance sheet sense, other factors would also need to be considered. First, we need to determine the extent to which assets and liabilities are in the same currency. If they are substantially the same, a Class 1 setting, as defined in the previous section, is appropriate. If assets and liabilities are substantially in different currencies, a Class 2 setting is appropriate. Recall, a Class 1 borrower is a special case of Class 2, with constant S equal to unity. Second, we need estimates of the inputs, including 1) the levels of non-domestic currency ("dollar") liability B, local non-dollar assets $V^\star$, and exchange rate S, 2) the volatility of $V^\star$ and S, and 3) the correlation between $V^\star$ and S.

While these parameters cannot be estimated for the late 1980s period covered by Guidotti and Kumar (1991), we can begin to think about the situation in terms of Class 1 and Class 2 borrowers. The data in Table 2 provide insight to the extent of asset-liability mismatch in FX exposure. As can be seen, the three G-7 countries have negligible amounts of debt issued externally in non-domestic currencies, despite having high ratios of total public debt to GDP. In contrast, the G-15 debt exposure is 70% external. Thus, it seems a reasonable approximation to view the three G-7 countries as Class 1 and the G-15 as Class 2.[2]

Viewed from the perspective of Class 1 vs. Class 2 borrowers, the noted pricing differences make more sense. In the previous section, it was shown that Class 2 borrowers would always have higher credit-spread term structures than otherwise identical Class 1 borrowers (e.g., Figure 3). Given the high likelihood that markets perceived the local asset value of G-7 sovereigns as less volatile than G-15 local asset value, the scope for difference increases.

It was also shown in the previous section that positive correlation between $V^\star$ and S made the difference between Class 1 and Class 2 term structures more extreme (e.g., Figure 4), *ceteris paribus*. While we cannot estimate what this correlation was directly, it is not unreasonable to assume it was positive for the G-15, given the association of financial distress and currency depreciation or devaluation, and

Table 2. Ratio of external debt to total debt

	1983	1984	1985	1986	1987	1988
U.S.	0	0	0	0	0	0
Japan	0.0048	0.0058	0.0057	0.0053	0.0054	0.0054
Italy	0.0298	0.0342	0.0312	0.0254	0.0296	0.0315
G-15	0.707	0.7038	0.705	0.703	0.7034	0.6981

Source: Government Finance Statistics Yearbook 1993, IMF: Guidotti and Kumar (1991).

Table 3. Monthly volatility of log FX changes (local currency/USD)

January 1982–January 1989

Italy	Argentina	Brazil	Mexico	Venezuela
0.013769	0.052901	0.029952	0.040005	0.040393

Source: Author's calculations based on International Monetary Fund data.

rather less so for the G-7. One way to consider this issue is to proxy changes in sovereign asset value with those of the national equity market. There is an observed tendency for EM stock markets to plunge in the wake of sharp currency depreciation, while advanced markets tend to gain an offsetting amount.

It is possible to confuse the role played by external borrowing in credit pricing. The portrayal of G-7 sovereigns as Class 1 borrowers and G-15 as Class 2 is not tantamount to saying the relative *level* of *external* debt to GDP is a crucial explanatory variable in pricing, as many regression-based analyses suggest. It would be a mistake to conclude that the observed price differences are necessarily a result of the advanced countries having negligible amounts of external debt outstanding. Even if both groups were Class 2, ample scope for pricing differences would remain. One reason is that a crucial parameter to the bi-currency balance sheet framework, the volatility of S, was lower in the G-7 than in the G-15. This can be seen in Table 3, which shows monthly exchange rate volatility over the time period. A second reason is that large differences in relative asset volatility would remain. A third is that correlation between asset value and exchange rate was probably lower and even negative in the G-7.

Thus, the gross differences in 1988 debt prices had a number of justifications. First, markets likely perceived G-15 asset values as highly volatile while viewing G-7 asset values as having little to no volatility. Second, the G-7 had basically no external debt and thus zero S volatility, while G-15 debt had perceived volatility in both $V^\star$ and S. Third, probable positive correlation between $V^\star$ and S in the G-15 would have made the pricing difference more extreme. These differences which arise from bi-currency optionality in the capital structure would lead to discounts for EM debt even if we ignored expectations of future primary surpluses and the trade-off between default windfalls and long-term business opportunities. No assumptions were necessary about relative ratios of total-debt-to-asset-value (i.e. leverage in the balance sheet sense as opposed to the debt/GDP sense) or external-debt-to-asset-value between the groups. The results would still hold even if these ratios were identical. In addition, these results were derived without resorting to arguments about expropriation and politically motivated issuer behavior.

Pricing differences between EM and standard corporate debt

Cantor and Packer (1996) present evidence that EM external debt which rating agencies classify below grade "A" trades at higher spreads than identically rated corporate debt. Their sample consists of U.S. corporate spread data reported by Bloomberg, L.P. and observed spreads of sovereign bonds issued in U.S. dollars. Comparisons were made as of September 29, 1995 at the five-year maturity level. Yields observed from sovereign bonds with a different maturity were adjusted to the five-year level by adding the difference between the identically rated corporate spreads observed at the five-year maturity and at that sovereign's maturity.

Following a similar procedure, we collected data for four borrowers of decreasing credit quality rankings: Mexico, Argentina, Brazil, and Venezuela on the five-year maturity as of January 27, 1997. These data were presented in Figure 1. An interpretation of these data suggested by Cantor and Packer (1996) is that investors are more pessimistic than rating agencies about sovereign credit quality below the A level, though in agreement with the agencies' relative rankings. Going one step further, some financial institutions recommend investment strategies anticipating a convergence between the spreads of similarly rated EM and U.S. corporate issuers.

While rating agencies could be less pessimistic than the markets in their assessment of EM issuers, the issue may be rather richer. Looking at spread term structures, rather than one horizon only, it appears the differences are narrower at the short horizon than at longer horizons. But viewed from the perspective of the bi-currency balance sheet, the spread patterns are not surprising. Credit ratings are driven by leverage considerations. As noted in Sarig and Warga (1989), Ederington and Yawitz (1987) empirically document an inverse relationship between ratings and leverage. Assume that the rating agencies mainly considered the leverage (again in the balance sheet sense, debt to assets) of the EM issuers during the rating-assignment process. Spread differences of the kind observed could not be ruled out. Recall that in Section 2, it was shown that Class 1 and Class 2 borrowers, having identical leverage, could have very different term structures of credit spreads. View the U.S. corporate issuers as Class 1 borrowers and the EM issuers as Class 2 with identical debt to asset value ratios. If we allow asset volatility to differ, while adding exchange rate volatility and positive correlation between changes in the exchange rate and asset value in terms of domestic currency, there is ample scope for such spread differences.

Such an interpretation seems consistent with the credit spread term structure data from January 27, 1997 presented in Figure 2 for Mexico and Figures 9, 10, and 11

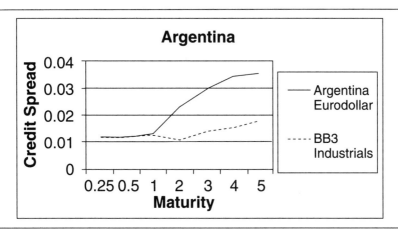

Figure 9. Yield Spreads Relative to U.S. Treasuries for Argentine Eurodollar Bonds and BB3 U.S. Corporate Industrials at Various Maturities

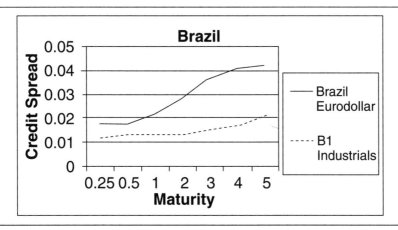

Figure 10. Yield Spreads Relative to U.S. Treasuries for Brazilian Eurodollar Bonds and B1 U.S. Corporate Industrials at Various Maturities

for Argentina, Brazil and Venezuela. If markets were *uniformly* more pessimistic than the rating agencies, the EM credit spread term structure would be consistently higher than the corresponding corporate one. However, considering the credit spread term structure as a whole from a bi-currency balance sheet perspective, another interpretation arises. The market view seems consistent with U.S. corporate and EM issuers having similar credit ratings, if these ratings are in fact mainly leverage-based. The difference is term structures arise from the non-leverage parameters of credit risk, such as asset and currency volatility.

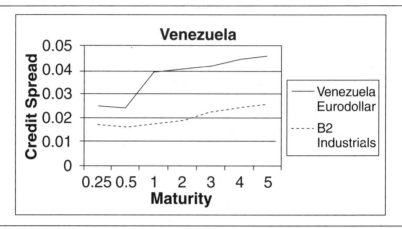

Figure 11. Yield Spreads Relative to U.S. Treasuries for Venezuelan Eurodollar Bonds and B2 U.S. Corporate Industrials at Various Maturities

5. COMMON INVESTMENT PRACTICES IN LIGHT OF THE CCA FRAMEWORK

The results of the previous section provide an opportunity to consider implicit assumptions underlying common investment analysis practices in light of this modeling framework. Implicit in the view that identically rated EM and corporate debt should have similar spreads is the assumption that a credit rating can characterize the term structure of credit spreads.

Many market participants believe that credit ratings provide pricing guidelines for the term structure of credit risk. However, credit ratings cannot fulfill that purpose, and probably were not intended to. A term structure of interest rates, be it riskless or risky, reflects investor expectations of how a given interest rate will evolve over time. Appropriate modeling of such dynamic expectations requires some form of stochastic characterization, and a stochastic model requires at least two parameters if it is to be anything other than driftless Brownian motion. (Recall that in the Merton framework, the credit spread term structure was a function of two variables, which were sufficient to characterize a risk-neutral constant drift diffusion process.) A traditional credit rating, as a scalar variable, cannot provide enough information to dynamically model a credit risk term structure.

Admittedly, models of the term structure explicitly based on a scalar credit rating are uncommon. However, a more common procedure involves a subtler form of the same principle. This is the practice of constructing term structures associated with each credit rating class by fitting a curve to large numbers of identically rated issues at different maturities, and then assuming identically-rated issuers will fall on or near the same curve. This raises the following difficulty: if the term structure of credit risk reflects a stochastic process governed by at least two variables, why should the debt of two separate issuers trade on the same curve because they share one variable in common? Taking a simple case, assume a scalar rating correctly identifies one of the two variables. Even then the credit curves of two identically rated issuers could differ owing to the second unidentified, non-identical variable.

The issues raised by such credit pricing practices are analogous to a point made by Cumby and Evans (1995). That article showed that a credit-pricing model commonly used by practitioners, which assumes constant conditional probability of default, mis-specifies the term structure of credit risk. Such an assumption implies that investors do not expect credit quality to evolve over time. However, the authors found evidence that investors distinguished between present and future credit quality, and that the term structure of credit risks reflected such *dynamic* expectations. Nevertheless, one of the attractions of such models is that the constant credit quality assumption is a convenient one, simplifying the solution by reducing credit risk to a single scalar variable—the constant conditional default probability. In this sense, expecting the term structure of credit risk to be adequately characterized by a scalar credit rating is akin to assuming credit quality will not evolve over time. Both of these views impose unjustifiably restrictive conditions on the pricing of credit risk.

6. CONCLUSIONS

In this study, we analyzed the role of latent currency risk in the pricing of emerging market external debt. We posited that a fundamental difference between emerging market and standard corporate borrowers was the potential for the former to hold severe asset-liability mismatches in FX exposure, and that this leads to a latent currency risk in emerging market sovereign debt. The bi-currency balance sheet model served as a theoretical framework for examining the impact of this latent currency risk. The model provides a richer perspective on the pricing of emerging market debt and helps to account for the empirical pricing patterns emerging market debt.

NOTES

1. See *Risk*, December 1996, Latin America Supplement for details about Latin American currency hedging.
2. Strictly speaking, the G-7 countries are not even Class 1, given that Class 1 describes a particular kind of risky borrower and the debt of the three countries concerned is perceived as riskless. However, riskless debt could be thought of as a special case of Class 1 with near-zero asset volatility, which leads to pricing tantamount to the riskless curve. For illustrative purposes only, we consider the G-7 debt as risky to facilitate comparisons with the G-15.

REFERENCES

Black, F., and J. Cox, 1976, "Valuing Corporate Securities: Some Effects of Bond Indenture Provisions," *Journal of Finance*, 31, 351–367.
Black, F., and M. Scholes, 1973, "The Pricing of Options and Corporate Liabilities," *Journal of Political Economy*, 83, 3, 637–654.
Boehmer, E., and W.L. Megginson, 1990, "Determinants of Secondary Market Prices for Developing Country Syndicated Loans," *Journal of Finance*, 45, 1517–1540.
Cantor, R., and F. Packer, 1996, "Determinants and Impact of Sovereign Credit Ratings," *Economic Policy Review*, Federal Reserve Bank of New York, 2, 37–53.

Claessens, S., and G. Pennacchi, 1996, "Estimating the Likelihood of Mexican Default from the Market Prices of Brady Bonds", *Journal of Financial and Quantitative Analysis*, 31, 109–126.

Cumby, R., and M.D.D. Evans, 1995, "The Term Structure of Credit Risk: Estimates and Specification Tests," Working Paper S-95-21, NYU Salomon Center.

Ederington, L.H., and J.B. Yawitz, 1987, "The Bond Rating Process," in E. Altman, ed., *Handbook of Financial Markets and Institutions*, 6th ed., New York, Wiley.

Edwards, S., 1986, "The Pricing of Bonds and Bank Loans in International Markets," *European Economic Review*, 30, 565–589.

Fisher, L., 1959, "Determinants of Risk Premiums on Corporate Bonds," *Journal of Political Economy*, 67, 3, 217–237.

Guidotti, P.E., and M.S. Kumar, 1991, "Domestic Public Debt of Externally Indebted Countries," International Monetary Fund, Occasional Paper 80.

Hull, John. C. *Options, futures, and other derivatives*, Prentice-Hall, Saddle River, NJ, 1993.

Jones, E.P., S.P. Mason, and E. Rosenfeld, 1984, "Contingent Claims Analysis of Corporate Capital Structures: an Empirical Investigation," *Journal of Finance*, 39, 611–627.

Longstaff, F., and E. Schwartz, 1995, "A Simple Approach to Valuing Risky Fixed and Floating Rate Debt," *Journal of Finance*, 50, 789–819.

Merton, R.C., 1974, "On the Pricing of Corporate Debt: The Risk Structure of Interest Rates," *Journal of Finance*, 29, 449–470.

Sarig, O., and A. Warga, 1989, "Some Empirical Estimates of the Risk Structure of Interest Rates," *Journal of Finance*, 44, 1351–1360.

13. DOES CONTAGION EXIST?

ROBERTO RIGOBON

Sloan School of Management, MIT and NBER

The Russian crash in August 1998 was followed by several stock market and currency collapses around the world. It was, as Yogi Berra would say, "déjà vu all over again". During the Mexican and the Asian crises the markets behaved similarly. In general, these events have been called "contagion". However, there does not seem to be an agreement on what exactly contagion means.

In the literature, it is possible to find at least three definitions of contagion:

1. First, contagion can be interpreted as the concurrence of crises: a collapse in one country generates a speculative attack in another one. A very good example was the massive attack Brazil suffered during late 1998 after Russia crashed.
2. Second, based on the fact that countries in crisis experience increases in the volatility of their returns, contagion can be characterized as the transmission of volatility across countries. For example, during the Mexican crisis, the variance of daily returns in Argentina increased by almost 10 times, and this cannot be attributed to news generated in Argentina. This shift in the volatility is what some authors have rendered as contagion.
3. Finally, contagion can be defined as a change in the propagation of shocks across countries. For example, shocks from one country to another are transmitted with higher intensity during crises.

However, these definitions of contagion have some problems: The first two make sense only in particular cases, while the third one is not found in actual data.

R.M. Levich and S. Figlewski (eds.). RISK MANAGEMENT. Copyright © 2001. Kluwer Academic Publishers. Boston. All rights reserved.

Let us first concentrate on the problems with the first two definitions. Assume we are interested in studying if there is contagion between the NYSE and NASDAQ. Suppose very bad news about IBM is announced, and a crash in the NYSE and in the NASDAQ is observed. Are we willing to call this contagion? Furthermore, what if there is a simultaneous increase in the volatility of the two indices, are we willing to call this contagion? Probably not. We would call the event something that is part of a single economy and both stock indices part of that economy. This example is a bit extreme because indeed it is the same economy, but what about Canada and the U.S., or Germany and the Netherlands? Are not these economies so interrelated in practice that their stock markets behave as if they are almost the same economy? Are we willing to call events between very interrelated countries contagion? Again, I think the answer is no. On the other hand, this question makes more sense when the two markets analyzed are, in principle, "not related", for example, Mexico and Morocco. In this case, besides them both starting with the same letter, our prior is that the economies have nothing in common. Therefore, observing that they suddenly co-move is surprising. The problem with these definitions is that they only makes sense when we believe, *ex-ante*, that the countries are not interrelated. However, this requires defining what classifies as being interrelated. Should it be how much the countries trade with each other, how close they are geographically, or whether or not they have similar exchange rate regimes? This leaves a zone for *subjective* interpretation.

Now, let's turn our attention to the last definition of contagion. In this case, contagion implies that crises are inherently different from periods of tranquility. A very important strand in the literature that started with King and Wadhwani[1] (1990) measures the change in the transmission mechanism as increases in the correlation. The following table shows the correlation between daily stock market returns in dollars for Mexico and Argentina during the Mexican 1994 and the Hong Kong 1997 crises. The tranquil period in the six months prior to the crisis, and the crisis period is the month after the abandonment or the crash takes place.

The test that the coefficients are the same is rejected in both crises. Thus, we might be tempted to conclude that the propagation of shocks changed during those crises. However, as is shown in Forbes and Rigobon[2] (1998) this conclusion is incorrect. The reason is that the correlation estimate is biased, and it tends to increase when the variance of the shocks rises. In our paper, we use careful statistical

Table 1. Correlation of daily stock returns between Mexico and Argentina

	Correlation		
	Tranquility	Crisis	Is the correlation statistically the same?
Mexican Crisis	41.2	65.1	No
Hong Kong Crisis	44.3	86.0	No

techniques to show this, however a simple coin flipping game should illustrate the intuition to this result. Suppose there are two coin flipping games that are interrelated. In the first game we flip a coin: heads we win the coin, tails we lose it. The game can be played either with a penny or a special $100 coin. In the second game, we also flip a coin (in this case it is always played with a quarter), but the payoff in the game also includes the payoff from the first game (for simplicity assume it pays 10 percent of the outcome of the first game). When the first game is played with a penny, the returns to the second game are a quarter plus or minus a tenth of a penny. Therefore, the outcome of the first game is negligible for the outcome of the second one and hence the two gambles have a correlation of almost zero (in fact the true correlation is 0.4 percent). One the other hand, assume that the first game is played with the $100 coin. The returns in the second game are the quarter plus or minus 10 dollars! In this case, the outcome of the second coin is negligible to the second gamble. The correlation between the two gambles is almost 1 (the correlation is 97 percent). As can be seen, the propagation of shocks is always 10 percent from one gamble to the other one, yet the correlation coefficient moves from zero to one.[3] We can think of Mexico as the first game and Argentina as the second one. We can interpret the crisis as the time when volatility increases (thus moving from the penny to the $100 coin). Forbes and Rigobon (1998) study the correlation between Mexico and 28 other countries and show that when the correlation is adjusted by taking into account the shifts in the variance, less than 5 percent of the cases traditionally classified as contagion experienced significant correlation changes when correcting for the bias. These results are generalized to situations when there are problems of endogeneity and omitted variables in a study of 36 stock markets and more than 1,200 pairs of relationships.[4] In this larger study, I find that in less than 10 percent of the cases does the transmission mechanism change.

In conclusion, the first two definitions of contagion make sense only when we believe *ex-ante* that the markets are not related, while the third definition does not seem to be found in the data when we correct for the bias inherent in simple correlations.

Therefore, there are two questions one must resolve in understanding contagion. The first is what is a sensible definition of contagion? The second is does it exist or does it not? There has been more success in answering the first question. The facts indicate that contagion is not a short-term phenomenon, and that if it exists, it is reflected in an unusually high interdependence across countries; unusually high with respect to what we think it should be. This interpretation of contagion, however, will always have the problem of how beliefs are constructed in the first place. It is subjective, and hence some person may find the fact that Mexico, Morocco and Argentina are highly correlated to be normal (i.e. just like the IBM example). Therefore, answering the second question is not independent of one's beliefs. So does contagion exist? This is a very sensible economic question, and for the moment, I'll give a very sensible economic answer: *it depends*.

NOTES

1. King, Mervyn and Sushil Wadhwani. "Transmission of Volatility between Stock Markets." *Review of Financial Studies*, pp. 5–33, 1990.

2. Forbes, Kristin and Roberto Rigobon. "Not Contagion, Only Interdependence: Measuring Stock Market Comovements." *MIT Mimeo*, 1998.

3. This result is known as the Normal Correlation Theorem. The first one to highlight this result (as far as I know) was Rob Stambaugh in a discussion of the paper: Karolyi, Andrew and Rene Stulz. "Why do Market Move Together? An Investigation of US-Japan Stock Return Comovements." *The Journal of Finance*, pp. 951–986, 1996.

4. Rigobon, Roberto. "On the Measurement of the International Propogation of Shocks." *MIT Mimeo*, 1999.

14. AN ANALYSIS AND CRITIQUE OF THE BIS PROPOSAL ON CAPITAL ADEQUACY AND RATINGS[*]

EDWARD I. ALTMAN[†], ANTHONY SAUNDERS

1. INTRODUCTION

In June 1999, the BIS released its long awaited proposal on reform of the 8% risk-based capital ratio for credit risk that has been in effect since 1993 (see Basel Committee on Banking Supervision, 1999).[1] The 8% ratio has been criticized on at least three major grounds. First, it gives an equal risk-weighting to all corporate credits whether of high or low credit quality. Second, it fails to incorporate potential capital savings from credit (loan) portfolio diversification. The latter is a result of its simple additive nature. And third, it has led to extensive regulatory capital arbitrage which adds to the riskiness of bank asset portfolios.

In its June 1999 draft, the BIS proposed a three-stage reform process.[2] In the first stage, the 8% risk based ratio (where all corporate loans receive the same 100% risk-weighting) would be replaced by weightings based on the external credit agency rating of the borrower (we discuss this proposal in more detail in Section 2 of the paper). In the second stage, at some unspecified time in the future, when some sophisticated banks have developed their own internal rating systems for loans, a

[*] This paper's drafts have been prepared for two symposia on the proposed new guidelines; the first held at the University of Frankfurt on 2 December 1999 and the second at the NYU Salomon Center's Stern School of Business forum, held on 25 February 2000.
[†] The authors are respectively the Max L. Heine and John M. Schiff Professors of Finance, Stern School of Business, NYU. They wish to thank several individuals from Standard and Poor's and Moody's for their data assistance. The computational assistance of Vellore Kishore and Sreedhar Bharath are also acknowledged as well as the coordination by Robyn Vanterpool. The opinions presented are solely of the authors.

transformation may be made to calculating capital requirements based on a bank's allocation of its loans to the various grades/ratings in its own internal loan rating system. Finally, in the third stage, given appropriate model and data base development and testing, some banks may be able to use their own internal credit risk models to calculate capital requirements. Importantly, these internal models allow for portfolio diversification effects (see Saunders, 1999).

A number of issues have been raised about stages two and three of the reform proposal e.g., how will the internal rating systems of different banks—especially if they continue to develop independently of each other—be grouped into some standardized set of capital risk weights; that is, will a rating of 1 for Citigroup be the same as a 1 for BankAmerica,[3] or will a rating of 1 for a bank in the United States be equivalent to a 1 for a bank in Germany? Also, what is the appropriate mapping of the internal rating model with external ratings? While these are important issues, this paper concentrates on the first stage of the proposal. In particular, we raise a number of concerns (backed by data) regarding the use of rating agencies rating systems in a reformed capital adequacy system in the manner that the 1999 BIS proposal stipulates.

Section 2 of this paper briefly outlines the BIS stage-one proposal. Section 3 presents some empirical evidence that questions the proposal and shows that similar "risk-shifting" incentives (i.e., regulatory capital arbitrage) exist under the new plan as under the current 8% risk-based capital ratio. These empirical tests are supplemented by simulations on sample data to better assess expected and unexpected losses from actual corporate bond portfolios. We will show that the current Basel "one size fits all" approach is not sufficiently modified in the new approach. Finally, Section 4 provides our recommendation to enlarge the number of "buckets" with different risk weightings to better approximate actual loss experience and risk categories.

2. THE BIS STAGE 1 PROPOSAL

Table 1 shows the proposed reform of the 8% ratio in stage 1 of the new plan. As noted in Section 1, currently all corporate loans have the same 100% risk-weight (for risk adjusted assets) implying the same minimum capital requirement (e.g., 8%). Under the new proposal, corporate borrowers rated AAA to AA—by S&P, or the equivalent authorized rating agencies (see Table 2), will have a risk weight of 20%. This implies a capital ratio of $0.2 \times 8\% = 1.6\%$; much lower than at present for "high quality" loans. In what follows, we shall label this category "bucket 1." For corporate borrowers rated A+ to B−, the risk weight will remain at 100%, i.e., they will continue to have a capital ratio of 8%; we will call this group of borrowers "bucket 2." For those borrowers rated below B−, the risk weighting increases to 150%, implying a capital ratio of $1.5 \times 8\% = 12\%$. It might be noted that, somewhat paradoxically, unrated corporate borrowers are given a lower 100% risk weight and thus an 8% capital requirement. A similar, but less broad bucketing approach is adopted for sovereigns and banks. In particular, the current system of a zero risk

Table 1. Proposal BIS risk weighting system for bank loan credits

Claim		Assessment (%)					
		AAA to AA−	A+ to A−	BBB+ to BBB−	BB+ to B−	Below B−	Unrated
Sovereigns		0	20	50	100	150	100
Banks	Option 1[a]	20	50	100	100	150	100
	Option 2[b]	20	50	50[c]	100[c]	150	50[c]
Corporates		20	100	100	100	150	100

[a] Risk weighting based on risk weighting of sovereign in which the bank is incorporated.
[b] Risk weighting based on the assessment of the individual bank.
[c] Claims on banks of a short original maturity, for example less than six months, would receive a weighting that is one category more favorable than the usual risk weight.

Table 2. Rating agencies extreme credit quality categories[a]

Credit assessment institution	Very high quality assessment	Very low quality assessment
Fitch IBCA	AA− and above	Below B−
Moody's	Aa3 and above	Below B3
Standard and Poor's	AA− and above	Below B−
Export insurance agencies	1	7

[a] Source: Basel Committee on Bank Supervision (1999).

weight for OECD countries and a 100% risk-weight for all other countries is replaced by four new buckets based on agency ratings.

In Section 3, we use data on bond ratings, defaults and loss rates to more closely examine the three-bucket approach for corporate borrowers. We do this with two questions in mind. First, does this approach lead to bank capital reserves rising prior to recessions, i.e., before the realization of loan losses typically occurs—as should happen under an "ideal" system? In particular, a well-designed regulatory system should see capital reserves rising during periods of high profitability and earnings for banks (which normally coincides with periods of business expansions) and falling during recessions as "unexpected losses" are written off against capital. At the very least, the size of the capital reserve should be coincident with the business cycle even if it does not lead it.

Second, does the bucketing system make economic sense? That is, how homogeneous in terms of risk are the different buckets. For example, bucket 2 encompasses both investment grade debt (A and BBB) as well as below investment grade debt (BB and B). Moreover, if they are not homogenous, what relative risk-weighting scheme would these data suggest?

3. EMPIRICAL RESULTS

In this section we use data from Moody's (1999) and Standard and Poor's (1999) and from the NYU Salomon Center's data base on Corporate bond defaults[4] and losses on defaults in order to gain insight into these two questions.

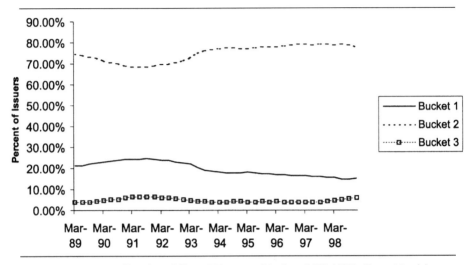

Figure 1. Proportion of bonds in different BIS proposed buckets (1989–1998). (*Source*: Moody's Investor Services, New York.)

3.1. The Lead–Lag Relationship of Capital Reserves

As discussed above, ideally, capital reserves for unexpected losses should be accumulated during periods of high bank profitability and business expansion. Banks find it much more difficult, if not impossible, to add substantially to their capital reserves when profits are low and the economy is in recession. And, reserves should be adequate prior to, not after defaults and losses increase.

In Fig. 1, we have used Moody's bond ratings to group bonds outstanding over the March 1989 to March 1999 period into the three buckets implied by the Moody's equivalents to the S&P ratings shown in Table 1. The period 1989–1991 is a period of recession while the period of the current expansion begins post-1992. Although these data include only one recession, they are representative of a number of recent critiques that have found that rating agencies move slowly and their ratings are often inflexible. As a result, external ratings' ability to predict default with a long (if any) lead has been questioned. Indeed, Fig. 1 suggests that a capital adequacy system built around traditional agency ratings might even follow, rather than lead, the business cycle. As can be seen, the proportion of bonds in bucket 2 appears to fall continuously over the March 1989 to March 1991 period, while those in buckets 1 and 3 appear to rise continuously. Specifically, the proportion of bonds in bucket 3, with the 150% risk weight, peaks in September 1991, near the end of the recession rather than at the beginning.

Figure 2 shows a similar result for S&P ratings. As can be seen, while the percentage of bonds in bucket 3 is small, its proportion still rises over the 1990–1991 period. If risk weights and capital requirements were tied to these buckets, this could

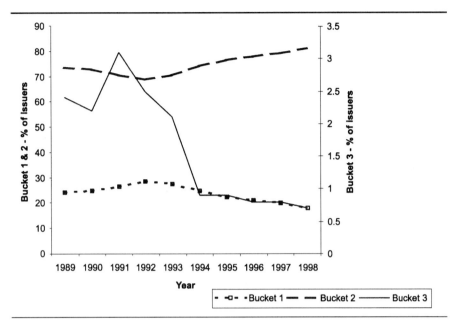

Figure 2. Proportion of bonds in different BIS proposed buckets (1989–1998). (*Source*: Standard & Poor's, New York.)

have meant (had the new proposal been in effect during the 1989–1991 recession) that some banks would have had to build up their minimum reserve requirements during the recession with a peak minimum capital ratio being achieved at or near the recession's end.[5] That is, rather than leading the recession, minimum capital requirements would have been lagging it and also the rising wave of loan defaults.

This suggests that alternatives to the rating agencies' bucket approach be assessed. For example, there are a number of rating and default forecasting approaches that have been developed in the last decade. These include ones by Jonsson and Fridson (1996), Moody's (1999), and Altman (1989). The first two utilize the existing rating proportions and add macroeconomic variables to the forecasting regression. The latter assumes a stable default aging frequency by original rating, and forecasts defaults based on the previous 30 years of default aging experience, in essence a regression-to-the-mean approach.

A second possibility is that the individual issuers of loans be subjected to a micro-default probability model and the aggregate of this bottom-up approach be assessed for expected and unexpected (capital) losses of the loan portfolio. Approaches with this objective include equity value option models (expected default frequencies) and multivariate models which involve financial statement and market equity variables.[6]

A final idea exploits the use of credit spreads to define the buckets. It can be empirically demonstrated that credit spreads were particularly accurate forecasters of subsequent default rates at the start of 1990 and again at the start of 1991 (see Table

3).[7] The credit spread indicator is a commonly used barometer of risk in financial systems and for economic cycles by both the government and banks.

3.2. Bucket Risk Homogeneity

To analyze the second question, bucket risk homogeneity, we examined data on bond issues (and issuers) over the 1981–1999 (September) period. Our focus of attention was the degree of homogeneity (heterogeneity) of unexpected loss rates over the sample period. Following most approaches of economic capital and loan loss reserve calculations, loan loss reserves are meant to cover expected (or mean) losses while economic capital reserves are meant to cover unexpected losses.

To undertake this study, we collected data on bond issues and issuers that did and did not default, the ratings of those defaulting issues one year prior to default, the price and coupon of the bonds one year prior to default and the price of the bonds just after default. The price (and coupon) one year prior to default (P_{t-1} and C_{t-1}) and the price (and lost coupon) on default (P_t and C_t) allowed us to calculate a loss

Table 3. Annual returns, yields and spreads on 10 year treasury (TREAS) and high yield (HY) bonds[a] (1978–1999)[b]

Year	Return (%)			Promised yield (%)		
	HY	TREAS	SPREAD	HY	TREAS	SPREAD
1999	1.73	(8.41)	10.14	11.41	6.44	4.97
1998	4.04	12.77	(8.73)	10.04	4.65	5.39
1997	14.27	11.16	3.11	9.20	5.75	3.45
1996	11.24	0.04	11.20	9.58	6.42	3.16
1995	22.40	23.58	(1.18)	9.76	5.58	4.18
1994	(2.55)	(8.29)	5.74	11.50	7.83	3.67
1993	18.33	12.08	6.25	9.08	5.80	3.28
1992	18.29	6.50	11.79	10.44	6.69	3.75
1991	43.23	17.18	26.05	12.56	6.70	5.86
1990	(8.46)	6.88	(15.34)	18.57	8.07	10.50
1989	1.98	16.72	(14.74)	15.17	7.93	7.24
1988	15.25	6.34	8.91	13.70	9.15	4.55
1987	4.57	(2.67)	7.24	13.89	8.83	5.06
1986	16.50	24.08	(7.58)	12.67	7.21	5.46
1985	26.08	31.54	(5.46)	13.50	8.99	4.51
1984	8.50	14.82	(6.32)	14.97	11.87	3.10
1983	21.80	2.23	19.57	15.74	10.70	5.04
1982	32.45	42.08	(9.63)	17.84	13.86	3.98
1981	7.56	0.48	7.08	15.97	12.08	3.89
1980	(1.00)	(2.96)	1.96	13.46	10.23	3.23
1979	3.69	(0.86)	4.55	12.07	9.13	2.94
1978	7.57	(1.11)	8.68	10.92	8.11	2.81
Arithmetic annual average						
1978–1999	12.16	9.28	2.88	12.82	8.27	4.35
Compound annual average						
1978–1999	11.54	8.58	2.96			

[a] End of year yields.
[b] Source: Salomon Smith Barney Inc.'s High Yield Composite Index; Altman et al. (2000).

rate for each bond default (i.e., $[P_t - (P_{t-1} + C_{t-1}/2)]/P_{t-1}$. The total number of defaulting bonds over the 18 years sample period, for which we had full price and rating information, was 588. For an additional 104 bonds, we only had the rating and not the price, one year prior to default. For these bonds, we assumed that their default experience mirrored the distribution of losses of the bonds in each rating class for which we did have loss data. Finally, there were over 100 bonds that were unrated and for which we had no price data. We placed them in the unrated category (see Table 1). Since we are only looking at the relative loss experience for rated bonds, these unrated bonds played no further part in our study.

We then applied a number of models to calculate unexpected loss rates (or "economic" capital requirements) for bonds of different ratings one year prior to default,[8] so as to calculate loss rates at various confidence intervals. Three distribution models were used to initially calculate loss rates; (i) a normal distribution (ii) the actual distribution and (iii) a Poisson distribution (with a stable mean). The first two models are similar to those used in J.P. Morgan's 1997 CreditMetrics® approach and the third is a simplified version of the model assumed in CSFP's 1997 CreditRisk+®. Tables 4–9 show the results for the full sample period for rating classes A through CCC and below. Note that BIS bucket 2 is represented here by the ratings A, BBB, BB and B and bucket 3 is represented by the CCC and lower category. Bucket 1 is not shown because of non-existent defaults in the AAA to AA ratings range at one year prior to default.

In addition, we carried out a set of Monte-Carlo simulations. Since most formal credit-risk models—such as CreditMetrics® and CreditRisk+® contain certain parametric assumptions (e.g., about correlations) embedded in their structures, these formal models' results reflect, in part, untested assumptions. Monte-Carlo simulations, by contrast, allow estimation of the size of losses in the tail of loan loss distributions conditional only on assumptions made about the composition of bank portfolios. In the simulations, we follow Carey (1998) and look at a number of portfolios. The first reflects the allocation for US life insurance company privately placed bonds. In this allocation, approximately 13% are below investment grade. The second reflects the suggested allocation by Carey for US banks' commerical loan portfolios. This reflects, on average, a much lower credit quality than that adopted by life insurers, with some 50% being below investment grade. In addition to these two portfolios, we look at loss distributions for portfolios that contain respectively only AAA, AA and A bonds (portfolio 3), BBB bonds (portfolio 4), BB bonds (portfolio 5), B bonds (portfolio 6) and CCC and lower (portfolio 7).

In conducting the Monte-Carlo simulation, a portfolio aggregate size is chosen ($1 billion) and assets are drawn at random subject to the composition of the portfolios conforming to the representative portfolios discussed above (until the target aggregate portfolio size is reached). The loss rate on the portfolio is then calculated. For each portfolio (1–7) the simulation is repeated 50,000 times and the frequency distribution of losses forms an estimate of the relevant loss distribution. From that loss distribution, loss rates at different quantiles can be analyzed, and by implication the capital reserves needed to absorb the level of unexpected losses are determined.

Table 4. Frequency distribution of losses (principal and coupon) (1981–1999) by rating one year before default (normal and actual loss distributions)[a]

Range of default losses	Midpoint	A	BBB	BB	B	CCC & Lower	Total
0	0	12,115	7,529	5,311	4,997	294	30,246
0.01–0.10	0.05	2	26	11	81	43	163
0.11–0.20	0.15	2	16	15	89	18	140
0.21–0.30	0.25	2	4	18	81	36	141
0.31–0.40	0.35	0	1	8	62	24	95
0.41–0.50	0.45	0	0	8	29	24	61
0.51–0.60	0.55	1	0	3	17	18	39
0.61–0.70	0.65	0	0	1	10	21	32
0.71–0.80	0.75	0	0	0	2	5	7
0.81–0.90	0.85	0	0	0	4	6	10
0.91–0.94	0.92	0	0	0	0	0	0
0.95–0.98	0.96	0	0	0	0	1	1
0.99	0.99	0	0	0	0	0	0
1	1	0	0	0	0	3	3
Total default		7	47	64	375	199	692
Total non-default		12,115	7,529	5,311	4,997	294	30,246
Total		12,122	7,576	5,375	5,372	493	30,938
Mean (%)		0.012	0.067	0.298	1.734	14.079	0.598
Median (%)		0.000	0.000	0.000	0.000	0.000	0.000
S.D. (%)		0.628	1.027	3.181	8.066	29.890	5.001
3.43192σ-E(L) (%)		2.142	3.458	10.619	25.947	88.501	16.566
2.32634σ-E(L) (%)		1.448	2.323	7.102	17.030	55.455	11.037
1.64485σ-E(L) (%)		1.021	1.623	2.051	11.533	35.085	7.628
99.97%		14.988% 3.6	24.933% 2.3	54.702% 1.6	83.266% 1.6	85.921% 0.1	84.402% 9.3
99.00%		0.000% 121.2	0.000% 75.8	4.702% 53.8	43.266% 53.7	70.921% 4.9	24.402% 309.4
95.00%		0.000% 606.1	0.000% 378.8	0.000% 268.8	13.266% 268.6	50.921% 24.7	0.000% 1546.9

[a]Source: Standard and Poor's, NYU Salomon Center Default Data Base.

Table 5. Frequency distribution of losses (principle and coupon) (1981–1999) by rating one year before default (normal and actual loss distributions) (Based on number of issuers—one default per Issuer)[a]

Range of default losses	Midpoint	A	BBB	BB	B	CCC & lower	Total
0	0	12,115	7,529	5,311	4,997	294	30,246
0.01–0.10	0.05	0	0	0	14	4	18
0.11–0.20	0.15	2	1	0	11	8	22
0.21–0.30	0.25	0	1	1	18	11	31
0.31–0.40	0.35	0	1	5	19	11	36
0.41–0.50	0.45	0	1	2	22	11	36
0.51–0.60	0.55	0	3	3	32	9	47
0.61–0.70	0.65	0	0	3	33	17	53
0.71–0.80	0.75	0	4	1	28	12	45
0.81–0.90	0.85	0	0	1	19	7	27
0.91–0.94	0.92	0	0	2	11	1	14
0.95–0.98	0.96	0	0	1	1	2	4
0.99	0.99	0	1	0	0	0	1
1	1	0	0	0	0	0	0
Total default		2	12	19	208	93	334
Total non-default		12,115	7,529	5,311	4,997	294	30,246
Total		12,117	7,541	5,330	5,205	387	30,580
Mean (%)		0.002	0.091	0.205	2.126	12.078	0.574
Median (%)		0.000	0.000	0.000	0.000	0.000	0.000
S.D. (%)		0.193	2.454	3.658	11.529	24.521	6.028
3.43192σ-E(L) (%)		0.659	8.332	12.351	37.440	72.077	20.114
2.32634σ-E(L) (%)		0.446	5.619	8.306	24.694	44.967	13.450
1.64485σ-E(L) (%)		0.314	3.946	5.813	16.837	28.256	9.342
99.97%		0.000%	74.909%	91.795%	89.874%	83.922%	91.426%
99.00%		0.000%	0.000%	0.000%	72.874%	72.922%	14.426%
95.00%		0.000%	0.000%	0.000%	0.000%	62.922%	0.000%
		3.6	2.3	1.6	1.6	0.1	9.2
		121.2	75.4	53.3	52.1	3.9	305.8
		605.9	377.1	266.5	260.3	19.4	1529.0

[a]Source: Standard and Poor's NYU Salomon Center Default Data Base.

Table 6. Frequency distribution of losses (principle and coupon) (1981–1999) by rating one year before default (normal and actual loss distributions) (Based on number of issuers)—Poisson process for defaults[a]

Range of default losses	Midpoint	A	BBB	BB	B	CCC & lower	Total
0	0	12,115	7,529	5,311	4,997	294	30,246
0.01–0.10	0.05	0	0	0	14	4	18
0.11–0.20	0.15	2	1	0	11	8	22
0.21–0.30	0.25	0	1	1	18	11	31
0.31–0.40	0.35	0	1	5	19	11	36
0.41–0.50	0.45	0	1	2	22	11	36
0.51–0.60	0.55	0	3	3	32	9	47
0.61–0.70	0.65	0	0	3	33	17	53
0.71–0.80	0.75	0	4	1	28	12	45
0.81–0.90	0.85	0	0	1	19	7	27
0.91–0.94	0.92	0	0	2	11	1	14
0.95–0.98	0.96	0	0	1	1	2	4
0.99	0.99	0	1	0	0	0	1
1	1	0	0	0	0	0	0
Total default		2	12	19	208	93	334
Total non-default		12,115	7,529	5,311	4,997	294	30,246
Total		12,117	7,541	5,330	5,205	387	30,580
Mean (%)		0.002	0.091	0.205	2.126	12.078	0.574
Median (%)		0.000	0.000	0.000	0.000	0.000	0.000
S.D. (%)		0.193	2.454	3.658	11.529	24.521	6.028
99.97%		1 0.000%	2 0.091%	3 0.409%	12 23.391%	42 495.178%	6 2.869%
99.00%		0 0.000%	1 0.000%	2 0.205%	9 17.011%	35 410.636%	4 1.721%
95.00%		0 0.000%	1 0.000%	1 0.000%	7 12.759%	32 374.403%	3 1.148%
Default rate *m* per 100 loans in the portfolio		0.017	0.159	0.356	3.996	24.031	1.092
		99.997%	99.965%	99.949%	99.976%	99.979%	99.979%
		99.178%	99.194%	99.421%	99.671%	99.182%	99.001%
		99.178%	99.194%	94.972%	96.975%	96.454%	94.921%

[a] Source: Standard and Poor's NYU Salomon Center Default Data Base.

Table 7. Frequency distribution of losses (principle and coupon) (1981–1999) one year before default by rating one year before default (normal and actual loss distributions) (Based on number of issues)[a]

Range of default losses	Midpoint	A	BBB	BB	B	CCC & lower	Total
0	0	67,507	34,525	12,137	8,187	487	122,843
0.01–0.10	0.05	2	26	11	81	43	163
0.11–0.20	0.15	2	16	15	89	18	140
0.21–0.30	0.25	2	4	18	81	36	141
0.31–0.40	0.35	0	1	8	62	24	95
0.41–0.50	0.45	0	0	8	29	24	61
0.51–0.60	0.55	1	0	3	17	18	39
0.61–0.70	0.65	0	0	1	10	21	32
0.71–0.80	0.75	0	0	0	2	5	7
0.81–0.90	0.85	0	0	0	4	6	10
0.91–0.94	0.92	0	0	0	0	0	0
0.95–0.98	0.96	0	0	0	0	1	1
0.99	0.99	0	0	0	0	0	0
1	1	0	0	0	0	3	3
Total default		7	47	64	375	199	692
Total non-default		67,507	34,525	12,137	8,187	487	122,843
Total		67,514	34,572	12,201	8,562	686	123,535
Mean (%)		0.002	0.015	0.131	1.088	10.118	0.150
Median (%)		0.000	0.000	0.000	0.000	0.000	0.000
S.D. (%)		0.261	0.286	1.421	4.573	20.549	2.488
3.43192σ–E(L) (%)		0.892	0.967	4.747	14.605	60.406	8.390
2.32634σ–E(L) (%)		0.604	0.651	3.176	9.550	37.687	5.639
1.64485σ–E(L) (%)		0.427	0.456	2.207	6.434	23.683	3.943
99.97%		0.000% 20.3	0.000% 10.4	54.869% 3.7	83.912% 2.6	89.882% 0.2	64.850% 37.1
99.00%		0.000% 675.1	0.000% 345.7	0.000% 122.0	33.912% 85.6	74.882% 6.9	0.000% 1,235.4
95.00%		0.000% 3,375.7	0.000% 1,728.6	0.000% 610.1	0.000% 428.1	54.882% 34.3	0.000% 6,176.8

[a]Source: Standard and Poor's NYU Salomon Center Default Data Base.

Table 8. Frequency distribution of losses (principal and coupon) (1981–1999) by rating one year before default (normal and actual loss distributions) (Based on number of issues)—Poisson process for default[a]

Range of default losses	Midpoint	A	BBB	BB	B	CCC & Lower	Total
0	0	67,507	34,525	12,137	8,187	487	122,843
0.01–0.10	0.05	2	26	11	81	43	163
0.11–0.20	0.15	2	16	15	89	18	140
0.21–0.30	0.25	2	4	18	81	36	141
0.31–0.40	0.35	0	1	8	62	24	95
0.41–0.50	0.45	0	0	8	29	24	61
0.51–0.60	0.55	1	0	3	17	18	39
0.61–0.70	0.65	0	0	1	10	21	32
0.71–0.80	0.75	0	0	0	2	5	7
0.81–0.90	0.85	0	0	0	4	6	10
0.91–0.94	0.92	0	0	0	0	0	0
0.95–0.98	0.96	0	0	0	0	1	1
0.99	0.99	0	0	0	0	0	0
1	1	0	0	0	0	3	3
Total default		7	47	64	375	199	692
Total non-default		67,507	34,525	12,137	8,187	487	122,843
Total		67,514	34,572	12,201	8,562	686	123,535
Mean (%)		0.002	0.015	0.131	1.088	10.118	0.150
Median (%)		0.000	0.000	0.000	0.000	0.000	0.000
S.D. (%)		0.261	0.286	1.421	4.573	20.549	2.488
3.43192σ-E(L) (%)		0.892	0.967	4.747	14.605	60.406	8.390
2.32634σ-E(L) (%)		0.604	0.651	3.176	9.550	37.687	5.639
1.64485σ-E(L) (%)		0.427	0.456	2.207	6.434	23.683	3.943
99.97%		0.000% 1	0.015% 2	0.393% 4	13.055% 13	485.668% 49	0.449% 4
99.00%		0.000% 0	0.000% 1	0.262% 3	8.704% 9	414.841% 42	0.300% 3
95.00%		0.000% 0	0.000% 0	0.131% 2	7.616% 8	374.369% 38	0.150% 2
Default rate m per 100 loans in the portfolio		0.010	0.136	0.525	4.380	29.009	0.560
		99.996%	99.971%	99.979%	99.967%	99.979%	99.987%
		99.115%	99.288%	99.792%	99.629%	99.037%	99.862%
		99.115%	88.303%	98.368%	97.098%	94.853%	98.790%

[a]Source: Standard and Poor's NYU Salomon Center Default Data Base.

Table 9. Monte-Carlo simulation of loss rates using
data 1981–1999, simulated loss rates (%) confidence level

Portfolio	Portfolio size ($b)	Mean	95%	97.5%	99%	99.5%	99.9%	99.97%
1. 13% < BBB (P.P.)	1.00	0.109	0.468	0.55	0.673	0.767	1.007	1.112
2. 50% < BBB (Loans)	1.00	0.409	1.106	1.28	1.486	1.657	2	2.18
3. AAA, AA, A	1.00	0.003	0	0	0.05	0.25	0.55	0.55
4. BBB	1.00	0.015	0.15	0.15	0.25	0.3	0.4	0.4
5. BB	1.00	0.131	0.55	0.7	0.9	1	1.25	1.35
6. B	1.00	1.085	2.2	2.5	2.85	3.05	3.6	3.8
7. CCC & Lower	1.00	10.119	13.6	14.35	15.2	15.95	17.1	17.56

Unexpected losses are the difference between the loss rate at a given quantile and the mean, or expected, loss rate.

3.3. Empirical Results of Loss Distributions

Table 4 shows that, for A-rated bonds, 12,115 issuers did not default over this period, while seven (7) A rated issues defaulted within one year of being rated A. Of the seven, two defaults had a loss rate in 1–10% range, two had loss rates in 11–20% range, two had loss rates in 21–30% range and one had a loss rate in 51–60% range. The mean loss rate (the expected loan loss reserve) for the entire A-rated sample was 0.012%. Recall, we do not observe any one year losses for AAA or AA rated bonds; hence, no tables are presented.

For capital or unexpected loss calculations, different quantiles were used to describe extreme losses. The more conservative the banker or the regulator, the higher the quantile chosen. For the normal distribution, we calculated the 95% (1.64485σ), 99% (2.32634σ) and 99.97% (3.431925σ) unexpected loss rates. As can be seen for single A bonds, these unexpected loss rates were respectively, 1.021%, 1.448% and 2.142%. These are well below the current 8% capital requirement (actually quite close to the proposed guideline for AAA/AA credits). However, as is well known, the loss distribution of loans is highly non-normal, so the second calculation, also shown in Table 4, uses the actual distribution of bond losses. To calculate a particular quantile's loss rate involves counting backwards under the actual default distribution and finding the loss rate coincident with the default that just matches the quantile. For example, to find the unexpected loss rate consistent with the 99.97% quantile (i.e., where capital is sufficiently large to meet all but 3 losses out of 10,000,[9]) we calculate that 0.03% of 12,122 is 3.6 issues. We then count backwards under the A-rated bond distribution and find that 3.6 defaults are coincident with a loss range of 11–20%. In all cases, we take the mid-point of the loss range (here 15%) to reflect the unexpected loss. To net out the loan loss reserve, we deduct from 15% the expected or mean loss rate (here 0.012%) to get an unexpected loss rate at the 99.97% quantile of 14.988%. This is clearly much larger than the current

8% ratio of the BIS. Note, however, at the less conservative quantiles of 99% and 95%, the unexpected loss rates (and hence capital ratios) are actually zero.

Table 4 carries out a similar exercise to the one discussed above for BBB, BB, B and CCC (and lower) bonds. In addition, a "total" column aggregates across all of the rating classes.[10]

We can use these calculations to examine the degree of homogeneity (hetero-geneity) across the four rating grades A, BBB, BB and B entering into bucket 2. Using the 99th percentile, or its equivalent, as a standard for comparison, we can see that, under the normal distribution assumption, the capital requirements for the four ratings classes are respectively 1.448%, 2.323%, 7.102% and 17.030%. Even under the highly unrealistic assumption of normally distributed loss rates, B rated bonds' risk is more than 10 times that of A rated bonds.[11] Looking at the actual distribu-tion of losses at the 99th percentile, a similar degree of heterogeneity emerges. Specifically, the capital requirements are respectively, 0%, 0%, 4.7% and 43.266%, indicating a very clear distinction between unexpected loss rates of investment grade borrowers (those rated A and BBB) and below investment grade borrowers (those rate BB and B). Thus, Table 4 suggests that if we use external rating agency buckets, as the current proposal suggests, for capital requirement risk-weights, the degree of granularity is far too coarse.

Finally, what can be said about the relative risk weightings of buckets 2 and 3. Under the BIS proposal, bucket 2 has a 100% risk-weight while bucket 3 has a 150% risk weight-implying that loans in bucket 3 are $1\frac{1}{2}$ times "more default risky" than those in bucket 2. As can be seen from Table 4, even where we use, for bucket 2, the lowest rating grade (B), and unexpected loss rates are used to compare with bucket 3 loss rates, the *normal* distribution suggests a risk-weighting ratio of 3.2 times (i.e., 55.455% divided by 17.030%) at the 99% level. The equivalent 99% rel-ative risk-weighting was 1.64 times using the *actual* distribution. Of course, these relative risk-weightings are far larger when either A, BBB, or BB are used to compare to loss rates in bucket 3. Overall, these results suggests that for the new BIS proposal, the credit risk of loans in bucket 3 is relatively underpriced (under capitalized) to that of a loan in bucket 2.

3.4. Robustness Checks

We decided to carry out a number of additional robustness checks to examine how the degree of heterogeneity in bucket 2 changes under "alternative" assumptions. In Table 5, we recognize that Table 4's findings are biased towards finding higher capital ratios and may be confounding loan losses with bond losses (the latter is what we actually measure). Both biases occur, in part, because for non-defaulters we have used the number of issuers (i.e., implicitly assuming one bond per issuer), while the defaults reflect the number of defaulted issues (i.e., one issuer may default on a number of bonds).[12] This bias is corrected in Table 5 where we only analyze the loss rate on the most senior bond or note of each defaulting issuer. As a result, the total number of defaults falls from 692 to 334.[13] This has the additional advantage of making bonds look more like loans, since most bank loans have covenants and/or collateral backing that make them highly senior in the debt repayment structure—especially on default.

Again we find a considerable degree of heterogeneity persisting. For example, at the 99% quantile (2.3264σ), and assuming the normal distribution, the unexpected loss rates vary widely: i.e., 0.446% (A), 5.619% (BBB), 8.306% (BB), 24.694% (B). At the same 99% percent quantile, under the actual distribution, the unexpected loss rates are respectively, 0%, 0%, 0%, and 72.874%.

Table 6 repeats a similar exercise as Table 5 but assumes defaults follow a Poisson distribution with a stable mean.[14] For bucket 2, the simple Poisson model produces similar results as those in Tables 4 and 5. In particular, the unexpected loss rates at the 99% quantile are respectively: 0% (A), 0% (BBB), 0.205% (BB) and 17.011% (B).

Finally, Table 7 repeats in similar exercise to those above except that it replaces the number of issuers in the no default category with an estimate of the number of issues.[15] This considerably increases the number of non-defaults and reduces the mean or expected loss rate. The unexpected loss rates are also affected because of the larger total sample size. As can be seen from Table 7, however, using estimated issues instead of issuers for the non-defaulting class leaves the basic conclusions unchanged. Specifically, again using the 99th percent quantile, the unexpected loss rate under the normal distribution is 0.604% for A rated borrowers versus 9.550% for B rated borrowers, while using the actual distribution the relative unexpected loss rates for A versus B are respectively, 0% vs. 33.912%. Table 8 shows a similar "lack of granularity" using the Poisson distribution. In this case 0% vs. 8.704%.[16]

3.5. Simulation Results

Table 9 looks at the loss rates generated from Monte-Carlo simulations of the seven different portfolios discussed earlier (US life insurer-type portfolio, US bank-type portfolio, and different agency ratings). Each loss distribution is based on 50,000 simulations and an aggregate portfolio size of $1 billion. In recent years, $1 billion in asset size has been viewed as representative of medium-sized US banks.[17]

From Table 9, it can be seen that at the 99% quantile, the unexpected loss rates suggest capital requirements much lower than 8% in all cases, even the most risky rating class. For the insurance company portfolio (portfolio 1), the unexpected loss rate (99% loss rate minus the mean loss rate) suggests a capital ratio of 0.673 − 0.109 = 0.564%. For the riskier bank loan portfolio (portfolio 2), the implied capital ratio is 1.077%. Looking at the question of bucket homogeneity, which is the key focus of this paper, it can be seen that unexpected loss rates for BBB vs. BB vs. B differ significantly, i.e., specifically, 0.235% vs. 0.769% vs. 1.765%.[18] The simulation results clearly show that the unexpected loss rate of the investment grade components (A and BBB) of bucket 2 is much lower than the below investment grade components of bucket 2 (BB and B). Even for the CCC and lower portfolio (bucket 3) the unexpected loss rate is 15.2 − 10.119 = 5.08%. This may imply that the suggested BIS capital ratio for bucket 3 (12%) is perhaps too high.[19] Overall, the Monte-

Carlo simulations confirm the results of the parametric approaches discussed in Tables 4–8—especially the heterogeneity of bucket 2.

4. SUMMARY AND PROPOSAL

This paper has examined two specific aspects of stage 1 of the BIS's proposed reforms to the risk-based capital ratio. It has been argued that relying on "traditional" agency ratings could produce cyclically lagging rather leading capital requirements, resulting in an enhanced rather than reduced degree of instability in the banking and financial system. In addition, even if risk-weights were to be tied to traditional agency ratings, the current bucketing proposal lacks a sufficient degree of granularity. In particular, lumping A and BBB (investment grade borrowers) together with BB and B (below investment grade borrowers) severely misprices risk within that bucket and calls, at a minimum, for that bucket to be split into two.

Table 10 repeats the calculations of Table 5, but groups together A and BBB for comparison with BB and B. If we take the most conservative regulatory view and require capital to be sufficient to meet the 99.97% quantile test, then we can calculate some relative risk-weightings as examples for a split bucket 2. Specifically, in Table 10, which is based on senior bond defaults, (the bond default data that most closely resembles loans), we observe 14 defaults out of 19,658 observations in the A/BBB investment grade bucket and 227 out of 10,535 in the non-investment grade BB/B bucket within the one-year time horizon. At the 99.97% level, for the actual distribution results, the ratio of unexpected losses between the two buckets is 1.65 (90.846/54.96). Under the normal distribution assumption for all levels of confidence (95–99.97%), the ratio is about 5.4 (e.g., 28.240/5.208 for 3.43σ or the 99.97% quantile).[20] Hence, we find a considerable difference in risk between these buckets, as expected. The CCC and lower bucket is considerably more risky under the normal distribution assumption—about 2.5 times the BB/B bucket.[21] Since the CCC and lower category has so few observations (387), we cannot be as confident as we would like to be about its exact risk compared to other buckets.

4.1. A Revised Bucket Proposal

A bucket system with four categories, and with a weighting system something like that shown in Table 11, would accomplish much of what the BIS proposal is attempting to do, and also comes closer to capturing the reality of actual relative default losses by ratings.

We constructed this table based on the following logic. We felt constrained to choose a non-zero weighting for the first bucket (AAA/AA), although our results (over the last 19 years) clearly show that no defaults have actually taken place within one year for bonds in these two highest ratings. The choice of 10% for bucket 1 is therefore arbitrary but still less than the BIS proposal's 20%. A second consideration was that we felt it appropriate to give the new BB/B non-investment grade bucket a full 100% weighting.[22] This left us with a decision as to the appropriate A/BBB classification. We decided to use a ratio of about 3.33–1 when comparing the BB/B

Table 10. Frequency distribution of losses (principal and coupon) (1981–1999) by rating one year before default (normal and actual loss distributions (Based on number of issuers)[a]

Range of default losses	Midpoint	A&BBB	BB&B	CCC & lower	Total
0	0	19,644	10,308	294	30,246
0.01–0.10	0.05	0	14	4	18
0.11–0.20	0.15	3	11	8	22
0.21–0.30	0.25	1	19	11	31
0.31–0.40	0.35	1	24	11	36
0.41–0.50	0.45	1	24	11	36
0.51–0.60	0.55	3	35	9	47
0.61–0.70	0.65	0	36	17	53
0.71–0.80	0.75	4	29	12	45
0.81–0.90	0.85	0	20	7	27
0.91–0.94	0.92	0	13	1	14
0.95–0.98	0.96	0	2	2	4
0.99	0.99	1	0	0	1
1	1	0	0	0	0
Total default		14	227	93	334
Total non–default		19,644	10,308	294	30,246
Total		19,658	10,535	387	30,580
Mean (%)		0.036	1.154	12.078	0.574
Median (%)		0.000	0.000	0.000	0.000
S.D.		1.528	8.565	24.521	6.028
3.43192σ-E(L) (%)		5.208	28.240	72.077	20.114
2.32634σ-E(L) (%)		3.519	18.771	44.967	13.450
1.64485σ-E(L) (%)		2.477	12.934	28.256	9.342
99.97%		54.964%	90.846%	83.922%	91.426%
		5.9	3.2	0.1	9.2
99.00%		0.000%	53.846%	72.922%	14.426%
		196.6	105.4	3.9	305.8
95.00%		0.000%	0.000%	62.922%	0.000%
		982.9	526.8	19.4	1,529.0

[a]Source: Standard and Poor's, NYU Salomon Center Default Data Base.

Table 11. An alternative risk weighting
proposal for bank corporate loans

	AAA to AA–	A+ to BBB–	BB+ to B–	Below
Corporates (%)	10	30	100	150

bucket with this A/BBB bucket. This is about the midpoint between the normal distribution and actual distribution's results at the 99.97% quantile (1.65 and 5.40), Hence, the designation of 30% for our bucket 2. Note that this 30% weighting is considerably lower than the BIS proposal and the 100% weighting for bucket 3 is the same as their earlier proposal. Finally, we adopt the same 150% weighting for below B-credits (bucket 4).

4.2. The Unrated Class

Note that we do not propose any specific weighting for the category "unrated." We feel that the appropriate weighting system that bank regulators sanction will be based on a combination of external and internal ratings. Using internal ratings obviates the need for an "unrated" class since banks should be rating all customers. Also, the currently proposed BIS unrated class is essentially a classification that assumes no clear risk analysis. That is not very helpful in a world where most assets are unrated by external rating agencies; hence, the inevitable sanctioning of internal systems.

4.3. Final Comment

We are aware that our proposals are not perfect, but they appear to resemble more closely the existing data on unexpected losses. Although we do not expect regulatory capital arbitrage to cease completely, we are convinced that it will be reduced with our modifications and will bring regulatory capital closer to economic capital estimates.

NOTES

1. The 8% ratio was phased-in over the 1988–1992 period, following the 1988 Basel Accord. Some countries have actually adopted a capital adequacy ratio of over 8% (e.g., Brazil uses 11%). In all cases, the level of capital is to help to ensure a bank's solvency against unexpected losses.

2. The discussion period for the proposal runs until March 2000. A revised proposal will then be distributed with a subsequent second, probably shorter, discussion and commentary period.

3. See Tracey and Carey (1998, 2000) for a discussion and survey of banks' internal ratings systems. A more recent discussion paper by the Basel Committee on Banking Supervision (2000) examines the range of Banks' internal rating systems.

4. The data includes defaults on straight (non-convertible) corporate bonds over the period 1971–1999, ratings and prices on the defaulting issues at birth, one year and one month prior to default as well as just after default.

5. The years 1990 and 1991 saw defaults rise dramatically in both the corporate loan and bond markets. Indeed, corporate bond default rates in each of those years were over 10% of the outstanding

bonds at the start of each year (see Altman et al., 2000). Moreover, Carey (1998) notes that more than 50% of large bank corporate loan portfolios are comprised of below investment grade borrowers, i.e., the proportion of below investment grade loans is significantly higher than the proportions of below investment grade bonds shown in Figs. 1 and 2.

6. A survey of these methods can be found in Altman and Saunders (1997) and Caouette et al. (1998).

7. On 31 December 1989 the yield-spread between high yield corporate bonds and 10 years US Treasury bonds was 7.24% and one year later it was 10.50% (Table 3). These were the highest levels for several decades and the subsequent annual default rates (10.1% and 10.3%) were the highest default rates on high yield "junk" bonds ever recorded. It should be noted that the highest dollar amount of defaults ($23.5 billion) in this market, perhaps in the commerical loan market as well, occurred in the most recent year (1999), see Altman et al. (2000). Of course, the size of these markets are much greater in 1999 than in the early 1990s. Still recent default experience highlights the cyclical nature of default rates and marks the end of the benign credit cycle of most of the 1990s.

8. The one year horizon is consistent with the horizon adopted by most internal credit risk models.

9. Alternatively, where the bank will have sufficient capital to survive all but 3 years out of the next 10,000 years.

10. Interestingly, the total mean or expected loss rate of 0.598% is quite close to the level of banks' average loan loss reserve holdings in recent years.

11. This compares to an expected loss rate ratio of about 100 times greater for B vs. A rated bonds (see the cumulative loss rates in Altman et al. (1999)). For example, the 5 years cumulative loss rate for bonds rated A upon issuance is 0.12%, while the B rated bonds' loss rate is 13.9%. The fifth year's marginal (one year) loss rate is 0.04% for A rated bonds compared to 3.36% for B rated bonds.

12. The rating agencies only report the number of issuers for each grade rating category in each of the years in our sample period. See, for example, Table 16 in Standard and Poor's (1999).

13. The most senior bond is defined as the one with the highest price one year prior to default.

14. The CreditRisk$^{+®}$ model assumes defaults follow a Poisson distribution around a shifting mean. Specifically, the mean default rate is assumed to follow a gamma distribution. The Poisson distribution is a simple distribution in that its mean equals its variance. Assuming a stable mean will tend to underestimate the "fat-tailedness" of the distribution and thus unexpected loss rates will be understated.

15. This was done by taking three monthly samples (for December 1987, December 1992 and February 1999) on the number of issues per issuer from S and P bond guides, calculating an average number of issues per defaulting issuer in each rating category and multiplying the number of issuers row in Table 4 by the resulting average number of issues per issuer.

16. Similar conclusions, regarding the relative risk weights of buckets 2 and 3, are also reached by analyzing Tables 5–8. The large risk weighting differences between rating classes are particularly evident.

17. Interestingly, the results of our simulations were quite insensitive to asset portfolio size assumptions beyond the $1 billion size range.

18. In this test, A was combined with AA and AAA to be comparable with the Carey (1998) paper.

19. This assumes that appropriate reserves for the high expected losses (e.g., over 10%) are deducted from the profit and loss accounts.

20. The 99.97% level is actually not shown but is essentially identical to the 99.9% level.

21. The results for the CCC and lower bucket was about the same as BB/B for the actual distribution, since both were near the maximum loss possible at the 99.97% level.

22. One could actually argue for a higher weighting in this bucket but this would almost surely cutoff most lending to firms in this bucket—a bucket which we believe now represents a very high proportion of current loans outstanding.

REFERENCES

Altman, E.I., 1989. Measuring corporate bond mortality and performance. Journal of Finance 64 (4), 909–922.

Altman, E.I., Saunders, A., 1997. Credit risk measurement: Developments over 20 the last years. Journal of Banking & Finance 21 (11), 1721–1742.

Altman, E.I., Cooke, D., Kishore, V., 2000. Defaults and returns on high yield bonds: Analysis through 1998 & Default outlook for 1999–2001, NYU Salomon Center Special Report, January 1999 (updated in January 2000).

Basel Committee on Banking Supervision, 1999. A New Capital Adequacy Framework, Basel.

Basel Committee on Banking Supervision, Range of Practice in Banks Internal Ratings Systems, January 2000. Basel.

Carey, M., 1998. Credit risk in private debt portfolios. Journal of Finance, 1363–1387.

Caouette, J.B., Altman, E.I., Narayanan, P., 1998. Managing Credit Risk: The Next Great Financial Challenge. Wiley, New York.

Credit Metrics, 1997. J.P. Morgan, New York.

Credit Suisse Financial Products, 1997. Credit Risk⁺: A Credit Risk Measurement Framework, London.

Jonsson, J.G., Fridson, M., 1996. Forecasting default rates on high yield bonds. Journal of Fixed Income.

Moody's predicting default rates: A forecasting model for Moody's issuer-based default rates, 1999. Special Comment, Global Credit Research.

Saunders, A., 1999. Credit Risk Measurement. New Approaches to Value at Risk and Other Paradigms. Wiley, New York.

Standard and Poor's, 1999. Rating performance 1998: Stability & Transition, S&P Special Report.

Treacy, W., Carey, M. 1998. Credit rating systems at large US banks. Federal Reserve Bulletin.

Treacy, W., Carey, M., 2000. Credit rating systems at large US banks. Journal of Banking and Finance 24 (4), 167–201.

15. HEDGE FUND TRANSPARENCY IS NO SILVER BULLET!

BRUCE BRITTAIN

Lyster Watson & Company

THE HEDGE FUND ADVISORS' DILEMMA

In September 1998, a consortium of sixteen banks and US broker-dealers restructured the ownership of the hedge fund, Long Term Capital Management (LTCM). Among the biggest, best-known and most respected hedge funds, LTCM held positions that had fallen so far in value that calls for collateral had virtually exhausted the firm's capital. LTCM was not alone. Other hedge funds were also printing double-digit red ink. The consensus holds that a global widening of credit spreads did this damage and that the Russian government's moratorium on debt payments (announced on August 17th) was a catalytic event. As the magnitude of hedge fund exposures to global credits became clear, the funds' bankers sharply increased collateral calls. Throughout September and October some funds were pushed into bankruptcy and many more were pushed to the brink. Trading desks at money center banks and their counterparts in the broker-dealer community held positions that mirrored those of their hedge fund clients. They suffered equivalent mark to market losses as well. Credit in the interbank market became so tight that the U.S. Federal Reserve Bank injected substantial new reserves into the banking system and abandoned its tightening bias in monetary policy. These actions were designed to bring order to the credit markets and to avert a global credit crunch. By November, order had returned to the markets and a process of evaluation began. The post morterm is now nearing completion.

Assessing the harm done in the summer and fall of 1998, the hedge fund community finds itself both hurt and embarrassed by these developments. Totals reflect-

R.M. Levich and S. Figlewski (eds.). RISK MANAGEMENT. Copyright © 2001. Kluwer Academic Publishers. Boston. All rights reserved.

ing the financial damage are hard to come by, but investors in LTCM and other internationally oriented fixed income arbitrage firms lost billions. Based on reported declines in the many hedge fund performance indices that occurred between the end of June 1998 and the end of December 1998, investors could easily have lost *tens* of billions of dollars.

Professional hedge fund advisors suffered the greatest embarrassment. Throughout 1997 and into 1998, investors that held portfolios of hedge fund managers and the groups that advise them popularized the concept of multi-advisor portfolios of market neutral hedge fund managers. These products offered the prospect of yearly returns in the range of 10 to 15% with attractive volatility characteristics. Investors expected these portfolios to produce returns with Sharpe ratios of 1.0 or more and correlation coefficients with returns on stock and bond markets of 0.3 or less. Skeptical investors worldwide, who held that this could not be true, became believers when presented with a vast array of historical return statistics showing that such portfolios could indeed have been constructed. Despite the positive hype, the proof of the pudding was a bitter taste. By the end of 1998, realized Sharpe ratios had turned negative and correlation coefficients with broad markets appeared near 1.0.

Particularly damning to the professional advisor community, few explanations surfaced of what had gone wrong. Professional advisors normally demand of themselves a deep understanding of a manager's personnel, performance, investment philosophy and investment process. They develop this understanding to discharge the fiduciary obligations to clients implied by their consulting contracts. In the case of certain star investment managers, the advisors had stopped after evaluating people and performance—both of which were extremely good in the case of these high visibility hedge funds—and did not develop (indeed, the disclosure policies of these funds ensured they could not develop) a deep understanding of philosophy and process.

Reacting to the advisory disaster of last year, hedge fund consultants are moving rapidly towards consensus on how they were hurt last year and how they can avoid repeating this painful experience. The emerging conventional wisdom incorporates the several themes. Major hedge fund losses came from a one off credit event, the Russian debt moratorium, which led to a widening of credit spreads in all markets and to losses in all hedge fund portfolios. Excessive use of leverage and excessive position size magnified the effects of these market developments. Lack of transparency kept hedge fund advisors from understanding both the degree of leverage and credit risk factor that was common to many funds.

The emerging consensus has been reinforced by the ongoing public policy debate, which is currently focused on the proceedings of the President's Working Group on Financial Markets entitled "Hedge Funds, Leverage and the Lessons of Long Term Capital Management." The Counterparty Risk Management Policy Group, an industry initiative, continues to sift through the history of the period and to develop market practices that will minimize the chance of future debacles. The main policy conclusions of this debate were, however, anticipated by U.S. Federal Reserve officials even in the heat of last September's battles.

Alan Greenspan, Chairman of the Federal Reserve System Board of Governors, in testimony before the House Committee on Banking and Financial Services on October 1st of last year most strongly advanced the case that excessive use of leverage by hedge funds was a central feature of the crisis. The Chairman argues: "In its search for high return, LTCM (Long Term Capital Management) leveraged its capital through securities repurchase contacts and derivative transactions . . . the very efficiencies that LTCM and its competitors brought to the overall financial system gradually reduced the opportunities for above normal profits. . . . To counter these diminishing opportunities, LTCM apparently reached further for return over time by employing more leverage and increasing its exposure to risk, a strategy that was destined to fail."

William J. McDonough, President of the Federal Reserve Bank of New York, in testimony on the same day and before the same subcommittee, echoes the hedge fund advisor's demand for transparency. He argues that, "... it was the extraordinary events of August in Global markets that appears to have tripped them. . . . The abrupt and simultaneous widening of credit spreads globally, for both corporate and emerging-market sovereign debt, was an extraordinary event beyond the expectations of investors and financial intermediaries." In his post mortem on the events of the fall, the Reserve Bank's President questions the adequacy of bank's credit analysis of LTCM. He upbraids the banks for not having been rigorous and conservative enough in measuring LTCM's future exposures. He cautions that LTCM's counterparties did too little stress testing of the firm's portfolios.

Together the Chairman and President argue that hedge fund leverage was too large, that their operations lacked transparency, that bank and broker dealer counterparties were lax in understanding the latent risks in hedge fund portfolios and that all were overtaken by an externally imposed widening of credit spreads. These are heartening themes to the hedge fund advisory community, which wants fervently to believe that a "perfect storm" hit the markets in the third quarter 1998. The storm was impossible to forecast and unlikely to recur. To hedge against the residual risk of a storm recurring—or at least to identify the managers who are likely to be badly hurt if the experience repeats itself—advisors are beginning to demand transparency from hedge funds. By doing this, they hope to avoid funds that are excessively leveraged. They also hope to do a better job of understanding hidden risk factors that are unknowingly shared by managers with superficially different investment styles.

As advisors, we should closely examine the emerging consensus because its understanding of events is not complete and its conclusions are partly erroneous. Would transparency have helped advisors avoid money-losing managers? I don't think so. Set aside the issues raised by the complexity of some hedge fund books. (LTCM is reported to have had upwards of 70,000 positions on its books in mid September. Digesting, let alone analyzing, such masses of data is beyond the capacity of virtually the entire advisory community.) However, with some help from the managers, most advisors would have concluded that their portfolios were highly diversified and could withstand most adverse developments. Indeed they would probably have been convinced that these portfolios were likely to do quite well. Some advisors might have avoided funds that were holding very large positions. Other advisors would have viewed large size as good. Some advisors would have avoided domestic fixed income arbitrageurs that had strayed into the overseas fixed income markets and even into domestic merger arbitrage. Other advisors would have applauded the migration of skilled traders from a traditional sector to other areas of potentially greater opportunity. After all, opportunism is the hallmark of some successful hedge funds.

Had we been able to predict the Russian default, would we have declined to invest? I don't think so. The Russian market was small and developments there were only indirectly connected with developments in the markets for other emerging credits. Many market participants thought that the Russian challenge was to reestablish the rule of law while other developing nations confronted different challenges. The contagious nature of the Russian problem was *not* evident before the fact and needs to be explained as well.

If direct knowledge of hedge fund positions and the ability to predict the Russian default were not enough, what would we have had to know? The answer is that we would have had to understand systemic issues that an individual hedge fund's books would not have revealed, including:

1) Mark-to-market losses from mortgage arbitrage, short equity volatility and long stock positions in June and July produced large collateral calls. These reduced the hedge fund community's ability to deliver collateral in subsequent months and aggravated the effects of forced liquidations in August and September.
2) Although LTCM's positions were large, the hedge fund community's collective book was even larger. The banking community piggy backed on the hedge fund community's idea flow and was also positioned in parallel with the hedge funds.
3) Banks and broker dealers upped their estimates of hedge fund position volatility in August and September. Equally interesting, they appear to have ceased believing that arbitrage positions were uncorrelated and that portfolio diversification reduces risk. Both changes led to huge demands for additional collateral and both produced a degree of disorder in the process of position liquidation. Russian developments and the purely credit aspects of the hedge fund market explain much of the deterioration of hedge fund returns in August. September and October's developments are the results of the system imploding on itself.

**A CLOSER LOOK AT HEDGE FUND DEVELOPMENTS
IN THE SUMMER AND FALL OF 1998**

Figure 1 presents an eclectic set of arbitrage positions that represent a sampling of risks that were being run by different hedge funds during the second quarter of 1998. Most hedge funds would have restricted themselves to a particular subset of these transaction types, although a few ere surely running positions in all these areas. Each example is a simple expression of positions that can be complex in the extreme. The mortgage arbitrage position, for example, features credit risk and

A. Mortgage arbitrage. Long current coupon GNMA mortgage securities and short US Treasuries. Position held to benefit from a narrowing in the credit component of mortgage spreads to US Treasury securities.

B. Volatility arbitrage. Short 3-month straddles on S & P 500 futures, delta hedged. Position managed to benefit from decline in equity index volatilities implied by the pricing of short-term options on S & P futures. Volatility arbitrageurs could have similar positions in non-US stock markets and in the global fixed income markets.

C. International fixed income arbitrage. Long Russian GKOs and short rubles. Position designed to produce a dollar asset yielding several hundred basis points in excess of funding rate.

D. Merger arbitrage. Long common shares of Ciena and short common shares of Tellabs. Position constructed to produce a short-term investment yield well in excess of funding rate as the Ciena stock price converges to Tellabs take-out price. Merger arbitrageurs would typically be running large portfolios of such positions in order to spread the risk of loss from broken deals.

E. Domestic fixed income arbitrage. Long off-the-run US government 30-year short the duration-weighted equivalent of on-the-run 30 year US government bonds. Position seeks to exploit narrowing in yield spread between the off and on the run 30 year US government bond issues.

F. International fixed income arbitrage, relative value. Receive position in 5-year sterling interest rate swaps and duration weighted short position in 5-year UK government gilt-edged stock. Position seeks to profit from a decline in yields on single "A" sterling credits relative to the yield on UK government credits.

G. International fixed income arbitrage, relative value. Pay position in 5-year Deutsche mark interest rate swaps and duration weighted long position in 5-year German federal government bonds. Position seeks to profit from an increase yields in single "A" German credits relative to the yield on German government bonds and to hedge sterling position, F.

Figure 1. Potential Arbitrage Positions

excludes a variety of other risks that mortgage arbitrageurs would willingly accept under appropriate conditions. A mortgage arbitrageur could, for example, include duration, yield curve, prepayment, convexity and implied options volatility risk as well as risks created by spreads between different collateralized mortgage obligation structures. Similarly, the risk arbitrage position (long Ciena, short Tellabs) crudely oversimplifies a book of "merger arbitrage" positions. More typical would be a portfolio of forty to forty-five announced deals with a high likelihood of closing within some short period of time. Not included in Figure 1 are examples of leveraged long position in U.S. stocks which are characteristic of traditional equity hedge funds.

Figure 2 details a possible allocation of positions in a hypothetical hedge fund with $500 million of capital and which approaches position management using a Value-at-Risk (VAR) framework. The columns, moving from the left to the right of the figure present rough estimates of the underlying volatility of the principal

Position	Estimated Standard deviation of principal factor driving value	Sensitivity of position value (in %) to a one standard deviation change in principal factor	Dollar value of position for which one standard deviation move produces a one percent change in fund value	Dollar Value of position employing 10% of capital with no allowance made for effect of diversification, or 4% with zero correlation
Mortgage Treasury Spread	6 basis points	.78%	$6 million	$60 million
Short equity volatility	.30 volatility points	.05%	$100 million	$1 billion
Hedged GKOs	500 basis points	2.5%	$2 million	$20 million
Long Ciena— Short Tellabs	$.50	1%	$5 million	$50 million
U.S. Treasury off-the-run, on-the-run spread	1 basis point	.13%	$38 million	$380 million
Sterling credit spread	2.9 basis points	.24%	$21 million	$210 million
Deutsche mark credit spread	.6 basis points	.05%	$100 million	$1 billion

Figure 2. Potential distribution of hedge fund positions

risk factor implicit in the relevant position, the effect a one standard deviation change in the factor would have on the value of the position, the dollar value of the position for which such a change would represent one percent of the value of the fund, and the size of the position that would be allowed if the fund manager were willing to risk four percent of the value of the fund on any given day and was also allowed to assume that all positions were perfectly uncorrelated. Thus the spread between mortgages and US treasuries is estimated to have a standard deviation of 6 basis points. A six basis point change in this spread would cause the value of the long mortgage short treasury position to change by .78%. A position of $6 million changing by .78% would produce a one percent change in the value of the fund. A position of $60 million would produce a 10 percentage point change, but this effect would be scaled down by the square root of seven (the number of positions) in the case of zero correlation of returns with other positions.

A BRIEF CHRONOLOGY OF MARKET DEVELOPMENTS

Figure 3 includes plots of price levels, yields and spreads relevant to valuing the arbitrage positions of Figure 1 on a daily basis for the period from April 30th to November 30th of 1998. The vertical lines are drawn at month end July, August, September and October. Capital letters A through D identify four phases in the development of the demand for collateral from hedge funds. Phase A, comprising the months of May, June and July, is the period of increasing collateral demands from markets that are demonstrably not Russian. Phase B, August, captures the effect of the Russian event. Phase C, September, is the initial phase of reaction to LTCM and of forced liquidation. Phase D, October, is post McDonough/Greenspan testimony, the start of a new accounting quarter for many banks and broker dealers and the month of a true scourging of hedge funds through more forced liquidation.

Phase A. Second quarter 1998. Losses on positions in mortgage spreads—the yield on current coupon, thirty-year GNMA mortgage bonds rose by 25 basis points relative to yields on 30 year US Treasury bonds during the quarter—led to collateral calls on hedge funds from their bank and broker dealer counterparts. Additional collateral calls on leveraged stock positions also educed hedge funds' ability to meet collateral calls in subsequent periods. Far from international in origin, the weaknesses in June markets were home grown.

Phase B. August 1998. After a brief respite in July, mortgage spreads resumed widening, adding to collateral demands. The initial effects of the Russian crisis appear in the sharp widening of UK gilt-sterling swap and German Bund-Deutsche mark swap spreads. From early August to just before the August 17 moratorium on interest payments, the Bund-Deutsche mark swap spread had widened by 5 basis points to 19 basis points and then spiked to about 35 basis points in the last several days of the month. The sterling spread equivalent did not move early in the month but spiked 30 basis points from 68 to 98 basis points in the immediate aftermath of Russian developments. US stocks sold off sharply and the volatility implied by stock options pricing rose dramatically from 30% to 48% virtually overnight. All these changes increased hedge fund collateral requirements.

Not the least important source of these demands was the decision by certain money center banks to declare *force majeure*, after the Russian debt moratorium and nullify forward ruble contracts. Although I have no firm estimate of the damage done by this last development, I believe the impact was significant. As of early August the value of GKOs outstanding was in the neighborhood of $9 billion at a dollar-ruble exchange rate of 6.25 rubles per dollar. Hedge funds were probably the single biggest holder of these obligations. These funds lost money as the value of Russian GKOs fell towards zero but, in principal, should have recouped a significant portion of these losses as the ruble declined from pre-debt debt moratorium levels to 10 to the dollar by the end of August. (Recall that their GKO positions had been hedged back to dollars with forward sales of rubles.) Western money center banks were the principal providers of forward ruble contracts to the hedge fund community and

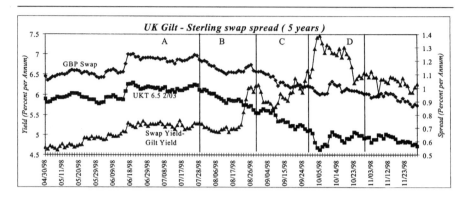

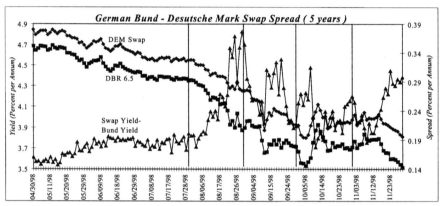

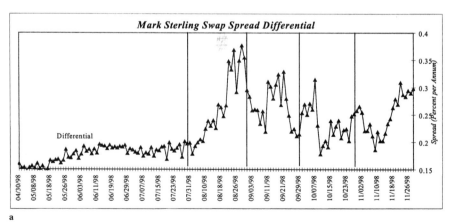

a

Figure 3.

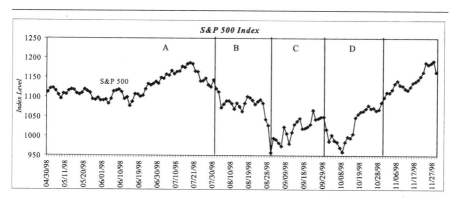

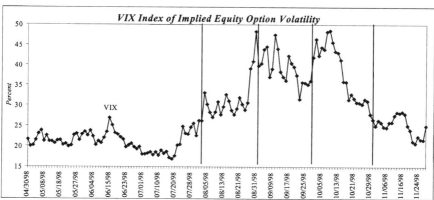

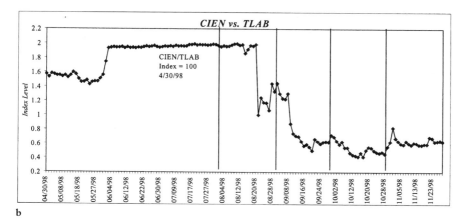

b

Figure 3. *Continued*

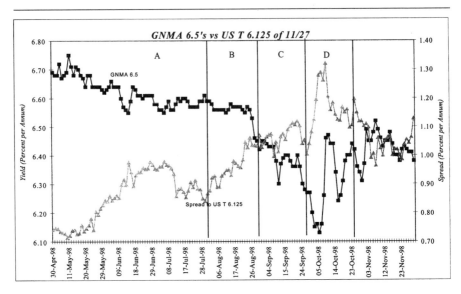

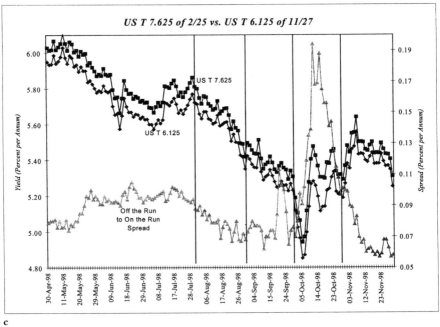

c

Figure 3. *Continued*

were, in turn, hedged by offsetting contracts struck with local Russian banks. Russian banks began to default in August, exposing the money center banks to very serious potential loses. Declaring *force majeure*, voiding ruble contracts and seizing collateral was a means to avoid financial damage. What would have been money center bank losses on their ruble forward contracts were transferred to hedge funds, putting even more stress on the troubled collateral markets.

The coincident sell-off in US stocks, the sharp upward move in options volatility and the spectacular collapse of the Ciena-Tellabs deal (in turn, accompanied by a widening of all merger arbitrage spreads) did their part to worsen conditions in the market for collateral.

Phase C. September 1998. By the beginning of September, the widening of mortgage and other credits spreads, increases in levels of implied volatility—not to speak of Russian and other emerging market spread trades—had done serious damage to hedge fund books. Troubled hedge funds were seeking new capital arguing that spread movements had been exaggerated and that current levels had created real opportunities.

Supported by exhortations from hedge fund managers to step forward and seize opportunity, the markets displayed uneasy calm for about a fortnight. Most spread positions rallied briefly. At about this time, takers of collateral in the market for credit were beginning to revise upwards both their estimates of position volatility and to increase their estimates of the correlation of returns on positions, which were previously thought to be uncorrelated. The revelation of Long Term Capital Management's positions during the weekend of September 21st confirmed massive position size and high degrees of duplication among hedge funds and between hedge funds on the one hand, and their broker dealer counterparts, on the other.

Phase D. October 1998. August ushered in a new quarter and a concerted effort among the banks and broker dealers to achieve an appropriate balance between the demand for and supply of collateral. Three pieces of evidence suggest that takers of collateral increased demands by orders of magnitude—forcing hedge funds to liquidate positions and creating extreme market anomalies. The first example is the sharp increase in mortgage spreads to Treasuries. Current coupon GNMA spreads to U.S. Treasuries gapped by more than 30 basis points during the first two weeks of October. More startling, off-the-run 30 year U.S. Treasury bond spreads to on-the-run 30 year issues moved from about 7.5 basis points to an astounding 19.5 basis points during the first two weeks of October. Most surprising of all, while UK gilt—sterling swap spreads continued to widen in line with the general perception of that credit spreads were expanding, German Bund—Deutsche mark swap rates narrowed on average in both September and October! All these moves suggest that the dominant market factor for most of October and much of September was a sharp increase in demand for collateral from hedge funds that were met with a wave of forced liquidations.

The magnitude of the increase in collateral demand is hard to estimate, but some simple calculations can be made.[1] A doubling of the expected volatilities of the positions described in Figure 2 would have doubled estimates of the portfolios value at risk; and, had VAR models been widely embraced at the time, to a corresponding increase in collateral demands. Collateral requirements would also have risen as takers of collateral revised their estimates of the correlation of returns among various positions in hedge fund books. In theory, collateral requirements on a hedge fund with a diversified book of positions similar to those in Figure 2 and displaying zero correlation would have seen collateral requirements rise by the square root of the number of positions in the portfolio if estimated correlation coefficients rose to a value of one—in the case of the portfolio in Figure 2 by a factor of more than 2.5.

CONCLUDING COMMENTS

The job of the hedge fund advisor is to help his client construct a portfolio of hedge fund investments that produce an appropriate mix of risk and expected return. The concept of market-neutral multi-manager portfolios emerged during 1997 and 1998 as a particularly popular fund-of-fund format. These portfolios were constructed to produce moderate levels of return and to exhibit low levels of volatility and essentially no correlation with stocks and bonds. Advisors failed to achieve this objective in 1998 as market neutral funds-of-funds declined in value during the summer and fall in line with the overall market and in response to the same factors that produced wider spreads over that same period.

The emerging consensus holds that advisors would have done better if hedge fund managers had embraced transparency and disclosed their portfolio holdings in detail and if better stress testing techniques been employed. Developments in the market for collateral imply that transparency and stress testing would not have been enough. Understanding individual manager risks would not have produced an understanding of the systemic risks being run by the community as a whole. Hedge fund advisors would have had great difficulty discovering the proliferation of copycat trades that pervaded the books of hedge funds and their bank and broker dealer counterparts. Furthermore, it is almost inconceivable that more complete knowledge of managers' portfolios or greater stress testing would have predicted the massive increase in risk estimates embraced by banks and broker dealers in the September-October period.

Equally disturbing for the hedge fund advisor is the unevenness of the common ground between hedge funds and their counterparties on the one hand, and between these two and central banks on the other. The September-October period shows that the three communities do not share well developed and well tested views on the nature of financial risks and on appropriate risk management approaches. As long as this situation persists, the market for collateral and thus hedge fund returns will be unnecessarily subject to arbitrary and potentially damaging shocks that stem from a sudden change in risk management paradigms.

Transparency *could* have helped individual advisors make the transition from purely returns based analysis of hedge fund performance, an approach that relies on a manager's historical returns and the relation of his returns to certain passive benchmarks, to a more compelling approach. The more compelling approach includes a qualitative appreciation of the manager's trading style and a detailed quantitative understanding of his portfolio of risks. At the very least, last fall's events will force hedge fund advisors to understand the specific risks their managers are running and, based on the manager's trading style, how these risks might change. Transparency of investment portfolios is a critical element in this understanding, but transparency on its own, and at the level of the dialog between advisor and hedge fund manager cannot anticipate systemic events like those of last summer and fall.

Transparency might, however, have been a powerful tool in the hands of policy makers. Detailed knowledge of hedge fund positions might have produced an earlier policy reaction and have avoided the serious dislocations that occurred last year. Communications technology should allow close to real time reporting by banks and broker dealers of derivative and financing positions to a very high level of detail. One could easily imagine the U.S. Federal Reserve reviewing bank exposures to particular hedge funds and of all banks to all hedge funds in particular trades. With some effort, one could also imagine a high degree of collaboration among regulatory agencies within the United States (so that broker-dealers as well as banks were covered) and among regulators in other countries. With more effort, one could even imagine a commitment from central banks to model the detailed characteristics of the market for collateral. Our central bank would help clarify issues if they helped us understand in detail how the force of external events was compounded by the workings of a market which is central to our financial system but which is poorly understood by many market participants. A related natural progression for our central bank would be to move beyond modeling the level of stock market prices (and occasionally opining on the exuberance of investors) to formulating a view on a variance covariance matrix of expected returns from the major asset classes. Propagating that view would surely produce a healthy debate among professional risk managers. A final related development would be for our central bank to embrace and consistently propagate an internally consistent view of risk management methodology. Central bank testimony to Congress in the midst of the crisis emphasized the perils of leverage and thus promoted the concept. This came at the cost of de-emphasizing Value-at-Risk concepts, even though these had, with Fed acquiescence, begun to take hold in the financial community. October was a month of frenzy and forced liquidation in the market for collateral. Would that our Fed had balanced the cry of excessive leverage with at least a hint that collateral markets were irrationally pessimistic!

APPENDIX. A MORE DETAILED MODEL OF MARKET FOR COLLATERAL

Bank or broker-dealer demand for collateral from hedge funds:

$$C_{i,j,d} = f_d(\sigma_{i,j}, MV_{i,j} - IV_{i,j}, C_{i,d}/C_d, C_d/E_i) \tag{1}$$

Where:

$C_{i,j,d}$ = bank or broker-dealer i's demand for collateral from hedge fund j;

$C_{i,d}$ = bank or broker-dealer i's demand for collateral from all hedge funds;

$\sigma_{i,j}$ = expected volatility of hedge fund j's portfolio of "credit" positions with bank or broker dealer i;

$MV_{i,j}$ = mark-to-market value of hedge fund j's positions with broker-dealer i;

$IV_{i,j}$ = the initial value of hedge fund j's positions with broker-dealer i;

E_i = the equity capital of bank or broker-dealer i.

Mark-to-market considerations dominated increased demands for collateral in Phases A and B. The Russian crisis and non-performance by Russian banks threatened to impair equity at a number of banking institutions, prompting a large increase in collateral demands. Changes in the estimated variance-covariance matrix of returns among hedge fund positions and revelations of the size of the Long Term Capital Management Book dominated in Phases C and D.

NOTE

1. A more detailed model for market collateral is sketched in the Appendix to this paper.

16. CAPITAL ADEQUACY IN FINANCIAL INSTITUTIONS: BASEL PROPOSALS

DARRYLL HENDRICKS*

Federal Reserve Bank of New York

The Basel Committee's proposal for a new capital adequacy standard was released in June 1999, with comments due by the end of March 2000.[1] There is a desire to issue another proposal around the end of the year. The approach is based on three pillars. First, there are minimum capital requirements that banks have to meet; second, there is a supervisory review of capital; and third, there is market discipline. Another key aspect of the proposal in addition to introducing the three pillars is the desire to move to a more risk sensitive approach to the minimum requirements. Earlier in this conference volume, Professor Altman explained well why the broad-brush approach to minimum capital requirements of the current Basel Accord has created perverse incentives to shed low risk assets and hold more high-risk assets.[2]

Over time, these incentives have affected bank behavior to the point that capital ratios are significantly less meaningful. There has been quite a lot of "capital arbitrage" in various ways. In terms of the goals of the 1988 Basel Accord, I wasn't there at the time, but I believe an important mission at that point was to get something established. Once the idea for common ground for capital was begun, it could obviously be improved and refined over time. I also think that 8% capital as an unconditional measure of risk for the average set of bank portfolios may have been reasonable at the time. But of course, once something that makes sense in an overall

* The views expressed here are those of the author and not necessarily those of the Federal Reserve Bank of New York or the Federal Reserve System.

R.M. Levich and S. Figlewski (eds.). RISK MANAGEMENT. Copyright © 2001. Kluwer Academic Publishers. Boston. All rights reserved.

average way gets put into place, firms are going to react to it and begin to take action that will undermine its effectiveness. In fact, it has taken only about ten years to get to that point.

In the three pillars approach, there is also recognition that the current system focuses the market place exclusively on only a few key ratios—the total capital ratio and the tier one capital ratio. Broader disclosure of risk measures, elements of the bank's capital structure, and so forth would therefore be helpful in giving the marketplace a better view of capital adequacy.

The last introductory point I would like to make is that in spite of the drawbacks, there remains a great deal of support for the idea of common international capital adequacy standards. The view from many finance ministries around the world, including our own, has been that capital standards have helped to constrain leverage in the financial system, and thus have contributed to the ability of banking systems, especially in Europe and the United States, to weather recent financial crises. There is also a general sense that a successful effort to achieve greater risk sensitivity in capital requirements will be beneficial, including in emerging markets where this will reinforce the development of improved risk management practices.

The supervisory review pillar is the second pillar of the proposal. Different people have different views on exactly how this may work in practice. I believe that the key focus should be on the methods that banks are using internally to assess risk relative to the capital available to support those risks. The emphasis on these methods in the Basel proposal will increase pressure in two areas. One is on bands to further develop their internal methods for looking at how much capital they need to support the risks that they are taking. There has been substantial emphasis on risk measurement methods within banking organizations and some of the most sophisticated banks have taken that a step further to think about their overall capital strategy relative to their risk taking. But that process is something that needs to occur more systematically at a broader range of institutions. The second area of increased pressure will be on supervisors to develop a greater understanding of bank's internal processes for evaluating risk in relation to capital. Those processes are central to a bank's ability to manage risk and to survive in turbulent times. At the Federal Reserve, we try hard to focus on those processes and thus part of what the second pillar will do is encourage supervisors around the world to take a similar approach. It is not intended to replace bank judgments about risk and capital, but to provide a more sophisticated basis for assessing the risks that banks are taking.

The third pillar of the new proposal, the market discipline pillar, is just that. It is focused on improving bank disclosures and increasing the information that the marketplace has to assess banks and their soundness. A new paper will be issued in about a week that fleshes out some of these proposals. I will mention several of the most critical elements. First, what are the elements of a bank's capital structure? In many cases, these go beyond common equity and encompass a range of different innovative instruments that have been issued here and in other countries. Those elements need to be disclosed clearly to provide an accurate sense of what the capital structure looks like. Second, and it is almost impossible to overstate the importance of this topic, is accounting standards. The accounting conventions used are essential to understanding the numbers that banks report, for example, in relation to how they describe the condition of the loans they have on their books. Third, we need disclosure of measures of risk. In some sense this is an accounting topic as well, but it is a new type of accounting topic. More work will need to be done to develop comparable measures of credit risk, of market risk, of other kinds of risk if possible, to be able to give the marketplace a clear sense of how these compare relative to capital.

Moving into the proposals for revised minimum capital requirements, Professor Altman has well summarized the external ratings approach to credit risk capital contained in the June 1999 proposal. He touched on the internal ratings approach as well, but that is worth spending some more time on because we expect there to be quite a lot of support for that approach. First, it is worth noting that the internal ratings approach probably would not be targeted to fit within the small set of risk weights that are included in the external ratings approach. The point that was made earlier about the need for a mapping on the basis of "expected default frequency" and "loss given default" estimates is extremely well understood. That kind of internal ratings approach likely would lead to a much greater granularity of risk weights then was in the external ratings approach that came out in June.

There are a number of questions about internal ratings approaches. How can they be operationalized? How to maintain comparability across banks that are using different approaches? What are the appropriate qualitative standards for these approaches? This last question is a particularly important issue because we expect that quite a large number of banks within the G-10 are likely to want to use an internal ratings approach. Thus, it will be a challenge to define appropriate standards for usage of such an approach that are both open and rigorous.

On the external ratings approach, the comments that were made in the prior presentation are obviously something the Basel Committee on Banking Supervision has to consider very seriously. To talk about the treatment of unrated credits briefly, one point that did not come out fully in that discussion is the enormous difference in the percentage of firms that are rated in the United States relative to many of the other countries including other G-10 countries. There has been a view that the external ratings approach is part of a U.S. effort to enhance the role of U.S. rating agencies and to give our banks competitive advantages. Similarly, we hear concerns that the approach will require huge new expenditures to develop national rating agencies. Some emerging market countries have also been vocal about their concerns with rating agency performance in recent years. These countries are not eager to see themselves subject to higher capital costs on the basis of what they view as an imperfect process.

Finally on the external ratings approach, many comments have seconded those of Professor Altman that there are insufficient or inappropriate distinctions between the categories. Since it is unlikely that an internal ratings approach would be applicable to every bank operating in a country that would like to adopt the revised Accord, there is a strong need to develop a revised standardized approach that balances risk sensitivity with simplicity. Constructive suggestions are especially welcome here, and I see that Professor Altman has taken that advice strongly to heart and we very much appreciate that.

Moving on to the elements of the proposal not related to credit risk, interest rate risk is an area where many efforts have been made over the years to assess whether this is feasible to include within capital requirements. This debate continues although the proposal suggested the idea of an outlier approach to interest rate risks that could involve possibly quite a bit of national discretion to allow banks to use their own methods for calculating interest rate risks. The outlier approach would charge capital only to those banks that held more than some significant amount of interest rate risk. An outlier approach is a novel idea and I personally am interested in the incentives that this could create. For example, if the charge is significant, it could create an incentive to spread the interest rate risk around the system in such a way that no bank bears a charge. It may even be that this is beneficial in encouraging diversification of interest rate risk around the entire system.

One of the more controversial elements of the Basel Committee proposal is to focus on other, operational risks. Efforts to tackle this risk have strong support among different members of the committee. Part of their concern is that they see a potential for the credit risk part of the package to reduce required capital for many banks. Yet, there is a general sentiment among many supervisors that the aggregate amount of capital in the system should not be significantly reduced. Operational and other risks are seen as a potential reason to hold additional capital and indeed many banks report that these risks account for a large portion of their overall risk—25% or mare. At this stage, however, there is not a clear consensus on the measurement of other, operational risk, although pressure from the Basel Committee may be able to achieve faster progress in this area. A recent European Union paper that parallels the Basel Committee proposal went a little further on the operational risk point and proposed the use of some fairly simple measures based on a linear combination of size and income. That approach is likely to receive little support from the industry, but the question is whether they will be able to put forward anything that is more promising.

I will not have time to mention all of the other individual issues that are addressed in the Basel proposal, such as how to treat collateral and guarantees. One interesting issue I will mention briefly is the treatment of two-name paper, that is, a claim that is guaranteed by another party. Currently, the way the Accord treats that claim is to assign it the risk weight of the guarantor, assuming it is lower than the risk weight of the original obligor. There is some sentiment to say that because losses will result only if both the obligor and the guarantor default, a multiplicative risk weight should be assigned. For example, 8% times 8% would imply a risk weight of .64% in that instance. On the other hand, if that approach were adopted, there is a potential for bands to pass around claims basically in a daisy chain so that everyone has lowered their capital requirements but the system as a whole has no lower risk at all.

One important issue that I have been thinking about recently is the incentive effects of a more risk sensitive capital regime. There is a concern that risk-sensitive capital requirements will make the whole system more pro-cyclical. That is, when there is an economic downturn, banks will see their capital ratios get worse, leading them to reduce credit availability, making the downturn worse. I think that is the starkest way of putting the concern. My response is that capital itself is clearly pro-cyclical in the sense that losses occur during downturns and that's when capital is going to be depleted by taking the write-offs from those losses. Risk measures that properly reflect risk are also clearly going to be inherently pro-cyclical. Conditional measures of credit risks are clearly going to rise in the downward phase of the credit cycle, probably more at the leading edge then necessarily at the trailing edge and that's an important fact. But they will definitely go up. So the question then is should the regulatory capital measures track those inherent features, or should they try to hide them?

My sense is that if we look at cases where banks over time have been able to endure credit cycles, what we see is bank management that is good at recognizing problems early and good at dealing with problems once they occur. Rarely have we seen historical cases where failing to take true account of a bank's underlying condition—that is, forbearance—has served the interest of the bank or the system very well. Thus, in a board sense I believe more risk sensitive requirements are the way to go. With that being said, however, we should also make sure that we include incentives within the overall approach for banks to build capital during good times. A key element of such a strategy has been alluded to in prior presentations, namely, not letting banks base risk estimates excessively on recent experience. If that occurs in a normal credit cycle, banks will hold too little capital at the end of the boom period and the beginning of the recessionary period. This is therefore a key to avoiding a pro-cyclical impact to risk-sensitive requirements, as is the need to further develop the culture of addressing credit problems promptly as they appear.

In conclusion, the Basel Committee is in the midst of a major effort to revise the Capital Accord, with an increased emphasis on supervisory review, market discipline, and internal approaches to risk measurement. An over-riding goal is the achievement of more risk-sensitive minimum standards. The Committee is very interested in comments from all relevant parties by March 31, 2000.

NOTES

1. Basel Committee on Banking Supervision, "A New Adequacy Framework," Basel Committee Publications No. 50, Bank for International Settlements, June 1999.

2. Edward I. Altman and Anthony Saunders, "The BIS Proposal on Capital Adequacy and Ratings: A Critique," Chapter 14 in this volume.

17. RISK MANAGEMENT: WHERE ARE WE HEADING? WHERE HAVE WE BEEN?

LESLIE RAHL

President, Capital Market Risk Advisors, INC.

The universe of risks is large and goes way beyond the market risk that we generally focus on (Table 1).

Although I assume most of you share my personal interest in the quantitative, the quantitative components of a robust risk management program represent only about a third of what needs to be done.

It's really important not to forget the basics like policies and procedures, checks and balances, and all of the more mundane management 101 aspects of risks. I can assure you that the mundane can cost a fortune if you don't do it right.

Then there is always going to be this little wedge of risks that you can't control.

No matter how effective your risk management is, there is always going to be something beyond the influence of robust risk management. The only thing you can do is keep this wedge as *small* as possible.

The non-controllable includes clever new forms of fraud, paradigm changes in the market, new kinds of market moves (i.e., suppose the Fed came in and fixed interest rates), or an "act of God" equivalent.

Again, just for some humility, I think it's important to go back and see where we were 15 or 20 years ago. When I look back now at what we did, when I first started trading caps in 1983, I laugh. We used a Black Scholes Model—but rather than using the actual term structure of interest rates. I as the head trader picked which of the two different yield curve shapes we would use for the day (1) relatively flat or (2) relatively steep. I also had the same type of decision to make on

R.M. Levich and S. Figlewski (eds.). RISK MANAGEMENT. Copyright © 2001. Kluwer Academic Publishers. Boston. All rights reserved.

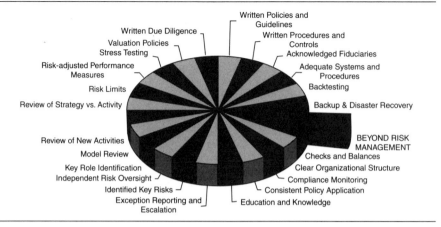

Figure 1. Risk Management Framework. Key Components

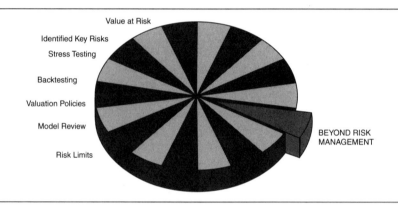

Figure 2. Risk Management Framework. Key Components—Only 1/3 are Quantitative

Table 1. Galaxy of risks

• Accountign risk	• Hedging risk	• Political risk
• Bankruptcy risk	• Horizon risk	• Prepayment risk
• Basis risk	• Iceberg risk	• Publicity risk
• Call risk	• Interest rate risk	• Raw data risk
• Capital risk	• Interpolation risk	• Regulatory risk
• Collateral risk	• Knowledge risk	• Reinvestment risk
• Commodity risk	• Legal risk	• Rollover risk
• Concentration risk	• Limit risk	• Spread risk
• Contract risk	• Liquidity risk	• Suitability risk
• Credit Risk	• Market risk	• Systemic risk
• Currency risk	• Maverick risk	• Systems risk
• Curve construction risk	• Modeling risk	• Tax risk
• Daylight risk	• Netting risk	• Technology risk
• Equity risk	• Optional risk	• Time lag risk
• Extrapolation risk	• Personnel risk	• Volatility risk
• Fiduciary risk	• Phantom risk	• Yield curve risk
	(Partial listing)	

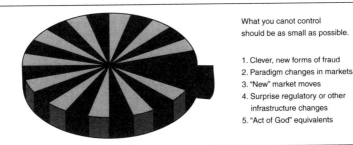

What you canot control
should be as small as possible.

1. Clever, new forms of fraud
2. Paradigm changes in markets
3. "New" market moves
4. Surprise regulatory or other
   infrastructure changes
5. "Act of God" equivalents

Figure 3. Risk Management Framework. Beyond Risk Management

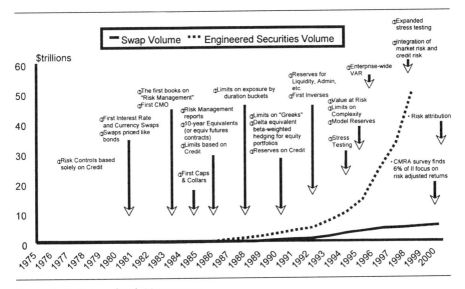

Figure 4. Evolution of Risk Measurement

volatility. I picked whether volatility was relatively high (a single volatility independent of moneyness or term of course) or relatively low. I remember well that we thought it was a real development when the concept that all mortgages had a twelve-year average life was introduced. We have been able to improve upon all of these methods that once seemed advanced, over time. So, however sophisticated the risk management tools we are using today may seem, I think it's very important to remember that we'll look back 10 or 15 years from now and probably laugh the same way. I believe we still have a long way to go.

LESSONS FROM THE 90's

One night about two weeks ago, I woke up in the middle of the night having some sort of anxiety attack and couldn't get back to sleep. We, at CMRA, were in the process of writing our annual newsletter, and so I decided to write down for the newsletter what some of my thoughts on the important lessons from the 1990s were.

- AAA is a measure of credit worthiness, not price volatility
- Saving your trading floor tapes can be dangerous
- Assuming that history will always repeat itself is a bad idea
- Purchasing credit protection from a Korean bank on a Korean counterparty is doubling your risk, not mitigating it
- Excessive leverage without deep pockets can kill you
- "Market Neutral" does not necessarily mean neutral to the market
- "Kitchen Sinks" and other scraps can be dangerous
- Never let your quants make short-sighted assumptions like "the Pound can never leave the Snake"
- Pegged currencies are no longer low volatility currencies once they de-peg
- Australia is an "emerging market"
- Whether the problems in Russia were credit risk, or market risk does not really matter
- "Default" means different things to different people

So many institutions spend a tremendous amount of effort analyzing questions like: What if interest rates go up 10 basis points? 25 basis points? 100 basis points? etc. Now who has really ever been badly hurt by a parallel shift in the yield curve? What generally cause massive problems are the *relationships* between markets, not small, parallel moves. I often think that the risk management community has the equation wrong and spend 80% of their time and effort on 20% of the problem (Table 2).

Table 2.   Categories of stress tests

Portfolio mix & markets	Model assumption	Product complexity	Credit/liquidity	Sea change
• Term structure and yield curve levels and shapes • Term structure and relationship of volatility • Price shifts in equities, sectors, indices • Currency, commodities price shifts • Spreads and basis relationships	• Yield curves building assumptions • Pricing models • VAR and Capital Models • Asset/Liability model	• Products with uncertain cash flows • Structured products & complex derivatives • Emerging markets and difficult to handle risks	• Concentrations • Linkages • Credit components of securities • Volatility of credit spreads • Default assumptions	• EMU • Y2K • Changing competitive structure

I have been asked to comment on what I think some of the big issues on the horizon are. I think the Internet will begin to change the way financial services are provided and will be a key issue/opportunity/risk, not only on the retail side but also on the wholesale side. I also think there are going to be tremendous reorganizations within financial institutions over the next few years that are triggered by the need to serve clients over the Internet by a client focus rather than a product focus. This is going to have a significant impact on risk management because organizational changes always create risks. I think that CBOs and CLOs are going to reach a much wider audience and I think that risk management is going to have to become more a prominent tool in the kit of the institutional investor. I think the recent increases in defaults makes it very clear that the basic stress tests that are being done don't necessarily tell what could happen under scenarios that are, or once were deemed to be, unlikely. Remember we have had at least one major market in the world that has moved by more than 10 standard deviations in each of the last 15 years. Once in a lifetime events happen much more frequently than once in a lifetime. I think that there will probably not be more regulation, but that regulatory fears will move hedge funds and others towards greater transparency. I think repo and securities lending, as I said in my opening remarks, will be a big risk issue. How many levered funds for instance, test their sensitivity to 'increased haircuts'? Advances in credit derivatives pricing and risk management have not yet percolated in many institutions to the repo department. The sophistication of quantitative techniques is going to be something that needs to be addressed. I think the whole concept of risk budgeting and risk allocation is eventually going to replace asset allocation on the buy side. I think the concept of putting capital against operational risk and trying to quantify operational risk will die a natural death. In the 1970's, I spent five years running the kind of businesses that have two hundred or two hundred fifty people who were largely clerical employees doing stock transfer, global investing, etc. I'm a firm believer that there are measures of operational risk that can be very important early warning signs (e.g., the number of exceptions, percent of risk on spreadsheets, etc.) but am not convinced that the statistical efforts to *quantify* operational risk will bear fruit. I think institutional investors are going to embrace and ultimately improve upon risk measures such as VaR and stress testing, that the dealer side has evolved. I think that the perspective of longer term investing is going to ultimately add immensely to the understanding of risk and will eventually create improved techniques that will feed back into the banking and dealer side. I think alternative investment and hedge funds will thrive (despite some of the well-publicized problems). As you probably all know hedge funds are going to start trading on the Bermuda stock exchange . . . and mere mortals like us are going to be able to participate in the hedge fund market.

There is going to be continued conflict between standardization of products and innovation. I think that the vast majority of risk still resides in a handful of "innovative" products. The "innovative" products change over time, but the 80/20 rule stays as a constant.

Figure 5. Continued Conflict

We at CMRA did a survey back in October 1999, a year after the Long Term Capital Management Debacle to identify how people and approaches have changed. What has been learned? I think the greatest impact of the crisis has probably been all the acceleration of the integration of credit risk and the market risk functions. Note that I say "functions" as opposed to integration of credit risk and market risk. I'm not sure anyone has the mathematics really worked out behind integrating credit risk and market risk. And I am not sure how important that is in my opinion. But to at least have the market risk functions and credit risk functions *communicate* and use the same basic disciplines is critical. Was the Russian debacle a market risk or a credit risk problem? There is still a lot of finger pointing on this issue. My opinion is: who cares? It is a risk that fell through the cracks in many institutions and we as an industry need to work towards minimizing the chances that such an oversight will occur again. Before the Russian/Long-Term crisis, CMRA's survey found that only 9% of large banks and broker dealers around the world said that they had the market risk and credit risk functions integrated and it was only up to 64% one year later. The whole issue of "documentation basis risk" seems mundane but can be a killer. It doesn't appeal to most quantitative folks but I can tell you there are some huge risks in liquidation between ISDA provisions and GRMA or RMA, etc., and even in how different dealers deal with the termination provisions. I've actually seen a trade where a hedge fund arbed two dealers and took out a healthy profit as the middleman in a long-dated credit derivatives trade. When they were liquidated, they ended up taking a fairly substantial loss because the two firms declared the liquidation on different dates and used two different methodologies to determine "losses". So it can get pretty interesting.

Another area on which the Russian/LTCM crisis has awakened the dealer community is the need for adjustments to margin for large and for illiquid positions. Only 25% of the banks/broker dealers in our survey focused on size and liquidity adjustment before the crises and still only 58% did so one-year post crisis. The "iceberg" effect of LTCM should be a chilling reminder to all of us as to the need for such adjustments.

Another key impact on risk management of the lessons from Russia/LTCM is the need for stress testing. While VaR is an important probabilistic measure, it doesn't address what happens when correlations go to $+1$ or -1 in a crisis or when *spreads* change dramatically or when markets move by 10 standard deviations. I think that management is beginning to recognize that their VaR of 12 is not necessarily equal to your VaR of 12, 12 is not 12. It depends on how you count. The need to elevate the importance of stress testing to at least the level of VaR has become better understood. Many institutions have also recognized that stress testing must go way beyond the evaluation of a portfolio's sensitivity to market changes and must also include stress testing of underlying models and assumptions. Eighty percent of respondents to our survey after the crises indicated that they are now focusing on the issue of stress-testing assumptions, as compared to 50% before the crisis.

Clearly one of the issues that crystallized in the aftermath of the crisis of 1998 is the misunderstanding, or perhaps the complete lack of understanding, by clients as to how haircuts are determined. I find that more and more dealers are recognizing that setting clear haircut and margining standards and methodologies and communicating those standards and methodologies to their clients is key to avoiding misunderstandings.

And when our survey queried as to whether dealers evaluated the impact of volatility curve twists (I have to tell you it's always the thing that causes you nightmares when short-dated volatility and long-dated volatility move in different ways), only forty-six percent did before the crisis and only 67% did so one year later.

Stress-testing potential credit risk exposure is still not where I believe it should be. Some dealers still use the static potential exposure calculated on the day a trade is done and in the extreme, although a currency is depegged and the volatility is 20 times what it was, still use the old static estimate. I believe estimating potential future credit exposure is still an area that needs significant work.

There is still a lot of work to be done to make robust risk management a reality. It is a daunting challenge but I think that when it is undertaken, most people find that attention to risk management can really make a difference on their bottom line.

PREDICTIONS

- 2000: Year of the Internet
- CDO's will take off
- More regulation or at least more transparency
- Collateral losses will continue
- Risk allocation will replace asset allocation
- Operational risk quantification will remain elusive
- Institutional investors will embrace risk measures
- Alternative investments will grow to record levels

AUTHOR INDEX

Almgren, R. 6, 13
Altman, E. 171, 185, 185n, 186, 203, 204, 205n
Ang, A. 144, 144n

Bertsimas, D. 6, 13
Best, E. 119
Black, F. 146, 147, 149, 161
Boehmer, E. 147, 161
Boyer, M. 144, 144n
Brenner, M. 118n, 119

Cantor, R. 145, 158, 161
Caouette, J. 185, 185n, 186
Carey, M. 184n, 185n, 186
Chen, J. 144, 144n
Chow, G. 130, 132, 134, 140, 142, 144
Chriss, N. 6, 13
Claessens, S. 147, 148, 149, 162
Cooke, D. 186
Cox, J. 146, 149, 161
Crouhy, M. 108n, 109
Cumby, R. 148, 149, 161, 162

Duffie, D. 24, 25, 98, 109
Dunbar, N. 4, 13

Ederington, L. 158, 162
Edwards, S. 147, 162
Evans, M. 148, 149, 161, 162

Fisher, L. 148, 162
Forbes, K. 144, 144n, 164, 165, 166n
Fridson, M. 171, 186
Froot, K. 51, 64, 65

Galai, D. 108n, 109, 118n, 119
Gibson, B. 144, 144n
Guidotti, P. 155–6, 162

Hamilton, J. 144, 144n
Hardle, W. 144, 144n
Henriksson, R. 144, 144n
Higinbotham, H. 80, 85
Hull, J. 153, 162

Jacquier, E. 130, 132, 134, 140, 142, 144
Jarrow, R. 6, 13, 98, 109
Johnson, N. 144, 144n
Jones, E. 147, 148, 162
Jonsson, J. 171, 186

Karlin, S. 144, 144n
Karolyi, A. 166n
King, M. 164, 166n
Kishore, V. 186
Kotz, S. 144, 144n
Krakovsky, A. 6, 13

Kritzman, M. 130, 132, 134, 140, 142, 144
Kumar, M. 155–156, 162

Lando, D. 98, 109
Latane, H. 118n, 119
Lo, A. 6, 13
Longin, F. 144, 144n
Longstaff, F. 147, 149, 162
Longstaff, F. 6, 13
Loretan, M. 144, 144n
Lowry, K. 130, 132, 134, 140, 142, 144

Mark, R. 108n, 109
Mason, S. 147, 148, 162
Megginson, W. 147, 161
Merton, R. 16, 18, 25, 87, 109, 140, 141, 144,
    144n, 146, 147, 148, 149–152, 162
Mordecai, D. 64
Mullarky, M. 51, 65
Murphy, B. 64

Narayanan, P. 186

Odier, P. 144, 144n

Packer, F. 145, 158, 161
Pennacchi, G. 147, 148, 149, 162
Perold, A. 16, 25

Rendleman, R. 118n, 119
Rigobon, R. 144, 144n, 164, 165, 166n
Rosenfeld, E. 147, 148, 162

Sarig, O. 158, 162
Saunders, A. 168, 185, 185n, 186, 205n
Scholes, M. 146, 161
Schwartz, E. 147, 149, 162
Seasholes, M. 65
Singleton, K. 98, 109
Solnik, B. 144, 144n
Stambaugh, R. 166n
Stern. A. 64
Stulz, R. 166n
Subramanian, A. 6, 13
Swift, C. 119

Taylor, H. 144, 144n
Telser, L. 80, 85
Terrile, J. 119
Treacy, W. 184n, 186
Turnbull, S. 98, 109

Usher, S. 64

Wadhwani, S. 164, 166n
Warga, A. 158, 162

Yawitz, J. 158, 162

SUBJECT INDEX

Baht 8–9
Bank for International Settlements (BIS) 3
Bank for International Settlements (BIS) capital
    adequacy requirements *see* capital
    requirements
Bankers Trust 36
Barings 35
Basel Committee on Banking Supervision *see*
    capital requirements
basis risk 29, 192
bid-ask spread 3, 5
Black-Scholes model 27–30, 32, 146, 207
bonds
    catastrophic ("cat") *see* catastrophic bonds
    pricing of 145–161
    rating of *see* credit ratings
    US dollar-denominated 152–155
Buffett, Warren 81–82, 84

Capital Asset Pricing Model 82
Capital Market Risk Advisors (CMRA) 209, 212
capital requirements
    and bias toward high-risk assets 15–16, 168,
      201
    and capital ratios 167, 182, 202
    and disclosure 202

Basel Accord 15, 201
    BIS proposals 13, 15–16, 167–169, 182,
      201–205
    violations of 3, 13
catastrophic ("cat") bonds 47–50, 53–63, 83
catastrophic event ("cat") insurance 37–38
catastrophic event ("cat") risk
    as event risk 38
    distribution of 37–40
    financing of 43–46
    transferring of 47–53
CIBC 88
closed-end mutual funds 38–40
contagion in financial markets
    definition of 163–164
    measurement of 164–165
contingent claims analysis 146–148, 156, 160
Continuous Linked Settlement (CLS) Bank
    124–125
credit derivatives 88
credit ratings 16, 20–23, 48, 84, 146, 158, 160,
    168–184, 185n, 203
credit risk
    and leverage 15
    and market risk 212
    and maturity 145

and return tradeoff 15
corporate 145, 148–161, 168–184
measurement of 16–24, 87–108
  buffer stock view of capital 16–17
  class of credit VaR models 16–17, 24
  credit migration approach (CIBC's
    CreditVaR model) 87–108
  Credit Risk+ approach 88
  insurance value approach 17–24
  structural approach 87–88
  sovereign 145–161
credit spread 112, 145–161, 185n
currency risk 9–10
currency risk latent 147, 155, 161

default risk *see* credit risk
delta hedging 28
derivatives traders 31
derivatives
  valuation of 27–34
  volatility of 29–30
diversification 16
dividend yields in options valuation 27–28
documentation risk 36

emerging markets 3, 147–161

Federal Reserve Bank 202
foreign currency (FX) *see* currency

Goldman Sachs 30

Hammersmith and Fulham 35–36
hedge funds 211
  and arbitrage 191
  regulation of 199
  transparency of 188–199
hedging 27–30
holding period *see* investment horizon

implied volatilities 112–115, 118
insurance risk securitization 79–82
interest rate risk 204, 210
interest rates in options valuation 27–30, 210
Internet, effect on capital markets 211
investment horizons 129–142

Japanese Yen *see* Yen

legal risk 35–36
Lehman Brothers 35–36
liquidity, cost of 5
liquidity risk 3, 212

endogenous 4, 5
  measurement of 6
exogenous 4, 5
  measurement of 6–12
measurement of 3–13
Long Term Capital Management (LTCM)
  187–190, 193, 197, 212–213

market volume 123
maturity impact of on credit risk *see* credit risk
moral hazard 17, 32, 65n

operational risk 211
options theory 27
Organization for Economic Cooperation and
  Development (OECD) 15
OTC options 29, 35
overconfidence 129

payment and settlement risk *see* settlement risk
Procter and Gamble 36

regime switching 132–142
regime-sensitive portfolios 129–142
risk,
  basis *see* basis risk
  catastrophic *see* catastrophic risk
  components of 4–6, 207–208
  credit *see* credit risk
  currency *see* currency risk
  documentation *see* documentation risk
  legal *see* legal risk
  liquidity *see* liquidity risk
  management of in the 1980s 208–209
  operational *see* operational risk
  settlement *see* settlement risk
  tolerance of 16
  value at risk *see* VaR
  weather *see* weather risk
  Y2K *see* Y2K risk
risk sensitive capital regime 204–205
Russian crisis 163, 187–190, 193, 212

settlement risk 124–127
  efforts to reduce 125
  in currency markets 125–127
settlement systems 123–124
stress testing 198, 213

Thai Baht *see* Baht
transaction costs 27–28

VaR (value at risk) 3, 213, 191
  failure to account for liquidity risk 4

credit VaR models *see* credit risk, measurement
    of
incorporating liquidity risk into 6–12
volatility, implied *see* implied volatility
volatility skew 32–33
volatility smile 28

weather derivatives
    design of 68–69

market for 69–78
weather risk 68–78, 79

Y2K problem 111–118
    estimates of associated upgrade costs
        111–112
Y2K risk market assessment of 112–118
Yen 8–9
yield spread *see* credit spread